REAL DEL MONTE

A British Mining Venture in Mexico

Latin American Monographs, No. 26
Institute of Latin American Studies
The University of Texas at Austin

Real del Monte

A BRITISH MINING VENTURE IN MEXICO

By ROBERT W. RANDALL

PUBLISHED FOR THE INSTITUTE OF LATIN AMERICAN STUDIES
BY THE UNIVERSITY OF TEXAS PRESS, AUSTIN & LONDON

Library of Congress Cataloging in Publication Data

Randall, Robert W   1925–
  Real del Monte: a British mining venture in Mexico.

  (Latin American monographs, no. 26)
  Based on thesis, Harvard University
  Bibliography: p.
  1. Company of Adventurers in the Mines of Real del
Monte. I. Title. II. Series: Latin American monographs
(Austin, Tex.) no. 26.
HD9536.M44C65   338.2'7'421   78-37944
ISBN 0-292-77000-6

Composition by G&S Typesetters, Austin
Printing by Capital Printing Company, Austin
Binding by Universal Bookbindery, Inc., San Antonio

TO JO ANNE

CONTENTS

MAPS

Maps 2, 3, 4, 6, 7, and 8 are based on drawings in John H. Buchan,
*Report of the Director, the Real del Monte Mining Company,
Mexico, March 1855.*

TABLES

PREFACE

The wave of capital that flowed from Great Britain to Latin America upon the disruption of the Spanish Empire and the special attraction that the mining of precious metals held out to English investors in the 1820's have been the subject of several investigations. The establishment of some half-dozen British silver-mining companies in Mexico alone between 1822 and 1825 and the failure of all but one of them by 1850 are at least mentioned in most of the standard histories of Mexico. But the reasons for those companies' failures, the impact they and the young, politically chaotic host country had on one another, and the extent to which their financially unsuccessful operations prepared the way for large and prosperous mining enterprises in the future are treated for the most part only in generalizations. By giving a full account of one of the British concerns—the Company of Adventurers in the Mines of Real del Monte—from its formation in 1824 through its dissolution in 1849, this study attempts to present a microcosmic view of foreign economic penetration into the Mexican mining industry in the first quarter-century after independence. I hope the inquiry will suggest concrete explanations for the historical problems mentioned above.

Established in London in 1824, the British Real del Monte Company was led by men convinced that the application of English capital and technology to the ancient, famous, and largely ruined silver mines of the former Spanish colony would not only reap them a handsome profit but also would have a salutary effect on the new nation's mining industry. The center of the firm's activi-

ties was the property owned by Pedro Romero de Terreros, the
third Count of Regla, in Real del Monte, one of the oldest and best
known silver districts of Mexico. During the twenty-five years that
the English concern existed, its overseas expenditures totaled
$16,218,490 and its income but $11,139,207. The loss of more than
$5 million makes it clear that the history of the British Real del
Monte is in one sense the story of a financial disaster. Accordingly, the factors that contributed most to the concern's downfall are
discussed in this work.

There is more to the history of the Company of Adventurers,
however, than the fact of eventual bankruptcy and the reasons for
it. The study, therefore, seeks answers to questions like the following: did the English make any significant changes in traditional
Mexican methods of draining water from deep mines, reducing silver ore, and paying mine labor; how could a company located in a
country virtually without industry keep its plant, and particularly
the part of it that depended on imported steam-powered machinery, supplied with the necessary equipment and stores; how was it
possible for a foreign economic enterprise to operate within the
context of the political turmoil that characterized Mexico between
1824 and 1849; to what extent was the English concern's failure
an investment in the future of silver mining at Real del Monte?

Yet another inquiry about the British Real del Monte Company,
one that stems from the last question asked above, must be made.
Was it in the fullest sense of the word a failure? The Mexican firm
that bought out the English company in 1849 proved to be a profitable endeavor, whose net earnings far exceeded the $5 million loss
sustained by its predecessor. Under the United States Smelting,
Mining and Refining Company, which in 1906 acquired controlling interest in the stock, the property yielded one of the most spectacular and sustained bonanzas in the history of Mexican silver
mining. And the agency of the Mexican government to which the
securities of Real del Monte were sold in 1947 continues to operate
the centuries-old mines at no loss. If, as this study should clearly
show, the foundation for that series of successful mining enterprises
at Real del Monte was built between 1824 and 1849, then the his-

tory of the British company must be interpreted as the story of, at most, an ironic failure.

The sources used in the preparation of this study are discussed in detail in the Bibliographical Notes. It is important to note at the outset, however, that the massive collection of unpublished manuscripts belonging to the Compañía Minera del Real del Monte y Pachuca are by far the most important. Moreover, the documents falling under the heading of Correspondencia General bulk large among the company's manuscripts used. In citing Correspondencia General (CG) records, therefore, I have employed a very abbreviated form, for example, 1838 CG 39, which shows only the year of the CG document and the number of the volume in which it may be found.

I wish here to express my sincere appreciation to Professor Ernest R. May of Harvard University, who offered invaluable suggestions on the preparation of the thesis upon which this book is based, and to Dr. Charles C. Griffin, who, as visiting professor of Latin American history at Harvard, awakened my interest in mining in newly independent Mexico as a topic for investigation.

My thanks go as well to all those in Mexico who made it possible for me to consult archival material without which this work could not have been written. The doors to the present Real del Monte and Pachuca Mining Company, where records of the British concern are housed, were opened to me by Mr. Salvador Peña Slane, the undersecretary for nonrenewable natural resources in the Ministry of National Patrimony, and by Mr. Oswaldo Gurría Urgel, the director of the Commission on Mining Development. My research in Pachuca was in no small measure facilitated by the kindness of the company's director, Mr. Arturo R. Geyne, and his cooperative staff. Special mention must be made of the generosity of Manuel Romero de Terreros, who granted me access to important papers in his family's collection.

A NOTE ON SPANISH WORDS AND ON WEIGHTS, MEASURES, AND CURRENCY

Throughout the text, the spelling of Spanish proper nouns follows the original, with these exceptions: first names of persons and names of places and mines are modernized; in accordance with present-day usage, accents are added where pronunciation demands. In quotations and bibliographical citations, however, the original form, including the use of diacritical marks, is retained.

Spanish words that have become Anglicized are neither accented nor italicized in the text. Spanish words, particularly mining terms, for which there are no adequate English equivalents, are italicized throughout and are explained the first time they appear.

In the documents on which this study is based, weights, measures, and currency are expressed in widely different terms. Without some standardization of terminology, references to depths and location of mines and to production, costs, and profit or loss would be confusing and comparisons difficult. Current American usage is therefore followed for the most part, the original terms being maintained only when appropriate in their context.

For the period covered by the main body of this study, 1824–1849, the Mexican peso and the American dollar were approximately equal in value; the British pound was worth about five pesos or dollars. The symbol $, which could mean either Mexican pesos or American dollars, signifies the latter throughout.

Some of the conversions to American units of weight, measure, and currency are probably not without a degree of error, owing to short-term fluctuations in exchange rates and to variations in the meaning of certain terms. In the calculation of United States equivalents, therefore, the time and place in which terms were used have been taken into account.

ABBREVIATIONS

AEM	Archivo del Estado de México
AGC	Annual General Court
AGN	Archivo General de la Nación
AMM	*Anales de la minería mexicana*
AN	Archivo de Notarías
ASGC	Annual and Special General Court
CG	Correspondencia General
LJ	*Law Journal*
MJ	*The Mining Journal and Commercial Gazette*
ODM	*Ordenanzas de minería otorgados por el Rey Carlos III*
PCR	Papelos de los Condes de Regla
QMR	*Quarterly Mining Review*
RdM	Real del Monte Company Papers
RT	Romero de Terreros Papers
SGC	Special General Court

REAL DEL MONTE

A British Mining Venture in Mexico

1. Introduction

SILVER WAS THE OBJECT OF THE MINING ADVENTURES UNDER-
taken by the British Real del Monte Company in early nineteenth-century Mexico. Silver had also been the object of that
firm's predecessor, the House of Regla, when it exploited the Real
del Monte–Pachuca district in the late colonial period. Indeed, to
speak of mining during that era of Mexican history is to speak of
silver. Of the other metals, only gold was as ardently sought. The
base metals, such as copper, lead, and zinc, which are today the
main support of the Mexican mining industry, were almost completely ignored. As Baron Alexander von Humboldt observed after
having visited New Spain in the first decade of the nineteenth century, a preference for products that could be exported was responsible for the mine owners' directing their attention almost exclusively to the extraction of precious metals. And it was silver, not
the intrinsically more valuable gold, that made up the major share
of the enormous mineral wealth that flowed from the colony to the

CHIHUAHUA

PARRAL

DURANGO
SOMBRERETE• •CATORCE
•FRESNILLO
ZACATECAS •

SAN LUIS POTOSI

BOLAÑOS • GUANAJUATO
• ZIMAPÁN
PACHUCA •• REAL DEL MONTE
TLALPUJAHUA • ☆ MEXICO CITY
• TEMASCALTEPEC
SULTEPEC • • TAXCO

OAXACA

N

1. Principal mining districts of New Spain.

mother country.[1] Today, despite impressive efforts on the part of the Mexican government to introduce diversified industry into the Real del Monte–Pachuca district, silver is still ardently sought—by men who look back with a combination of admiration and hostility to the exploits of the Regla family and the British company.

The Real del Monte–Pachuca District

Located no more than sixty or seventy miles northeast of Mexico City, in the present state of Hidalgo, the Real del Monte–Pachuca mining district is, of the major silver-producing areas, the one nearest the country's political and financial center (see Map 1). During the colonial period mining was for the most part confined to the town of Real del Monte and its environs; yet Pachuca, the seat of government for the region, also played a decisive role in the affairs of the concern with which this study deals. Another

[1] Alexander de [sic] Humboldt, *Political Essay on the Kingdom of New Spain*, III, 104–105, 434.

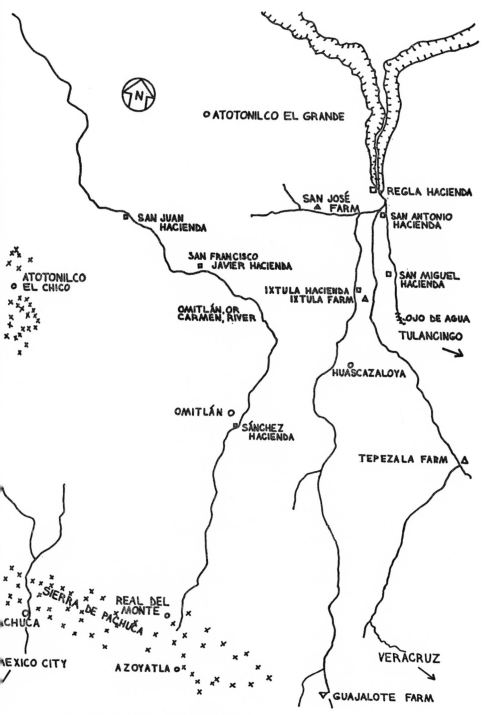

2. Real del Monte–Pachuca district.

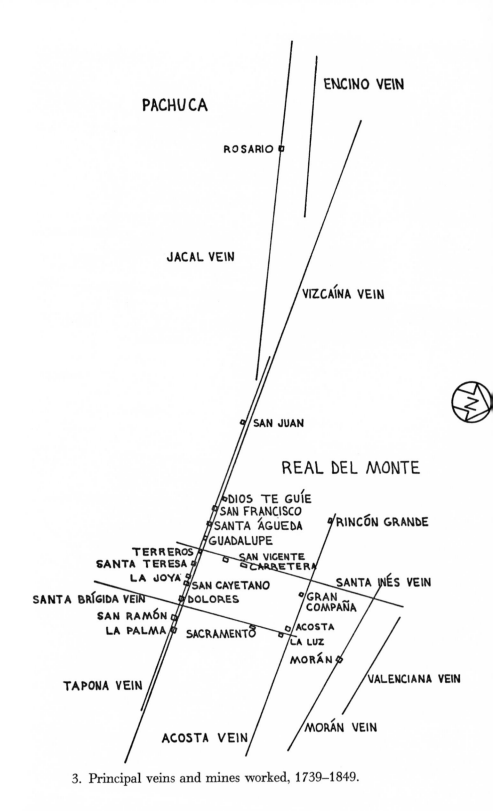

3. Principal veins and mines worked, 1739–1849.

nearby town of importance, Huascazaloya or Huasca, became the site of the main reduction haciendas (see Map 2).

The Real del Monte district itself forms a horseshoe, approximately seven and one-half square miles in area, opening to the northeast and surrounded on the three other sides by the high peaks of the Sierra de Pachuca. It is cut from the southwest by the small, dry valley of Azoyatla, and opposite is the deep valley of the Omitlán, or Carmen, River, which flows from south to north onto the plain of Atotonilco el Grande. To the west of the Real, the Pachuca district occupies an area of some twelve and one-half square miles. Three of its principal rivers, the Texinca, the Rosario, and the San Cristóbal (or Sabanilla), during the short period when they are not dry, drain into the Pachuca River, whose direction is north-south. The town of Pachuca lies at the southwestern base of the Sierra, whose northern slope extends to the plain of Atotonilco el Grande, on which both the district and the town of Huasca are located.

About 9,020 feet above sea level, the Real is some 1,060 feet higher than Pachuca and 1,670 feet higher than Mexico City. It receives an annual precipitation of approximately thirty-one inches, twice that of semiarid Pachuca. A summer-autumn rainy season is followed by a winter-spring dry period. In recent years the maximum temperature at the Real, recorded in May, averaged 83° F., and the minimum, recorded in December, reached 23° F. Pachuca has a slightly higher maximum and a slightly lower minimum, and Huasca tends to be warmer the year round.

The area's wood supply has come from the Sierra de Pachuca. Consisting mainly of firs, with some oak and pine, these forests were, and continue to be, more abundant at the crest of the range near the Real than on the southern, or Pachuca, slope. The depletion of wooded lands, noticeable at the present time, was probably not so advanced in the late eighteenth and early nineteenth centuries.

The silver-producing veins in the region as a whole are divided into a north-south system and a more productive east-west system (see Map 3). In colonial times, the most important veins in the latter group that were worked at Real del Monte were Valenciana,

Morán, Acosta, Vizcaína, and Tapona. In Pachuca the two principal east-west veins were Encino and Xacal. This district reported
no north-south lodes of significance at the end of the eighteenth
and the beginning of the nineteenth centuries, but several in that
system, especially Santa Brígida and Santa Inés, did receive attention at the Real. The mineralogy of the north-south system is not
basically different from that of the east-west system, the veins of
both losing their metallic content with depth; however, the ore
deposits of the former tend to decrease in width as they go deeper
underground, whereas those of the latter tend to widen.[2]

The Real del Monte–Pachuca district was the scene of important
mining enterprises long before the House of Regla or the British
Real del Monte Company were formed. Shortly after the Conquest,
and certainly before the middle of the sixteenth century, silver
mines were discovered and worked in Pachuca. According to an
early seventeenth-century account, the first formal *denuncio*, or
filing of a claim, in the Real del Monte–Pachuca district was made
in 1552.[3]

Following Bartolomé de Medina's discovery of the patio process
of amalgamation in 1555, the industry developed rapidly. Within
fifteen years, Pachuca, Real del Monte, El Chico, Ixmiquilpan, and
Zimapán had become the sites of significant mining operations.
The area attracted large numbers of Spanish mine owners, mer-

[2] The geographical sketch is based on the following sources: J[oseph] Burkart, "Memoria sobre explotación de minas de los distritos de Pachuca y Real
del Monte de México," *AMM*, 1 (1861), 7–15; José M. Romero, "Memoria
sobre el distrito de Pachuca," in Ramón Almaraz, ed., *Memoria de los trabajos
ejecutados por la Comisión Científica de Pachuca en el año de 1864*, pp. 75, 85–
88, 101, 121–122, 177–178; José G. Aguilera and Ezequiel Ordóñez, "Fisiografía
de la Sierra de Pachuca," in Instituto Geológico de México, *El mineral de Pachuca*, pp. 19–26; Ezequiel Ordóñez, "Descripción topográfica y geológica," in
Instituto Geológico de México, *El Real del Monte*, pp. 3–10; and A. R. Geyne et
al., *Geology and Mineral Deposits of the Pachuca–Real del Monte District, State
of Hidalgo, Mexico*, pp. 8–19, 125–127.

[3] Miguel O. de Mendizábal, "Los minerales de Pachuca y Real del Monte
en la época colonial," *El trimestre económico*, 8, no. 2 (July–September 1941),
254; Modesto Bargalló, *La minería y la metalurgia en la América española
durante la época colonial*, p. 63; *Descripción de las minas de Pachuca*, pp. 8–9,
23.

chants, and artisans, as well as native workers, who were able to offer themselves as salaried mine workers because for various reasons they had been freed from the necessity of paying tribute.[4]

The Real del Monte and Pachuca mines were somewhat less prosperous at the beginning of the seventeenth century than they had been a few decades earlier, partly because they were yielding a lower grade of ore. Further, and more important, they had been dug to a depth at which water was encountered, and the owners had not developed an adequate means of drainage.[5] The need for finding a way to keep the mines free of water—one of the most vexing technological problems with which the British Real del Monte Company was to struggle—had thus become evident in the district a full two centuries before the formation of that foreign enterprise.

Another recurring problem, that of a chronic labor shortage, also dates back to the sixteenth century. On three occasions between November 1579 and March 1580, for example, Viceroy Enríquez directed the mayor of Pachuca to furnish the owners of the Gran Compaña mine in Real del Monte with a *repartimiento* of forty Indians a week for three months. The subordinate official's failure to comply with the first order was apparently due to nothing more than a lack of Indians available for duty in the mines. At about the same time (November 1579), the viceroy instructed the mayor to grant a Pachuca mine owner a six-month *amparo*, a legal device to secure his property against *denuncio* by another party, on the grounds that a "well-known disease and pestilence" had killed a large number of "slaves and servants" and thus prevented his working the mines with the legally required labor force (four operators per mine).[6]

Owing to the labor shortage in the mines, the owners were, by the end of the sixteenth century, already holding out as an inducement a system of payment that was later to be known as the *par-*

---

[4] Mendizábal, "Los minerales de Pachuca y Real del Monte," pp. 258–259.
[5] *Ibid.*, p. 273.
[6] Silvio Zavala and María Castelo, eds., *Fuentes para la historia del trabajo en Nueva España*, II, 223, 227, 259, 278.

tido, whereby a portion of the workers' wages was paid in the form of ore. At the end of their regular shift, the Indians and mulattoes were given some of the ore they had extracted, called "sorted ore."[7]

During the early eighteenth century, mining in the Real del Monte–Pachuca district was in a state of depression, not because the lodes had become exhausted but because the mines had reached a depth at which their working was too costly for the average mine owner. The abundance of water in the veins and the crude methods of drainage had combined to cause the abandonment of most of the mines at the relatively shallow depth of approximately 130 yards. Of more importance than the technological backwardness of the industry was the lack of capital, which made it impossible for most proprietors to finance the large-scale drainage projects required to rehabilitate the area.[8] Although at least one attempt had been made, during the 1720's, to solve the twofold problem of insufficient capital and flooded mines,[9] the entire Vizcaína vein was abandoned by the late 1730's. Nonetheless the stage was set for the greatest mining enterprise of the colonial period in the Real del Monte–Pachuca district.

The House of Regla

The silver-mining pursuits of the three counts of Regla in the late eighteenth and early nineteenth centuries, themselves the subject of much romantic story telling and a few serious studies, are important to the present work because they bequeathed to the British Real del Monte Company three legacies. The first was a legend of success that served as a challenging model for the economic and human tragedy played out by the English adventurers. Indeed, Pedro Romero de Terreros, the third Count of Regla, acting as business partner, technical consultant, political advisor, and even occasionally antagonist, was on the scene until 1846 to remind the foreign enterprise of the saga enacted by his ancestors.

[7]Mendizábal, "Los minerales de Pachuca y Real del Monte," p. 275; *Descripción de las minas de Pachuca*, pp. 42–43.

[8] Mendizábal, "Los minerales de Pachuca y Real del Monte," pp. 283–284.

[9] Zavala and Castelo, *Fuentes para la historia del trabajo*, VIII, 256–258.

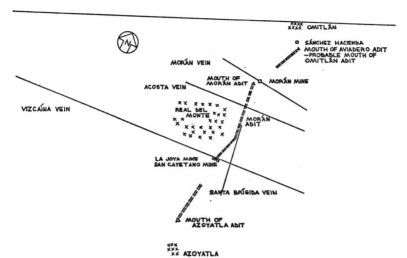

4. Adits, constructed or begun, 1739–1824.

The second legacy comprised two technological problems: the drainage of old and deep mines and the economical treatment of low-grade silver ore. The English struggled with these problems for twenty-five years: yet their success in finding the means of solution could not save their economic venture.

The third legacy was a tradition of militancy among the Mexican workers of Real del Monte and Pachuca. That tradition became well established under the proprietorship of the House of Regla, faded but reappeared during the English firm's early days to plague it to the end, and was passed on to the Mexican and American successors who controlled the huge Real del Monte–Pachuca silver enterprise for the next century.

The family that came to own, operate, and make both a fortune and a title of nobility from the Real del Monte mines entered the mining business, so to speak, from the side door. The elder Pedro Romero de Torreros, who became the first Count of Regla, began his noteworthy career in New Spain not as a mining entrepreneur but as a merchant in the agricultural-market city of Querétaro.[10]

[10] Manuel Romero de Terreros, *El Conde de Regla, creso de la Nuevo España,* p. 13.

Before the formation of his great mining enterprise, Romero de Terreros was a financial supporter and then partner of a well-known professional miner with foresight, José Alejandro Bustamante y Bustillo. Romero de Terreros was, therefore, a member of a class of financiers who helped provide funds to the chronically capital-poor mining industry of colonial Mexico. The famous Mining Ordinances of 1783, following the practice set forth in earlier codes governing mining in New Spain, recognized the fact that many mine owners worked their properties with the aid of outside capital. The persons who furnished those funds, and sometimes supplies as well, were known as *aviadores*. The ordinances made a distinction between *aviadores* who became part owners of the property and those who merely received metal from the mine owner at a discount from its legal price.[11] Pedro Romero de Terreros was one of the first, and obviously more adventurous, class of *aviador*.

In 1739 the prescient miner Bustamante developed a plan to resurrect mining in the virtually deserted Real del Monte district. His idea was to drain a large portion of the formerly active mining camp, in particular the Vizcaína vein, by means of an adit. Accordingly, he petitioned Viceroy Juan Antonio de Vizarrón for the right of possession over all the mines on the Vizcaína and such others as might be discovered between that vein and the proposed opening of the adit, a deep ravine in Azoyatla, to the southwest of the Real (see Map 4).[12]

On 1 June 1739 Viceroy Vizarrón approved Bustamante's claim of the Vizcaína vein. Consequently, at a formal ceremony held in Pachuca on 15 June, Bustamante took possession of the famous vein and, during the next ten or eleven days, staked out his individual claims in preparation for the digging of the Azoyatla adit.[13] Bustamante's object was not only to reach the great lode and drain

11 "Ordenanzas de minería," 1783 (cited hereafter as "Ordenanzas"), in *ODM*, titles 14, 15.

12 Bustamante's claim and specifications, n.d., Títulos de la veta Vizcaína (cited hereafter as Títulos), RT, fols. 2–2v; AGN, Ramo de Minería (cited hereafter as AGN Minería), vol. 29, fol. 320.

13 Viceroy Vizarron's concurrence in Bustamante's claim and specifications, 1 June 1739, Títulos, RT, fols. 6–8v; AGN Minería, vol. 29, fols. 340–355v.

the abandoned mines included in the general claim but also to exploit such new veins as might be encountered in the digging. The location of the Azoyatla adit, in relatively sterile ground and on the opposite side of the Vizcaína from most of the other veins in the Real del Monte district, might explain its lack of early success. For whatever reason, by 1741 Bustamante sensed failure and the imminent exhaustion of his resources and thus sought financial aid of the wealthy Querétaro merchant, Pedro Romero de Terreros.[14]

Within a few years the professional miner began to fade from the scene at the Real, and the *aviador* to dominate it. In September 1743 Bustamante and Romero de Terreros made a contractual agreement to act in company, in a formal partnership, for the driving not only of the Azoyatla adit but also another one from a point on the road between Real del Monte and Omitlán, north of the Vizcaína vein. The concept of joint ownership of everything that pertained to the adit drainage of the great lode was particularly stressed in the contract.[15] Yet Bustamante began to withdraw from the actual management of the undertaking, granting to his brother a power of attorney to handle all matters at the Real pertaining to the adits mentioned in the Romero de Terreros contract.[16] Until the time of his death in 1750, Bustamante enjoyed fame (though apparently little remuneration) for his capabilities as a professional miner and for his enterprise in attempting the rehabilitation of the Real del Monte mines. His expert opinion was sought on such matters as the price of quicksilver dispensed to Mexican miners through the government monopoly and a proposed company for the financing of mining ventures.[17] Yet he did not live to see the Vizcaína vein drained, and when this feat was accomplished, it was by an entirely different adit on the opposite side of the lode from Azoyatla. Instead, it was Pedro Romero de Terreros who

[14] Romero de Terreros, *El Conde*, p. 13. See Maps 3 and 4.

[15] AN, Juan Antonio de Arroyo, 1743, fols. 630v–632v.

[16] AN, Juan Antonio de Arroyo, 1743, fols. 636–637.

[17] Francisco Xavier de Gamboa, "Comentarios a las ordenanzas de minas," 1761 (cited hereafter as "Comentarios"), in *ODM*, ch. 2, Commentary 77, ch. 7, Commentary 65.

reaped all of the benefits—great personal wealth, a title of nobility, and legendary fame.

The founding father of the rich and powerful Romero de Terreros family was a legendary figure who far outshone his descendants, including the similarly named grandson most directly concerned with this work. Reputed to have been one of the richest men of his times, Bustamante's partner is said to have drawn more than $5.2 million from the Vizcaína by 1774; to have presented two warships to King Charles III of Spain; to have lent $1 million to the Court of Madrid, for which he was never repaid; to have purchased immense estates; and to have left to his children a fortune equalled in Mexico only by that of the Count of Valenciana.[18] Over the years, his wealth became the subject of numerous anecdotes. When his children were baptized, so one story went, the procession walked on bars of silver. According to another, he was so grateful to the Spanish king for having conferred upon him the title of Count of Regla that he invited the monarch to visit him at his mine, assuring His Majesty that his feet would not touch the ground during his stay in the New World, for it would be on a pavement of silver that he would alight from his carriage and his lodgings would be lined with the precious metal.[19]

In his biography of his ancestor, the present Marquis of San Francisco, Manuel Romero de Terreros, calls those stories exaggerations;[20] yet he does little to dispel them or, at best, replaces them with others. Subtitling his book "The Croesus of New Spain," the author supports the statement that the count was "one of the richest men in the realm and perhaps in the entire world,"[21] by citing

[18] Humboldt, *Political Essay*, III, 217–218. With slight differences, this abbreviated version of Romero de Terreros' wealth is repeated by a number of authors, including Benjamin Disraeli (*An Inquiry into the Plans, Progress, and Policy of the American Mining Companies*, pp. 74–76); H. G. Ward (*Mexico in 1827*, II, 362–363); and Frederick A. Ober (*Travels in Mexico and Life Among the Mexicans*, p. 461).

[19] Robert A. Wilson (*Mexico: Its Peasants and Its Priests*, p. 365) and Ober (*Travels in Mexico*, p. 461) are among the recounters of these anecdotes.

[20] Romero de Terreros, *Conde de Regla*, pp. 174–175.

[21] *Ibid.*, p. 16.

his gifts of cash ($100,000) and jewels to his bride; by devoting an entire chapter to one of the mine owner's several sumptuous residences, his "house of silver," in Mexico City; and by noting that the count's landholdings in large areas of what are now the states of Mexico, Hidalgo, Querétaro, Guanajuato, Michoacán, Jalisco, and Colima, though valued at merely $5 million in 1782 (a year after his death), would be of "incalculable worth today."[22]

On the death of the first Count of Regla in 1781, his property was divided among his several children (his wife having died in 1766). His eldest son, Pedro Ramón Mariano José, inherited not only the Regla title but also the mining concern at Real del Monte and Zimapán, which had been entailed in 1775. Born on 30 August 1761 in Pachuca, the second Count of Regla was throughout his lifetime considerably less prosperous than his father. Shortly before his death in 1809, he was forced to sacrifice a good deal of his landed property to satisfy his creditors. With his passing, the Regla title and mining concern went to his fourth and eldest surviving child, Pedro José María Ignacio Antonio Pascual Ramón Manuel Santos. The third Count of Regla was born in Mexico City on 1 November 1788. He served in the royal army during the liberation movements of Hidalgo and Morelos, but in 1821 he elected to remain in Mexico and signed Agustín de Iturbide's Act of Independence. Two years later he accepted a commission as brigadier general in the Mexican army. It was he who leased the Real del Monte mining concern to a group of British investors in 1824.[23]

How was the great wealth of the Romero de Terreros family amassed? That not all of it came from the Real del Monte mines is certain from facts already mentioned: the first Pedro was a successful businessman before he entered the silver-mining field, and the clan acquired and operated huge landed estates. But that a very

[22] *Ibid.*, pp. 40–41, 79–89, 170.
[23] Fundación del mayorazgo que . . . instituió el S. D. Pedro Romero de Terreros, . . . Conde de Regla, 7 de septiembre de 1775, and Testimonio del testamento que otorgó el Señor Don Pedro Romero de Terreros, Conde de Regla, el dia 9 de septiembre de 1775, PCR, folders 94, 95, 108; Manuel Romero de Terreros, "D. Pedro Romero de Terreros, Count of Regla" (unpublished translation), RdM, *passim*.

large portion of the family fortune was extracted from the argentiferous veins of the Sierra de Pachuca is equally certain.

The basic wealth was gained by Pedro I when he temporarily solved the dual problems of capital shortage and a method of draining the Vizcaína vein below the level at which mining had been carried out before about 1730. During the digging of what became known as the Morán adit, the third to be tried since Bustamante's 1739 general drainage plan and not completed until 1762, the first Count of Regla made a profit of slightly more than $1.5 million.[24] Between 1762 and 1781, the year of the first count's death, mining activities at the Real consisted mainly of taking ore out of the vast areas opened to exploitation by the general drainage of the district. Although operations were all but halted by labor strife that lasted from 1766 until 1775, the post-Morán–adit period saw Pedro Romero de Terreros make a profit of approximately $9.5 million from his mining activities.[25]

The second Count of Regla, on inheriting the mining properties from his famous and successful father, saw the profits decline drastically for a period of years, rise for a short period, and finally fall off sharply again. Between 1781 and 1794 the second count was compelled to carry out numerous dead works, including the reinforcement of the Morán adit. While this development work was in progress, ore production dropped appreciably, reducing mining profit to but about $600,000 for the entire 1781–1794 period.[26] At the end of those thirteen years, however, the mines at the Real were again ready for full production—for the last time until after the English adventurers arrived in 1824. Between 1794 and 1801,

[24] Statement made by Pedro Romero de Terreros, n.d., Títulos, RT, fols. 90v–93.

[25] *Ibid.*; "Report of Pedro José de Leóz, June 11, 1770" (cited hereafter as "Leóz Report"), in Luis Chávez Orozco, ed., *La situación del minero asalariado en la Nueva España a fines del siglo XVIII*, vol. 8 of *Documentos para la historia económica de México*, p. 41; José Rodrigo de Castelazo, *Manifiesto de la riqueza de la negociación de minas conocida por la veta Vizcaína*, pp. 9–10.

[26] Castelazo, *Manifiesto de la riqueza*, pp. 17–18; Burkart, *AMM*, I (1861), 23; Jorge L. Tamayo, "La minería de Nueva España en 1794," *El trimestre económico*, 10, no. 2 (July–September 1943), 292.

silver valued at some $6 million was raised.[27] In 1801 the count found it impossible to keep the lower workings of the central part of the Vizcaína free of water.

Having decided to abandon most of the deep levels of the mid-Vizcaína, Romero de Terreros, in 1801, directed that a map be drawn of the major productive areas below the Morán level. The plan, which was to figure prominently and perhaps disastrously in the scheme of mining operations of the British Real del Monte Company, was submitted to the count in December by Juan Bars, the chief administrator at the Real. It pictured an area some nine hundred yards in length along the Vizcaína vein, including the deep workings of Dolores, Guadalupe, San Cayetano, and Santa Teresa. From the point of view of future activities, its most significant information concerned grossly exaggerated estimates of the amount of rich and average-grade ore that was left underground.[28]

For the next eight years, the Spanish operation directed its main attention to the two extremities of the Vizcaína vein. The $500,000 worth of silver produced between 1801 and 1809, the year of the second count's death, came from the Dios Te Guíe mine, located in some new western Vizcaína claims, and from San Ramón at the eastern end of that lode.[29]

The third Count of Regla received fewer profits from Real del Monte than did either his father or his grandfather. When he assumed the management of the concern in 1809, he continued to exploit the works that had been laid open by his immediate predecessor.[30] But within two or three years the impact of the wars of independence in progress throughout much of New Spain was being felt. While testimony from the third count's mother in 1811 and from an anonymous reporter in 1816 makes it highly doubtful that insurgents caused any outright damage to the Romero de Te-

[27] Castelazo, *Manifiesto de la riqueza*, pp. 17–18; Burkart, *AMM*, I (1861), 23.

[28] Castelazo, *Manifiesto de la riqueza*, pp. 41–49; Burkart, *AMM*, I (1861), 23.

[29] AGN Minería, vol. 137, fols. 241–259; Castelazo, *Manifiesto de la riqueza*, pp. 19–20; Burkart, *AMM*, I (1861), 23.

[30] Burkart, *AMM*, I (1861), 23–24.

rreros mining properties at Real del Monte,[31] the pace of work in the Regla mines definitely slowed after the first, violent phase of revolutionary activity. In 1819 the exploitation of the third count's property, then in a state of nearly total decline, was suspended. During the 1809–1819 period as a whole, when mining operations were almost entirely confined to the new workings above the level of the Morán adit at both ends of the Vizcaína vein, Romero de Terreros netted merely $200,000.[32]

Before abandoning mining activities at Real del Monte altogether, the third count started driving a new drainage tunnel, which came to be known as the Aviadero adit and whose continuation would require no little investment of time, energy, and money by the British mining concern. The digging began in 1816 at a point some four thousand yards from the Vizcaína vein, near the road between Real del Monte and Omitlán, and was carried on intermittently for several years. When it became evident that ore production was insufficient to defray the cost of such an ambitious project, the Aviadero was abandoned.[33]

The question of mine drainage at Real del Monte was first explored by Bustamante, whose plan for an adit to reach the Vizcaína vein was a daring idea even as late as the 1730's, because adits (called *socavones* or *contraminas* in Spanish) were relatively uncommon in colonial Mexico. As the mid-eighteenth-century jurist and mining authority Francisco Xavier de Gamboa has pointed out, although mine owners benefiting from adits were required by law to help defray the expenses borne by the builders, individuals and companies were seldom willing to risk their capital in such an expensive undertaking.[34] The more common means of

---

[31] AGN Minería, vol. 29, expediente 1, no. 48; vol. 192, expediente 3, no. 3.

[32] Castelazo, *Manifiesto de la riqueza*, pp. 21–24; Burkart, *AMM*, I (1861), 24.

[33] Contract revision of 12 February 1829, in Libro en que se hallen, el preliminar con que la Sociedad de Aventureros formada en Londres convino celebrar una Compañia . . . con el S. D. Pedro Terreros Conde de Jala y de Regla . . . ; la escritura pública con que se afianzó el contrato, y los ynventarios judiciales . . . , RT, p. 156; Castelazo, *Manifiesto de la riqueza*, pp. 21–22, 24.

[34] "Comentarios," in *ODM*, ch. 26, Comentaries 8–10.

drainage employed from the sixteenth century on—and this only in the minority of mines that had well-constructed, perpendicular shafts—was to drag the water out of the shafts in bags attached to ropes that were rolled up on the drums of horse- or mule-operated windlass hoists called *malacates*.[35]

Despite the fact that the first Count of Regla was able to exploit at a profit various ore-bearing veins as the first general drainage of mines at Real del Monte progressed, the digging of the Morán adit was a long and arduous undertaking. Begun in July 1749, it was not completed until August 1762. An inspection of the project within days of its termination revealed that the tunnel was approximately 2,640 yards long, braced with thick timbers, and ventilated by some ten adit shafts (*lumbreras*) constructed at intervals from one end of the adit to the other.[36]

While the much-praised Morán adit made a great inroad on the drainage problem at Real del Monte, it by no means completely answered the question of unwelcome underground water. What of the parts of the various mines beneath the level of that great tunnel? Although unaffected by the natural runoff of water through the adit, they were still subject to flooding. To solve that phase of the over-all problem the House of Regla took a step backward—to the sixteenth-century practice of employing *malacates*. In 1794 the second count was using 19 of the crude horse whims to aid in the general drainage so that he might exploit ore ground below the Morán level. By 1801 the magnitude of the ever-present water problem can be seen by the fact that 28 *malacates*, 400 men, and 1,200 animals were employed, at an annual cost of approximately $125,000 to lift the water from the main workings, then about 100 yards below the adit level.[37]

The problems of draining the Regla mines were, then, clearly

[35] Humboldt, *Political Essay*, III, 241–242.

[36] Pedro Romero de Terreros' announcement of completion of the Morán adit, 2 September 1762, Record of inspection of the Morán adit, 6 September 1762, Certification of adit inspection by royal scribe at Pachuca, 7 September 1762, Títulos, RT, fols. 54–54v, 59–62, 62v–64v.

[37] Castelazo, *Manifiesto de la riqueza*, pp. 10–11; Burkart, *AMM*, I (1861), 23.

troublesome from the formation of the Bustamante–Romero de
Terreros partnership until the third Count of Regla ceased all mining activities. On the other hand, economically extracting silver
from its ore was less evidently irksome to the Reglas. Although
they were aware that their method of ore reduction by amalgamation was inefficient, they could tolerate the process because it had
long been used, because ore supplies were plentiful most of the
time, and because the Spanish colonial government provided mercury to Mexican miners at a low price.

The House of Regla, like most other mining establishments in
colonial Mexico, separated most of its silver from ore by the patio
amalgamation process, developed in the Real del Monte–Pachuca
district in the mid-sixteenth century by Bartolomé de Medina.[38]
The patio process was used to great advantage in Mexico as a
whole, largely because it required no fuel, which was in short supply in most mining districts. While the Real was one of the exceptional camps that had ample fuel in the form of extensive forests,
the patio method was nonetheless eagerly adopted and retained
throughout the colonial period. It allowed the working of certain
kinds of average or poor grades of ore that could not support the
high cost of smelting,[39] usually referred to as *azogue* ore (that
normally reserved for amalgamation with *azogue*, or quicksilver).

In spite of its obvious advantages over smelting, patio amalgamation had serious drawbacks. First, it was slow; a month or more
might pass before the silver was removed from the ore. Second, on
certain ores, usually referred to as "rebellious" or "refractory," it
was ineffective. That is, a fairly large percentage of the silver was
not separated from the rock and was therefore lost. If that percent-

[38] Bargalló, *Minería y metalurgia*, p. 120. Whether Medina "invented" the
patio process in Pachuca or merely carried it from Europe to Mexico has long
been the subject of dispute. In his summary of the question, Bargalló arrives at
the convincing conclusion that Medina learned in Europe the rudiments of a
method for extracting silver from its ore by making use of the metal's known
affinity for mercury, and that in Pachuca he transformed what in the Old
World was little more than a curiosity into a practical method for reducing
some of the low-grade ores common to Mexico (*ibid.*, pp. 115–120).

[39] Mendizábal, "Los minerales de Pachuca y Real del Monte," p. 258.

age was high enough, the ore, no matter how abundant, was virtually worthless. Third, the mine owner depending heavily on the patio process was also heavily dependent on a steady and relatively inexpensive supply of mercury. All three of those drawbacks would eventually cause concern, and in some cases harm, to the British Real del Monte Company.

The first step in the reduction of ore, whether it was to be treated by the patio amalgamation process or smelted, was breaking it into pieces small enough to pass through a one-inch hole in a rough cowhide screen. This was frequently done by hand, even by women; in large establishments, however, rude braying or stamping machines, usually powered by animals, though sometimes by men, were in use by the late eighteenth century. Concerns located near an abundant source of water, like the mills in the Real del Monte area that belonged to the House of Regla, employed water-, rather than animal- or man-driven, equipment.

The high-grade ore, generally that yielding one hundred or more ounces of silver per ton, was reserved for smelting, and the remainder pulverized in grinding apparatuses called *arrastres*. These circular troughs, which were sometimes sunk below the floor of the mill, were from eight to ten feet in diameter and about three feet deep. The bottoms and sides were lined with the hardest rock available. Overhead, suspended from a pole sunk in the center, were large wooden booms on which heavy stones were hung, so as to pass through the *arrastre* in a circular motion. The somewhat elevated front edges of these grinding stones received the ore, and the rear portion pulverized it into a very fine powder. The motive power for the grinding was usually provided by mules walking in a circle and pulling or pushing the booms round and round. Toward the end of the second stage, which lasted some twenty-four hours, water was added to the powder, making it into a slime.

The ground, wet ore was then removed to the great patio of the hacienda, usually paved with flagstone and sometimes as large as two acres in area. There it was deposited in *montones*, or piles, containing from fifteen to thirty-five quintals. When enough of these piles were accumulated, some forty or fifty *montones*, to constitute a *torta* (the name given to a huge heap of argentiferous mud), salt was sprinkled over them, together with vegetable ashes, pine bark, or manure. Depending on the nature of the mixture, lime or roasted copper pyrites (*magistral*) would be added. If the action of the salt on the slime seemed to generate too much heat, the lime "cooled" it; if, on the other hand, the mixture was too "cool," the copper pyrites "heated" it.

After several days, during which time the salt was allowed to become evenly distributed throughout the slime, the *torta* was ready for the quicksilver. The amount of this key and expensive ingredient used depended on the quantity of silver the ore was thought to contain. Generally, the mercury weighed some six times more than the silver assumed to be in the ore; that is, three or four pounds of mercury were applied for each mark of silver. The mass was thoroughly mixed by horses, mules, or, on occasion, by barefoot workmen who trampled the metallic mud. The object of the mixing, which was speeded up or suspended for short periods of time according to the state of the *torta*, was to allow the mercury to amalgamate with the silver. The process took several weeks, even months, depending on the climatic conditions and the skill of the employee who supervised the operations; the average length of time was five weeks. The mass was tested from time to time by the observation of the color of the amalgam left in the bottom of a wooden spoon (*jicara*) after it had been dipped into the *torta* and the earthy refuse washed away. If the mercury took on the color of lead, it was assumed that the chemical action necessary to amalgamation was taking place, the particular shade determining whether the mixture was too "hot" or too "cold." Here again, lime or copper pyrites would be added to counteract either extreme, and sometimes more quicksilver would also be applied.

When the amalgamation process was finally judged complete, the mud was thrown into stone or wooden vats, the earthy parts being washed away and the amalgam and free mercury left at the bottom. To separate the unmixed quicksilver from the final mass, the amalgam was squeezed through bags. In a kind of plastic state, it was then shaped into pyramids, and, covered by copper or bronze bell-shaped crucibles (*capellinas*), heated over a charcoal fire. The mercury thus became vaporized, left the silver, condensed on the inside of the crucible, and ran down into small troughs, where it could be gathered up and used again in another *torta*. The remaining metal—either pure silver or silver containing a small amount of gold, copper, or other mineral, and resembling a large piece of Swiss cheese—was then cast into bars.[40]

Although patio amalgamation required the skill and perseverance of all the workmen engaged in the lengthy and complex process, it was above all on the *azoguero* (mercury man or mud chemist) that the success or failure of the entire chain of operations depended. Aware of their importance, these "aristocrats of the industry" became a close-mouthed group, jealous of their position and resentful of criticism or suggestion. Their technical proficiency was based less on a knowledge of the chemical process that took place in the *torta* than on experience and rule of thumb.

Long before the first agents of the British Real del Monte Company arrived in Mexico, mine workers in the Real del Monte–Pachuca district had established a tradition of labor militancy. Between 1753 and 1755, for example, *barreteros* (first class mine workers, able to locate, drill, and blast holes and work with a gad) employed by the first Count of Regla fought with one of the count's recruitment agents and killed four men from among a gang of some eighty mineworkers whom Romero de Terreros had brought in from Guanajuato.[41]

In the latter half of 1766, Real del Monte was the scene of a labor dispute that was to drag on for nine years, despite repeated efforts of the Spanish colonial government to bring about a settlement. Pitted against the strong-willed Pedro Romero de Terreros were hot-tempered, sometimes violent workers. Their clash shut down most of the mines of the Spanish Real del Monte and vir-

---

[40] The description of the patio process is drawn mainly from Clement G. Motten, *Mexican Silver and the Enlightenment*, pp. 22–24; and Humboldt, *Political Essay*, III, 256–265.

[41] Account of occurrences at Real del Monte, 1753–1755, Títulos, RT, fols. 9–15v.

tually halted silver production from the biggest producer in the district for the whole nine-year period. The trouble stemmed from the first count's attempt to modify, or even to do away with, the traditional *partido* method of paying the *barreteros* and to reduce the wages of the lesser-skilled peons employed in his mines.[42]

When trouble at Real del Monte first broke out, at the end of July 1766, the *partido* was at the heart of the matter. Most of the Regla mines' *barreteros* and peons quit work and presented a complaint to the viceregal government against Romero de Terreros. The main charge made by them was that the mine owner was whittling away the time-honored method of ore-sharing payment, essentially by increasing the amount of ore that a *barretero* had to break away and bag in a normal twelve-hour shift, called the *tequio* or *tarea* (task), and by lessening the amount of ore that they were allowed to break away and bag as their *partido*.[43]

The *barreteros* charged that Romero de Terreros was trying to

[42] In his introduction to a collection of documents on the early stages of the strife, Luis Chávez Orozco sees the conflict as the equivalent of a modern strike movement, cuts through the *partido* issue, and concludes that Romero de Terreros was attempting to concentrate in his own hands all of the elements of production; he leans heavily to the side of the workers, yet compliments the Spanish officials on their unexpected fairness in dealing with the situation ("Introduction," *Conflicto de trabajo con los mineros de Real del Monte, año de 1766*, pp. 9–21). Writing twenty years earlier but without the volume of Chávez Orosco's documentation, Mendizábal advances a similar interpretation; in his opinion, however, several royal officials ignored the injustices done the mine workers and, as if by affinity, favored the first Count of Regla, a title Pedro Romero de Terreros acquired while the labor dispute was still in progress ("Los minerales de Pachuca y Real del Monte," pp. 300–304). Walter Howe gives a straightforward but truncated account of the dispute, pointing up its importance in convincing the Spanish government of the need for a general reform in the administration of the mining industry of colonial Mexico (*The Mining Guild of New Spain and Its Tribunal General, 1770–1821*, pp. 24–26). Romero de Terreros defends his ancestor without reservation and attributes the trouble to the perversity of the mine workers (*Conde de Regla*, pp. 93–101). Bernard E. Bobb takes no sides in relating the story of the conflict; he relies almost entirely on Viceroy Antonio María de Bucareli's secondhand account of events that preceded his administration and reports of his efforts to settle the dispute (*The Viceregency of Antonio María Bucareli in New Spain, 1771–1799*, pp. 177–180).

[43] "Quejas dadas por los operarios del Real del Monte, ante oficiales reales de Pachuca," in Chávez Orozco, *Conflicto de trabajo*, pp. 25–34, 36.

cut the size of the *partido* from two bags of *partido* ore for every four bags of *tequio* ore, to one bag for four. That point was thrashed out at a direct confrontation between the mine owner and his employees. Held in the gallery of the Santa Teresa mine on 14 August 1766, the encounter developed into a lengthy and at times heated argument between Romero de Terreros, with several officers of his concern, and twelve *barreteros* chosen to represent their fellow workers, some two thousand strong, who were congregated outside. Nonetheless an agreement was reached, in which Romero de Terreros said that if the *barreteros* met their *tequio* requirement promptly and honestly (in other words, put the same quality of ore in the *partido* and *tarea* bags), they could take whatever *partido* they wished, "not only two bags but half the mine."[44]

Although the argument on the *partido* did not end the strike, the essence of that accord eventually received the official sanction of a government representative sent to settle the over-all dispute. It was after a second bitter clash between the mine owner and his workers (on the twin issues of his refusal to return peons' wages to four reals, or fifty cents, a day, from the three reals to which they had been cut, and the use of force by recruitment agents and mine administrators in trying to persuade both *barreteros* and peons to go underground[45]), that Francisco Xavier de Gamboa investigated the labor troubles and issued, on 13 September 1766, a set of regulations for the operation of the Real del Monte mines. Gamboa accepted the mine owner's position that his workers must be honest in raising *tequio* and *partido* ore, but he also accepted the *barreteros'* argument for a *partido* amounting to half the ore they raised over and above the task set for their twelve-hour shift.[46] There the *partido* matter stood for a number of years, although not unchallenged.

The labor peace based on Gamboa's regulations lasted little more

44 "Diligencias practicadas," in *ibid.*, pp. 51–57.

45 *Ibid.*, pp. 57–58; Viceroy Bucareli of New Spain to King Charles III of Spain, 24 December 1771, in Rómulo Velasco Ceballos, ed., *La administración de D. Fray Antonio Maria de Bucareli y Ursúa*, II, 361.

46 "Diligencias practicadas," in Chávez Orozco, *Conflicto de trabajo*, pp. 59–110.

than a month, but even after it was broken over the workers' refusal to accept a mine captain appointed by Romero de Terreros,[47]
the viceregal government left unaltered and still binding the code
drawn up by the famed jurist and mining authority. A full-scale
work stoppage then settled over most of the Real del Monte mines,
to last until 1775. During that period, the *partido* came under
heavy attack from several government officials. In 1770 Mayor
Pedro José de Leóz of Tulancingo prepared a report on the de-
pressed state of mining at the Real and a set of recommendations
for restoring good times. To Leóz the single, overriding cause for
the deplorable conditions was the *partido*, and he insisted that the
foremost requirement for bringing prosperity back to the Real del
Monte–Pachuca district was to bury forever the concept of the
partido.[48]

Notwithstanding the fact that Leóz's recommendations received
the enthusiastic approval and support of an Audiencia attorney
named Areche and Visitor-General José de Gálvez,[49] they were not
actually put into effect. Indeed, the viceroy was reluctant to sanction those general rules pressed by Gálvez that would have eliminated the *partido* from New Spain.[50] As a result, Gamboa's code
for the Real del Monte mines remained technically in force until
the settlement of the long strike. Viceroy Bucareli, who finally
accomplished labor peace in the Real del Monte–Pachuca district,
also concluded that it would be imprudent to attempt to do away
with the time-honored *partido* all over Mexico. As he had to ap-

[47] "Causa criminal a pedimento de Don Bernardino Díaz . . . contra Patricio
Nolasco, Juan Barbosa y Juan Luis, y los demas que resultaren culpados," in
ibid., pp. 123–143.

[48] "Leóz report," in Chávez Orozco, *Documentos para la historia económica de
México*, VIII, 1–48.

[49] "Areche report," in *ibid.*, pp. 50–89; "Oficio con que el Visitador Don José
de Gálvez remitió la instrucción para el restablecimiento de las minas de Pachuca y Real del Monte, 18 febrero de 1771," in Luis Chávez Orozco, ed., *Los
salarios y el trabajo en México durante el siglo XVIII*, vol. III of *Documentos
para la historia económica de México*, pp. 30–39 .

[50] Mendizábal, "Los minerales de Pachuca y Real del Monte," pp. 301–302;
Bucareli to Charles III, 24 December 1771, in Velasco Ceballos, *La administración de Bucareli*, II, 361, 363–364.

prove of regulations for the whole colony, not just one district, he accepted a provision whereby mine owners and their employees were free to make agreements for straight salary payments, mixed salary and *partido*, or *partido* alone.[51] Thus, when the first Count of Regla reopened his mines in 1775, the *partido* was still the rule. It remained so until the third count halted all work in the Regla mines many years later, and its concept had not been forgotten when the British operators arrived at Real del Monte.

The last major development work undertaken by the third Count of Regla—the Aviadero adit—eventually led him to look for outside financial assistance, first in Mexico and then abroad. With the other mining works at Real del Monte, the Aviadero was abandoned in 1819; a year later José Rodrigo de Castelazo, the administrator of the count's mines, published a treatise intended to attract investment in the Romero de Terreros concern. He pointed out that, inasmuch as the third count lacked the necessary capital to restore his mining establishment, he was considering the formation of a company of shareholders which, at a relatively small cost to each investor, would accomplish that end.[52] Castelazo emphasized the benefits to be gained from completion of the Aviadero adit, saying that once it was finished the government would be compelled to open another mint to handle the silver production of Real del Monte alone.[53]

Despite the inducements held out by Pedro Romero de Terreros, no capital was forthcoming and no company established in New Spain to revive his ruined mining concern. Doubtless the renewal of insurgent activity in the colony under Iturbide's leadership drew the count's attention away from Real del Monte. By the time he was again ready to seek outside financial assistance, Mexico had gained its independence. Moreover, the fledgling nation had already taken steps that were to make it possible for Romero de Te-

[51] Bucareli to Charles III, 24 December 1771, in Velasco Ceballos, *La administración de Bucareli*, II, 365–372; Bobb, *Viceregency of Antonio María Bucareli*, pp. 177–178.

[52] Castelazo, *Manifiesto de la riqueza*, p. 6.

[53] *Ibid.*, pp. 26–28.

rreros—and other mine owners as well—to obtain assistance from foreigners.

The first government of independent Mexico, the Regency, which held office from September 1821 to May 1822, showed a special interest in raising the mining industry from the decadence into which it had fallen during the period following Miguel Hidalgo's revolt in 1810. At least three of the members of its advisory board were, in fact, closely connected with mining matters: Juan Francisco Azcárate, José María Fagoaga, and Pedro Romero de Terreros.[54] The first and third of these influential men were later to lease mining properties to the British Real del Monte Company, and the second to its companion firm, the Bolaños Company.

The preamble to a February 1822 decree issued by the Regency noted the "urgent need to furnish this industry all available means to contribute to its increased prosperity, on which that of the empire depends."[55] Eliminating both the normal taxes of the colonial period and special ones imposed during the wars of independence, the order substituted a single 3-per-cent tax on the "true value" of silver and gold. It also limited the fees that the country's mints could charge for coining, assaying, and separating gold from silver. On paying the new mining tax, the owners of precious metals were free to dispose of the bullion in any way they wished. The decree also declared quicksilver, whether produced domestically or imported from abroad, absolutely free of tax, and it pledged the government to furnish blasting powder to mine owners at cost.[56]

During the period of Agustín de Iturbide's short-lived empire and of the provisional triumvirate that succeeded it, the Mexican government continued to display an interest in the re-establishment of mining prosperity and even looked to foreign participation in that industry. Immediately before his fall, in March 1823, Iturbide issued a decree clarifying the means by which the 2-per-cent

[54] Robert A. Potash, *El Banco de Avío de México: El fomento de la industria, 1821–1846*, p. 29; *Gaceta imperial de México*, 4 October 1821, pp. 14–15.

[55] Decreto de la Junta Provisional, 20 de febrero de 1822, "Ordenanzas, leyes y órdenes de minería," in *ODM*, p. 64.

[56] *Ibid.*, pp. 65–66.

tax on silver and gold was to be computed and collected.[57] In October of that year, the triumvirate published an order that opened the way for foreign participation. The decree suspended those articles of the *Recopilación de Castilla*, the *Recopilación de las Indias*, and the 1783 Mining Ordinances that had barred foreigners from the mining industry of colonial Mexico. The extension of rights to outsiders was, however, qualified. Nonnationals could help finance the rehabilitation of mines in exchange for a certain share of profits to be made, but they could not register claims on new mines or on old ones whose titles had reverted to the government because their former owners had not worked them continuously in accordance with mining law. A final provision in that important decree restated the exemption of mercury from all duties but required the payment of the *alcabala* (a sales tax imposed on many exchanges of goods) on all other articles used by the industry.[58]

In looking abroad for aid in reviving the mining industry, newly independent Mexico candidly admitted its desperate need for capital not available within its borders. Lucas Alamán, the man most directly responsible for opening the Mexican mining industry to foreign penetration and himself an organizer of the British-financed United-Mexican Mining Association, expressed what was probably a general opinion in government circles when he praised actions to allow "opulent foreigners" to participate as financiers in the hitherto closed mining industry.[59] To the chronic shortage of investment funds was added a flight of capital, precisely when money was badly needed to repair damaged mining properties and to bring about long-delayed technical improvements. That flight, which got under way immediately after the dissolution of the viceregal government in 1821, stemmed from the Spaniards' fear of reprisals at the hands of the Mexicans. Estimates of the amount of

[57] Decreto de 24 de marzo de 1823, "Ordenanzas, leyes y órdenes de minería," in *ibid.*, pp. 66–67.
[58] Decreto del Supremo Poder Ejecutivo, 8 de octubre de 1823, "Ordenanzas, leyes y órdenes de minería," in *ibid.*, p. 67.
[59] "Memoria que el secretario de estado y del despacho de relaciones esteriores e interiores presenta al . . . Congreso . . . [el] 8 de noviembre de 1823," in Lucas Alamán, *Documentos diversos*, I, 93–94.

capital withdrawn from Mexico in the first several years of its independence vary widely. The British consul at Jalapa wrote in 1824 that "it does not fall short" of $140 million.[60] Another estimate made that year placed the sum at $100 million.[61] On the other hand, Henry George Ward, the first British chargé d'affaires in newly independent Mexico, asserted that only $36 million had been withdrawn.[62] Whatever the true figure, the fact remains that influential members of the earliest governments of Mexico recognized their fledgling country's severe capital shortage and looked to foreigners for help.

In the context of the general Mexican willingness to accept foreign economic aid, especially if it were intended for the stagnant mining industry, the third Count of Regla's agent repeated his public appeal for assistance. In 1823 José Rodrigo de Castelazo published a second edition of his treatise on the mines of Real del Monte, again with the purpose of attracting investment in a rehabilitation scheme. The later manifesto restated the former wealth and future possibilities of the mines. The Aviadero adit played as prominent a role as it had in the 1820 document. For a second time, the proprietor of the mines of the Real announced his willingness to entertain investment proposals. Castelazo's second treatise included the 1801 description of the ore ground remaining in the deep workings of the Vizcaína vein.[63]

[60] Charles Mackensie to George Canning, 24 July 1824, cited by R. A. Humphreys, ed., *British Consular Reports on the Trade and Politics of Latin America, 1824–1826*, p. 203.

[61] Lionel Hervey to Canning, 18 January 1824, cited by Charles K. Webster, ed., *Britain and the Independence of Latin America, 1812–1830: Select Documents from the Foreign Office Archives*, I, 443.

[62] Ward, *Mexico in 1827*, II, 36.

[63] José Rodrigo de Cástelazo, *Manifiesto de las riquezas que han producido y actualmente contienen las celebradas minas de las vetas Vizcaína y Santa Brígida*, pp. 1–45. There is little difference in the contents of the two editions of Castelazo's work, but a striking one in language. The 1820 document is royalist, whereas the 1823 version is republican. The references to "His Gracious Majesty," "the royal treasury," and "the altar and the throne," so prevalent in the original, are absent in the revised edition. The earlier work, furthermore, emphasizes both Romero de Terreros' many titles and memberships in royal societies and Castelazo's own more modest connection with the royal Mining

Since Castelazo's 1823 manifesto attracted no capital investment in Mexico, Romero de Terreros turned to London, hoping to benefit by the modified mining ordinances. The third count commissioned the Robert Staples Company, a British commercial firm with offices in Mexico City, to propose investment in the Real del Monte mines to interested parties in London. As an inducement, Castelazo's document was carried to England by Vicente Rivafinoli, an Italian friend of the count. The entire matter was placed in the hands of Thomas Kinder, Staples' partner in London.⁶⁴

Guild; in the later edition most of the count's titles and his participation in associations are omitted, and Castelazo describes himself merely as a mining expert and administrator of the Real del Monte concern.

⁶⁴ William Parish Robertson, *A Visit to Mexico by the West India Islands, Yucatan and United States, with Observations and Adventures on the Way*, II, 168; "Cases Argued and Determined in the Court of Chancery . . . March 1825, Kinder v. Taylor," *LJ*, 3 (1825), 68–69.

2. Formation in London

WHEN PEDRO ROMERO DE TERREROS TURNED TO GREAT BRITAIN for help in the rehabilitation of his mines, he was approaching a nation that was not only extremely well disposed toward investing in foreign ventures but specifically interested in penetrating the hitherto closed Spanish American empire as a field for that investment. Ever since 1810, the year in which England secured the right to trade with the Spanish colonies, its manufacturers and shipping concerns had been pressing for closer commercial ties with that part of the New World. Nor were the British unaware of the importance that the mining of precious metals had for centuries assumed in the economy of the Spanish possessions. By 1821, when Mexico gained its independence, Great Britain was, moreover, on the threshold of a new economic era, in which the free-trade doctrine and overseas investment would exert an ever-stronger appeal and in which, partly because of a decline in the yield of government-funded securities, large amounts of idle capital would be in the hands of the merchant class. What both the British government and British capitalists were seeking, on the disruption of the Spanish Empire in America, was not territory but trade and bullion.[1]

The first step toward British exploitation of Mexican mines was necessarily a diplomatic one. Since Great Britain had become aligned with Spain in opposition to Napoleonic France, its citizens could not participate in mining ventures in the Kingdom of New Spain until that alliance was either reshaped or done away with. Between 1810 and 1820 the British government attempted to mediate the disputes between Spain and its straying colonies in America, but between 1820 and 1824 it shifted to a policy of preparing to recognize the independence of those colonies. In 1825 Great Britain formally recognized Mexico, Gran Colombia, and Argentina as independent nations.[2] Thus, at the time the Count of Regla sent his investment proposal to London in 1823, the political as well as economic climate favored British participation in his mining enterprise.

In the 1820's the migration of British capital to all parts of the world reached a peak, with a wave of speculative interest sweeping the country in 1824 and 1825. The enthusiasm was based on the belief, fostered by the promoters of insurance and mining firms, that much money could be made in a short time by the formation of joint-stock companies. Although the purpose of such concerns was of secondary importance, many of their backers thought that investment would be attracted by the possibility of using steam engines in some way. Not the least active of the promoters, especially those who singled out the steam engine as a means of gaining great wealth, were those who drew the attention of potential investors to the new nations of the Western Hemisphere. Numerous periodicals, including the reputable *Morning Chronicle, Times,*

[1] Newton R. Gilmore, "British Mining Ventures in Early National Mexico" (Ph.D. dissertation, University of California, 1956), pp. 1, 9; Charles K. Webster, ed., "Introduction," *Britain and the Independence of Latin America, 1812–1830: Select Documents from the Foreign Office Archives,* I, 9–10.

[2] Gilmore, "British Mining Ventures," p. 1; Webster, *Britain and the Independence of Latin America,* I, 12.

and *Quarterly Review*, devoted a large amount of space to Latin American affairs. In pointing out the investment possibilities in the former Spanish colonies, both the *Chronicle* and the *Times* stressed Mexico and its fabled mining resources.[3]

With such encouragement, it is not surprising that ventures for working foreign mines were organized between 1820 and 1824, once British recognition of the independence of the Spanish American nations seemed probable. By the end of 1825, at least twenty-eight separate concerns had been established for the exploitation of gold, silver, and other minerals in Latin America. Seven of them—Anglo-Mexican, Bolaños, Guanajuato, Mexican, Real del Monte, Tlalpujahua, and United-Mexican—proposed to work mines in Mexico.[4]

In their prospectuses those companies held out numerous inducements to potential investors. In general, they promised that their efforts would be confined to such Mexican mines as, in the past, had proved to be especially rich. Organizers of the enterprises recommended that interested persons read Humboldt's classic *Political Essay on the Kingdom of New Spain* in order to gain "detailed information" on the mining districts they proposed entering. Most of the concerns emphasized a close association between English and Mexican contributors to the mining ventures, and some even included Mexicans in their boards of directors; the United-Mexican Mining Association, for example, noted with pride that Lucas Alamán, the Mexican minister of foreign and domestic affairs, was a board member. In many instances blocks of stock were reserved for sale in Mexico. Finally, and probably most important, the companies proposed introducing modern European mining techniques and machinery, particularly steam engines for drainage, in the operation of the Mexican mines.[5]

[3] Leland H. Jenks, *The Migration of British Capital to 1875*, pp. 52–53; Gilmore, "British Mining Ventures," pp. 7–8.

[4] Henry English, *A General Guide to the Companies Formed for Working Foreign Mines, passim*; J. Fred Rippy, "Latin America and the British Investment 'Boom' of the 1820's," *Journal of Modern History*, 19 (June 1947), 128; Gilmore, "British Mining Ventures," p. 10.

[5] English, *General Guide*, pp. 5, 15, 32, 45, 55, 56, 68.

One of the seven enterprises seems to have failed almost immediately. Henry English made the following comment on the Guanajuato Company: "Of this Company little can be said: had the contents of the Prospectus been true, of which we entertain our doubts, the success of the Company was certain."[6] The other six at least placed an establishment in Mexico. According to Henry George Ward, all of the concerns included in English's 1825 list, except the Guanajuato Company, were still operating in 1827. Two companies not mentioned by English had, moreover, made a brief appearance: the Mexican Mine Company, which collapsed in 1826, and the Catorce Company, which was in a state of disorganization at the time Ward was writing. None of the original British concerns appears to have survived past midcentury except United-Mexican, and it was by then so reorganized that it could hardly be considered the same company.[7]

The Real del Monte Company

The authority to seek English investors in connection with the Count of Regla's plan to rehabilitate his Real del Monte mines, which had been granted to the Robert Staples Company in Mexico, was transferred in the fall of 1823 to Staples' London partner, Thomas Kinder. Having heard of the "great success and experience" of a John Taylor in mining ventures, Kinder approached him with the proposal. The two agreed that a company should be formed to work Romero de Terreros' mines, and perhaps others in Mexico as well, and from their association the British Real del Monte Company was born—and nearly dissolved in a legal dispute within a year and a half of their meeting.[8]

Aside from his participation in the establishment of the British Real del Monte and his part in an unsuccessful lawsuit against

[6] *Ibid.*, p. 88.

[7] H. G. Ward, *Mexico in 1827*, II, 64–68, 107; Gilmore, "British Mining Ventures," pp. 108–109, 182, 190; J. Fred Rippy, "British Investments in Latin America, End of 1913," *Journal of Modern History*, 19 (September 1947), 233.

[8] "Cases Argued and Determined in the Court of Chancery . . . March 1825, Kinder v. Taylor," *LJ*, 3, (1825), 68–69.

John Taylor in 1825, Thomas Kinder had little or nothing to do with the company's history. Taylor, on the other hand, not only played a key role in the formation of the concern but managed its affairs until shortly before its dissolution in 1848 and, during the subsequent two decades, maintained an active interest in the Mexican company that succeeded it. In his negotiations with Kinder, Taylor identified himself as the "treasurer and administrator" of the Mines of the Union and others in Cornwall and Devon, of the "privileged mines" of the Duke of Devonshire, and of the mines of the Earl of Grosvenor; as the inspector of the mines belonging to the Royal Hospital of Greenwich; and as a member of the council and the treasurer of the Geological Society of London.[9] While helping to found the British company, Taylor published in condensed form some of the data concerning Mexico that had appeared in Humboldt's *Political Essay* and *Geognostical Essay on the Superposition of Rocks*. In his introduction Taylor noted that as early as 1819 he had had occasion to "consider some circumstances connected with the Mexican mines," having been consulted by a British firm that was planning to send a steam engine to Mexico for use in a mine.[10]

The agreement between Taylor and Kinder called for an original capital of £200,000 ($1,000,000), divided into five hundred shares valued at £400 ($2,000) each. Taylor reserved the right to distribute three hundred shares between himself and his associates, and Kinder had claim to two hundred shares, fifty of which he might sell to interested parties in Mexico before being required to pay the first installment on their purchase price. At a preliminary meeting of persons desirous of forming the company, held in London on 16 January 1824, Taylor was authorized to negotiate with Kinder, who was acting on behalf of the Count of Regla, for the lease of the latter's mines, and also with a Colonel John Murphy for the acqui-

---

9 AN, Manuel García Romero, 1824, document 3, following fol. 78.
10 John Taylor, ed., *Selections from the Works of the Baron de [sic] Humboldt, Relating to the Climate, Inhabitants, Productions, and Mines of Mexico*, pp. viii–ix, xxiv.

sition of the Morán mine in Real del Monte, which was owned by the colonel's brother Tomás. On 4 February a second meeting was held, bringing into existence a corporate body to be known as the Company of Adventurers in the Mines of Real del Monte. The participants agreed to appoint a Committee of Management; to empower Taylor, on behalf of the company, to enter into contracts with Kinder and Murphy for the Regla and Morán mines; to raise £200,000 by the issuance of five hundred shares of stock; to authorize the subscription of those shares, requiring immediate payment of 5 per cent of the purchase price for each share taken; to instruct the law firm of Martineau and Malton to prepare a deed of settlement, or to apply for an act of Parliament, for the regulation of the company; and to charge the Committee of Management with submitting the deed to a general meeting of stockholders for approval and adoption.[11]

Armed with the powers conferred upon him by the Real del Monte proprietors, Taylor signed agreements on 6 March 1824 with Kinder, representing the Count of Regla, and with John Murphy, acting for his brother Tomás, for the company's lease of the numerous Real del Monte mines owned by the two absent Mexican parties. The contract with Kinder stated that the newly formed British company was to receive the "management and direction" of the mines of Guadalupe, Santa Teresa, San Cayetano, Dolores, and Santa Brígida, and of all others belonging to the Count of Regla in Real del Monte, "for the purpose of their being rehabilitated by means of steam engines or other machinery." The company was to retain control over those mines for twenty years, under certain specific conditions. The most important articles, which were ratified by a second agreement entered into by agents of the company and the count himself, had to do with the English firm's control over the mining property, the method of dividing profits, and

[11] *LJ*, III (1825), 69. Although the *Law Journal* gives the name of the owner of the Morán mine as "James Murphy, Esq.," the Real del Monte Company Papers consistently refer to him as "Thomas Murphy" and the Archivo de Notarías as "Tomás Murphy."

the company's obligation to introduce steam engines and English mining techniques in the working of the Real del Monte mines. The contract further stipulated that the British concern would immediately send agents to Mexico to inspect the count's mines and his titles to them. No provision was made for an advance payment to Romero de Terreros.[12]

The contract with Murphy entitled the British Real del Monte Company to work the Morán mine for twenty-one years. Though in most respects identical to the agreement between Taylor and Kinder, in one it was markedly different: the English firm was required to make an annual payment of £2,000 ($10,000) to the mine owner as an advance against his share of the profits. For his part Tomás Murphy was to see to it that his personal creditors and his former partners in the working of the Morán mine would in no way harass the company.[13]

During the period of contract negotiations and of the first meetings, a pamphlet was issued in London to publicize the aims of the new concern and to attract purchasers of shares. Entitled *Prospectus of a Company for Working the Regla Mines, in Mexico*, it followed the general pattern of other companies' advance notices that were brought out about the same time. In addition, the Real del Monte Company's preliminary statement mentioned a proposal received from Mexico for the rehabilitation of the Count of Regla's mines, according to which the Aviadero adit would be completed so as to drain the property in the Real well below the level at which the deep workings had been suspended in 1801. That scheme, the *Prospectus* said, was deemed inadvisable "in the opinion of those who have been consulted on the subject in England," and a "more

12 AN, Manuel García Romero, 1824, document 3, following fol. 78.
13 AN, Manuel García Romero, 1824, fols. 83v–86v; English, *General Guide*, p. 96. The document on file at the Archivo de Notarías is a copy not of the original contract signed in London by Taylor and John Murphy, acting on behalf of Tomás Murphy, but of a contract entered into by agents of the company and Tomás Murphy's representative on 1 July 1824 in Mexico City, and described in the document itself as a ratification of the earlier contract negotiated in London.

effective plan" would probably be used "to drain the Mines at once, and thus to bring them more rapidly into a productive state."[14]

Less than three weeks after the contracts for the Regla and Morán mines were signed, the founders of the British company dispatched the first group of officers and technicians who would conduct the concern's affairs at Real del Monte. On 25 March 1824 the fifteen men sailed from Liverpool for New York and Tampico. Led by James Vetch, who was to serve as the company's chief commissioner in Mexico, the party comprised the two other commissioners, John Rule, who would also be the mine manager at Real del Monte, and Vicente Rivafinoli; two mine captains; and ten others.[15]

The three commissioners were jointly granted power of attorney to act for the Committee of Management and for John Taylor, the instrument to that effect having been signed in London by the committee on 19 March and by Taylor on the following day. Besides being authorized to ratify the 6 March contracts with the Count of Regla and Tomás Murphy and to agree to any reasonable changes that might be desired by either of the parties in Mexico, the commissioners were permitted to cancel either or both of the contracts, should they find Romero de Terreros' or Murphy's titles to the Real del Monte mines to be defective, and to sign new agreements with those two parties or with the owners of other mines located in the Real or elsewhere in Mexico. They, and particularly Vetch, were also empowered to hire such persons as they considered essential, remunerating them as they saw fit; to dismiss and replace employees; to modify the regulations governing the conduct of the company's affairs and its personnel, when necessary;

---

[14] The *Prospectus* appears verbatim in English, *General Guide*, pp. 54–56.

[15] *Ibid.*, p. 96; Escritura de Compañía formada por el S. Conde de Jala y de Regla, de las minas y haciendas de beneficio de metales, de que es dueño en el Mineral del Monte y Zimapán, con la Sociedad Ynglesa Europea . . . , in Libro en que se hallan, el preliminar con que la Sociedad de Aventureros formada en Londres convino celebrar una Compañía . . . con el S. D. Pedro Terreros Conde de Jala y de Regla . . . ; la escritura pública con que se afianzó el contrato, y los ynventarios judiciales, RT, p. 56.

and to enter into such contracts or agreements as might further the effective working of the mines in the company's control.[16]

Of the three original commissioners, James Vetch and John Rule were to play important roles in the history of the English firm; Vicente Rivafinoli, on the other hand, remained with the company but a short time. A captain in the British Royal Engineers at the time of his Real del Monte Company appointment, Vetch had seen duty in Spain between 1810 and 1814. Even after his severance from the concern in 1827, he spent a good part of the next eight years in Mexico in the employ of the Anglo-Mexican and United-Mexican mining companies. On his return to England in 1835, he became associated with various public and private engineering enterprises. He died in 1869 at the age of eighty.[17]

John Rule's association with Real del Monte was to last nearly twenty years, during half of which time he held the highest over-seas position in the English company. In March 1824, on receiving power of attorney before his departure for Mexico, Rule gave as his residence the town of Camborne in the county of Cornwall. He later described himself as having been "brought up as a practical miner."[18] With his two brothers, he established in Mexico a branch of the Rule family whose descendants are still to be found in the Pachuca–Real del Monte district.

In a midcentury travel account of Mexico that sketches the history of the Real del Monte Company, Vicente Rivafinoli is referred to as an "Italian friend" of the third Count of Regla. Shortly after his arrival in Mexico with Vetch and Rule, he returned to London, where he helped form the Tlalpujahua Company, and within a year he was back in Mexico as its director.[19]

[16] AN, Manuel García Romero, 1824, docs. 4–6, 10–12, following fol. 78.

[17] Leslie Stephen and Sidney Lee, eds., *The Dictionary of National Biography*, XX, 292–293. It may have been in Spain, during the campaign against Napoleon's army, that Vetch acquired the knowledge of Spanish shown in his letters on file in the Real del Monte Company Papers.

[18] AN, Manuel García Romero, 1824, doc. 6, following fol. 78; John Rule to John Taylor, 27 January 1838, 1838 CG 39.

[19] William Parish Robertson, *A Visit to Mexico, by the West India Islands, Yucatan and United States, with Observations and Adventures on the Way*, II,

The British Real del Monte Company was given its corporate structure as a joint-stock company in London on 16 August 1824, when a deed of settlement was adopted. Provisions made in that instrument both specified the original capital of the company and defined the means by which additional money might be raised. Pursuant to earlier decisions of the founders, the initial capital was set at £200,000, divided into five hundred shares. Whatever funds might become necessary, after those first shares were fully sub-scribed and paid for, were to be derived from contributions by the proprietors or from the sale of additional stock. The amount that might be acquired by contributions was limited to £50,000 ($250,000). Should the sale of stock be decided upon, a special meeting of the proprietors was to determine the number, price, and method of payment of the new shares. Those proprietors would be entitled to pre-empt the new issue, in proportion to the number of shares each held in the capital of the concern.[20]

Important duties were assigned to the regular and special meet-ings of the proprietors. A regular meeting, known as the Annual General Court, was to be convened in February. Special General Courts might be called at any time. The ordinary business handled by regular meetings could be conducted on the basis of a simple majority of the proprietors present and voting. On the other hand, extraordinary matters, dealt with by special meetings, required a three-fourths vote for passage. The consideration of such issues as an increase in capital, the drafting of new regulations or the amending or repeal of existing ones, and the dissolution of the company was reserved for the Special General Courts.[21] The deed of settlement placed the management of the Real del Monte Com-

---

168; AN, Manuel García Romero, 1825, docs. 2, 3, following fol. 113; and fols. 114–121v; *Gaceta diaria de México*, 4 June 1825, p. 4.

[20] *LJ*, 3 (1825), 70–71. The deed of settlement being unavailable, the state-ments regarding its provisions are based on the issue of the *Law Journal* that covers the Kinder-Taylor suit and on transactions of company stockholders' meetings, which describe fully the scope of that instrument.

[21] *Ibid.*, p. 71; *Proceedings at the General Courts of Proprietors of the Real del Monte Mining Company* (cited hereafter as RdM *Proceedings*), SGC, 16 March 1842, pp. i–ii.

pany in the hands of a Court of Directors, composed of twelve members to be chosen from among the proprietors; that body was, however, to act "subject and without prejudice to the powers vested in the general courts." In establishing and defining the powers of the Court of Directors, the deed specified that the actions taken on behalf of the concern by the former Committee of Management or by John Taylor, including the signing of contracts and the granting of powers of attorney, were to continue in force and be binding on the proprietors. It appointed the members of the original court, under the chairmanship of Thomas Fowell Buxton, M.P., and named John Taylor as manager.[22]

Besides the deed of settlement, the company was governed by rules of procedure adopted the same year. Despite certain changes made in those regulations between 1824 and 1848—among the most important of which was a reduction in the number of directors, to nine in 1830 and to seven in 1842—the corporate structure was to remain basically the same throughout the life of the British concern. During the Kinder-Taylor lawsuit of 1825, the structure was praised by the Lord Chancellor, who suggested it as a model, should the Bank of England, the East India Company, or the South Sea Company want a new charter.[23]

The Bolaños Company

While the Real del Monte Company was being founded in London, John Taylor and Thomas Kinder had a falling out over the disposition of some of the latter's shares in the concern, and, more important, over the acquisition of rights to work certain mines in another of Mexico's fabled silver districts: Bolaños. The dispute eventually led to a lawsuit in which Kinder challenged the legal existence of the fledgling Real del Monte enterprise. Inasmuch as Kinder lost his case, however, the lawsuit's chief interest to this study rests in the light its records shed on the formation of both

---

[22] *LJ*, 3 (1825), 71; RdM *Proceedings*, SGC, 16 March 1842, pp. i–ii; English, *General Guide*, p. 53.

[23] RdM *Proceedings*, SGC, 16 March 1842, pp. i–ii; *LJ*, 3 (1825), 78.

Real del Monte and the not altogether separate Bolaños Company, whose history parallels that of the former concern.

The idea of working mines in the Bolaños district in what is to-day the Mexican state of Jalisco and described by Humboldt as the fifth richest in New Spain,[24] seems to have occurred to Taylor, Kinder, and the other founders of the Real del Monte Company sometime before the first English party was sent to Mexico. In the records of the trial Kinder reported Taylor's instruction to Captain Vetch and to the other two commissioners who led the group: in the event the contract with the Count of Regla was not confirmed, they should look for other mines to be worked by the company, among them the mines of Bolaños. Taylor denied that he had so instructed his agents and insisted that he had sought contracts for mines in the Bolaños district with the intention of having them worked by a company made up exclusively of "his own particular friends."[25] In other words, a corporation that quite pointedly did not include Thomas Kinder would be formed to profit from what-ever agreement regarding Bolaños Taylor's agents might make once they reached Mexico. Excitement at the prospect of reaping benefits larger than originally anticipated, then, split the English founders before an ounce of silver had been raised at Real del Monte, Bolaños, or elsewhere in Mexico.

In the Kinder-Taylor lawsuit, the former, plaintiff in the affair, charged that he had been denied a share in the Bolaños enterprise and asked the Court of Chancery not only to direct Taylor and his friends to grant him his fair portion of Bolaños but also to dissolve the Real del Monte Company if necessary in order to do that.

[24] Alexander de [*sic*] Humboldt, *Political Essay on the Kingdom of New Spain*, III, 138. The four districts that outranked Bolaños in Humboldt's list of thirteen are Guanajuato, Catorce, Zacatecas, and Real del Monte.

[25] *LJ*, 3 (1825), 74. The powers of attorney executed by Taylor and the Committee of Management for the three commissioners sent to Mexico did not mention Bolaños specifically. They merely authorized the agents to enter into contracts with "the owners and proprietors of any other mines situated in Real del Monte or elsewhere in the Province of Mexico," under terms similar to those of the agreements concluded with the Count of Regla and Tomás Murphy (AN, Manuel García Romero, 1824, docs. 6, 12, following fol. 78).

Taylor's defense was, in essence, that he had a right to establish a
new company for the working of the Bolaños mines and to include
or exclude such Real del Monte proprietors as he saw fit in the
second firm. After hearing a complex argument on the part of the
plaintiff and an equally complex argument on the part of the de-
fendant, the Lord Chancellor, in what appears to be a hair-splitting
judgment, agreed almost completely with Taylor. The result of
the lawsuit was, therefore, to allow both the Bolaños and Real del
Monte companies to exist as legal entities. Indeed, the Lord Chancellor sought to force a true separation of the two concerns; he
voided a resolution passed by a Real del Monte Company Special
General Court on 11 February 1825 that would have permitted the
employment of company officers in Mexico for the benefit of Bolaños.[26]

While it is beyond the scope of the present work to trace the
history of the Bolaños Company, it must be pointed out that Real
del Monte and Bolaños were closely intertwined throughout their
existence, that they struggled with similar problems in their Mexican operations, and that they failed at approximately the same time.
The Real del Monte management was tardy in complying with the
court order to disengage itself from the conduct of Bolaños' affairs
in Mexico. Both James Vetch and Charles Tindal, the first two
overseas chief officers of Real del Monte, held the same post with
Bolaños. Only in 1828 did Tindal relinquish his duties as director
of the Bolaños Company operations in Mexico. Separate manage-
ments in England as well as in Mexico seem to have evolved thereafter, but, according to a public charge made by a disgruntled
holder of Real del Monte and Bolaños stock in 1845, only a few
years before the collapse of both firms, one fifth of the registered
Real del Monte proprietors held shares in Bolaños and one fourth
of the registered Bolaños proprietors held shares in the Real del
Monte firm.[27]

Unlike its larger sister concern, the Bolaños Company achieved

[26] *LJ*, 3 (1825), 73–74, 75, 83–84.
[27] 1825 CG 8; 1828 CG 12; "Original Correspondence: Real del Monte and
Bolaños Mining Companies," *MJ*, 15 (8 March 1845), 85.

some temporary successes before joining Real del Monte on the route to bankruptcy, a road on which signs of hope and despair alternated with almost predictable regularity. Interestingly, Bolaños was most fortunate not in the district of that name, the subject of much dispute at the outset in 1825, but on the *veta grande*, or mother lode, at Zacatecas. According to the firm's onetime director at Zacatecas, between 1826 and 1834 the company realized a profit of nearly $4.5 million from its works on the *veta grande*.[28] By the middle of 1837, Bolaños had paid seven dividends to its English stockholders, and it remained reasonably solvent until 1839, at which time it reluctantly turned the *veta grande* mines back to their owners. Having to depend entirely upon the mines of the Bolaños district thereafter, the concern began its unsteady downhill trip into insolvency. Finally, in November 1849, at about the time that Real del Monte was meeting a similar fate, the Bolaños Company was dissolved.[29]

[28] Joseph Burkart, *Aufenthalt und Reisen in Mexico en den Jahren 1825 bis 1834*, II, 81.

[29] "Proceedings of Public Companies: Bolaños Mining Company," *MJ*, 5 (14 July 1837), 50; "Mining Correspondence, Foreign Mines: Bolaños Mining Company," *MJ*, 9 (2 September 1839), 110; "Proceedings of Public Companies: Bolaños Mining Company," *MJ*, 19 (24 November 1849), 562.

3. Establishment in Mexico

THE FIRST DETACHMENT OF OFFICERS AND TECHNICIANS ASSIGNED to set up the British concern in Mexico sailed from Liverpool on 25 March 1824. After a five-day stopover in New York the fifteen-man party reached Tampico on 25 May. Two days later it set off for the mine site, arriving on 11 June.[1] According to a member of the group, the overland journey from the coast to the Real was made in a caravan of more than forty mules. The "solemn and triumphal entry" into Real del Monte, or at least into the place where the town "once existed, and where it will ere long raise its head again," is described by that anonymous chronicler:

I say *once existed* because it now has the air of a village sacked by a horde of Cossacks, or of something yet more desolate. The *tempus edax* of the poets has here used his scythe with inexorable cruelty. The roofs are perforated and falling in, the walls crumbling down, and, in short, the whole village converted into a mass of ruins. . . . The cause of this

[1] "Review of the Real del Monte Mining Association: Annual Meeting, February 28, 1825," *QMR*, no. 4 (January 1831), p. 436.

decay is obvious enough. This district has no resources when the mines are not worked, which has been the case at Real del Monte for a long time past.[2]

Doubtless hoping that the newcomers would bring life once again to their ruined mining community, the villagers received them with the ringing of bells, thronged to church, and offered prayers for the success of the undertaking. Pedro Romero de Terreros returned from his San Javier estate to welcome his business partners and to lodge them in his house.

Despite the hospitality they were shown, the first arrivals must have found it difficult to adjust to a country whose climate, language, and customs were very different from those of the England they had just left. Still wearing summer clothes, they smarted at the raw cold characteristic of the rainy season at the Real, some nine thousand feet above sea level. As the author of the *Journal* wryly noted, within a day "we could bear the cold no longer, and were obliged to fortify ourselves in our winter clothes against the climate of the torrid zone."

Several members of the party were invited to the count's country house at San Miguel, where "in a delightful little grove" they saw "a beautiful display of fountains and jets d'eau." Of the reduction haciendas at Regla, San Antonio, and San Miguel the chronicler was less enthusiastic. It was clear that the buildings had been put up at great expense, but they were now in a state of decay. Moreover, their construction and placement had been poorly planned: "The architect, whoever he was, was a sworn enemy of right lines and angles."

Soon afterward the company officials were entertained at another house belonging to Romero de Terreros, this one in Pachuca.[3]

---

[2] *Journal Descriptive of the Route from New York to Real del Monte by Way of Tampico: By One of the First Detachment Sent by the Real del Monte Company*, p. 20. The original of this unsigned work was dated "Real del Monte, July 16, 1824." Its style and the personal references it contains suggest that its author was one of the company officers. The account of the first group's arrival and early days at the Real, given here, draws largely on the *Journal, passim*.

[3] The count's living accommodations were a matter of considerable interest to travelers of the period. In his *Notes on Mexico, Made in the Autumn of 1822*

The "perfectly fair" climate of this town, in contrast to that of the Real, was more to the visitors' liking. During their visit they were shown one of the two monasteries built by the count's father; "in this dwell, in holy ease, twenty Franciscan friars, who can look back to the good times when there were two hundred." Before leaving Pachuca, the chronicler and others in the group bade good-by to those who were going on to Mexico City, "launching them in an immense carriage faithfully copied from one of the first of the five hundred originally brought from Spain." The company officials so ceremoniously dispatched were probably the three commissioners, whose first tasks in the Mexican capital included negotiating a new contract with the count for working the Regla mines.

Acquisition of Mining Property

The contract governing the operation of Romero de Terreros's mines that had been negotiated in London in March 1824 was revised and ratified shortly after Commissioner Vetch arrived at Real del Monte. Signed in Mexico City on 1 July, the amended document lengthened the duration of the agreement from twenty to twenty-one years and incorporated two important new provisions: first, the count allowed an extension of the company's leasehold to include the argentiferous lead mines at Zimapán, a mining district some seventy-five miles northwest of Real del Monte, as well as the silver mines at the Real itself; and, second, the company agreed to pay the count an *alimento*, or subsistence allowance, of $12,000 per year, to be deducted from his share of the profits in the undertaking.[4]

(p. 56), Joel R. Poinsett described a visit to Romero de Terreros and his family at their home, "spacious and well furnished," in Mexico City. Edward T. Tayloe, a member of Poinsett's staff when the latter became United States minister to Mexico, was entertained by the manager of the count's San Javier estate, some forty-five miles from the capital, and by the count himself at San Miguel (*Mexico, 1825–1828*, pp. 133, 135). By 1840 Romero de Terreros had apparently given up his residence at San Miguel, for in that year Madame Calderón de la Barca found the establishment "entirely abandoned; the house comfortless and out of repair" (*Life in Mexico*, p. 180).

4 El preliminar con que la Sociedad de Aventureros en Londres convino celebrar la compañía por 21 años, in Libro en que se hallan, el preliminar con que

The commissioners then turned to the Morán mine. On 1 July 1824 Vetch and Rivafinoli, representing the Real del Monte concern, and Felipe Sáenz, acting on behalf of Tomás Murphy, ratified the contract that had been signed in London in March by John Taylor and the proprietor's brother. Besides restating the terms of the earlier document, the new agreement noted that only an additional £1,000 need be paid during the first year of the contract since the company had already advanced £1,000 toward the £2,000 *alimento* payment required annually.[5]

On 27 August 1824 Vetch and Antonio Cortezar, acting for his two brothers, concluded an agreement for leasing the Santa Inés and Carretera mines, also in Real del Monte. Similar to the Regla contract in most respects, this agreement placed a three-year limit on the $2,000 annual *alimento* to be paid the owners and on the company's obligation to continue working the mines.[6] After the Regla and Morán mines, the Santa Inés–Carretera group was to receive the most attention from the British concern.

During 1825 the chief commissioner leased a dozen additional mines, considered but rejected offers for several others, and gave casual attention to a few more properties.[7] He accepted Felipe Sáenz's offer of the Cabrera and Valenciana mines, for example, "to prevent their falling to the other English Company in Real del

---

la Sociedad de Aventureros formada en Londres convino celebrar una compañía . . . con el S. D. Pedro Terreros Conde de Jala y de Regla . . . ; la escritura pública con que se afianzó el contrato, y los ynventarios judiciales . . . , (cited hereafter as El preliminar), RT, pp. 1–3, 16–17; "Review of the Real del Monte Mining Association: Annual Meeting, February 28, 1825," *QMR*, no. 4 (January 1831), p. 436. The revised contract of 1 July 1824, which governed the operations of the company and served as a model for subsequent agreements between the British company and other Mexican mine owners, appears, in English translation, as Appendix A. Four subsequent revisions of the contract increased the court's annual allowance to $16,000 and extended the company's lease on the Real del Monte and Zimapán mines to perpetuity.

[5] AN, Manuel García Romero, 1824, fols. 83v–86v.

[6] Combenio de abilitación de las minas que se refieren entre Don James Vetch comisionado de la compañía inglesa, y Don Antonio Cortezar á nombre de sus hermanos Don José María y Don Manuel Mariano Cortezar, RdM, Contratos (1826–1893), pp. 20–33.

[7] For the location of the principal mines in the Real del Monte, see Map 3.

Monte." That other English concern was probably the Anglo-Mexican Mining Association, which for a short time controlled mining property in the Real.[8] In leasing the Cabrera and Valencia-na mines, Vetch might also have been trying to defend the Real del Monte Company against the acquisitive bent of Count Andrea Cornaro, of Venice, Italy, who, armed with a power of attorney granted him in London in February 1825 by Thomas Shingsby Duncombe, was by the end of that year seeking property in the Real del Monte–Pachuca area and elsewhere in Mexico.[9]

The question of extending the concern's operations to nearby Pachuca arose early. In February 1825 Vetch acknowledged that he was of two minds on the subject. Having been long abandoned, the mines of that district could not be rehabilitated without considerable expense; on the other hand, they had the advantage of proximity to Real del Monte. Two months later he considered their location to be a serious disadvantage. Even though some of those mines were attractive, he feared that "working them would paralyze our efforts at the better concern of Real del Monte."[10] Vetch had no way of knowing that he was rejecting the opportunity to enter a mining district that would prove to be one of the most productive in nineteenth-century Mexico.

El Chico, also near Real del Monte, received little of the chief commissioner's attention, and he made no recommendation that the company acquire property in that mining district. He did, however, make a concerted effort to examine, and in some cases obtain, mines far from the Real. At Ozumatlán, near what is today Morelia, Michoacán, he acquired for Real del Monte the San Pedro Barreno and Los Apóstoles mines and took steps to lease a third, La Machorra. In attempting to gain control of the management of San Pedro and Los Apóstoles, Vetch was compelled to deal with an intermediary named William Dollar.[11] Without realizing it the com-

8 1825 CG 8; H. G. Ward, *Mexico in 1827*, II, 65.

9 AN, Manuel García Romero, 1825, fols. 161–164v, 190–194v, 196v–200v, and 1826, fols. 216–219v and docs. 1–8, following fol. 215.

10 1825 CG 8.

11 *Ibid.* By the time Ward visited Ozumatlán, in 1826, the company had acquired La Machorra (*Mexico in 1827*, II, 681).

missioner was involving Real del Monte in a difficult situation, for a legal dispute with Dollar arose in 1829, when the concern decided to abandon its Ozumatlán operations, and continued throughout the British firm's existence in Mexico.

Acquiring mines for the Bolaños Company as well proved troublesome to the Real del Monte concern and to its chief commissioner. First, Vetch had not been granted power of attorney by Taylor to enter into contracts for the Bolaños mines on behalf of Real del Monte, and he therefore did so in his own name. Another problem stemmed from Vetch's attempts to gain complete control of the major vein in the Bolaños district. Although by the end of 1825 he had entered into contracts for several mines there, he was able to convince José María Fagoaga to lease his property on that lode only after threatening to divert the flow of the Bolaños River away from Fagoaga's property and thus prevent his using a water wheel to drain his mine.[12]

It was with considerably less difficulty that Vetch acquired Fagoaga's property on the *veta grande* of Zacatecas, a mine that proved to be more profitable than any of the others leased by either Real del Monte or Bolaños. For the first time Vetch was gaining access not to an abandoned mine but to a going concern. In June 1825 he estimated the annual production for the previous twenty years to have been $500,000, but with very little profit, and predicted that the expenses could be cut in half and the income doubled. Vetch recommended that the *veta grande* be operated by an entirely separate firm, which he proposed calling the London Company, "a name of utmost value here."[13] In the end, however, it was worked, and most profitably, by the Bolaños Company.

Under pressure from London to acquire valuable mining property, Real del Monte's first commissioner vied with a score of other Englishmen in seeking to control promising mines without entering into imprudent speculation. By late 1825 Vetch seems to have

---

[12] 1825 CG 8; 1828 CG 12; G. F. Lyon, *Journal of a Residence and Tour in the Republic of Mexico in the Year 1826, with Some Account of the Mines of That Country*, I, 287, 310.

[13] 1825 CG 8.

considered his search for new mines at an end. Noting that the "great fever" in Mexico was "fortunately subsiding," he said, "I now continue more in my former opinion than ever that we ought to prove 'ere we extend our operations & repeat that I know of no mines in this country that hold out the expectations of exorbitant gain."[14]

Transport of Equipment

One of the most dramatic, and tragic, episodes of the early years of the British Real del Monte Company was the transport of the first steam engines and other equipment and of a large group of English workers to the mining camp at the Real. According to the original plan, the men and material were to have left England in October 1824, so they would arrive in Mexico during the dry season. Instead, owing to a delay in the manufacture of the engines, the party was unable to set sail until the following spring and thus did not reach Mexico until the beginning of summer, the "sickly season." That "little miscalculation" was to prove costly, wrote the British chargé d'affaires in Mexico, for about a score of men died of fever and most of the machinery had to be abandoned until winter brought an end to the rains.[15]

The expedition was led by James Colquhoun, an officer in the British Royal Artillery, who served as the company's second commissioner in Mexico during the early years of its operations. Four ships were assigned to the operation: the *Courier* sailed direct for Tampico; the *Melpomene* and the *General Phipps* were destined for Veracruz or nearby ports; and the *Harriet*, conveying the remainder of the establishment and machinery, set sail soon afterward, also for the Veracruz area.[16] In all, the shipment weighed approximately 1,500 tons. It included 9 steam engines, 5 for pumping, 2 for stamping ore, and 2 for saw mills; various pumps; iron

---

[14] 1825 CG 8.

[15] Ibid.; Ward, *Mexico in 1827*, II, 250.

[16] John H. Buchan, *Report of the Director, the Real Del Monte Mining Company, March 1855*, p. 39; 1825 CG 8; Henry English, *A General Guide to the Companies Formed for Working Foreign Mines*, pp. 97–98.

works; tools and implements; 150 wagons; and 760 sets of mule harnesses. The equipment was accompanied by 123 officers, mechanics, artisans, and others. Seven women and 3 children were reported to be among the 63 passengers aboard the *Melpomene*, the vessel on which Colquhoun sailed.[17]

While Colquhoun was supervising the loading and sailing of the ships and himself making the long sea voyage to Mexico, Captain Vetch was preparing for the arrival of the transport party. His preliminary tasks included obtaining permission from the Mexican government for the English personnel to land in the country and to continue on to Real del Monte without undue immigration or customs difficulties; repairing the road from Veracruz to the Real so as to make it suitable for carriage traffic; and providing sufficient draft and pack animals for the trek from the coast to the central tableland. None was easily accomplished.

By April 1825 Vetch had persuaded the government to instruct the appropriate local officials not to embargo the company's wagons, carts, or mules to be used in carrying the machinery away from the coast. However, what was probably his most important request, addressed to Minister of Foreign and Domestic Affairs Lucas Alamán, was denied. Vetch sought permission to land the major part of the machinery and equipment at Antón Lizardo, some fifteen miles to the south of Veracruz, because use of the latter port was barred by the Spanish control of the harbor fortress of San Juan de Ulúa. Complaining bitterly to the British consul general, Vetch found it "absurd" of the Mexican government to "pretend to encourage & facilitate the importation of machinery if at the same time it will only admit of its being disembarked where it cannot be done in safety."[18]

Though considered by Real del Monte Company officials to be a minor matter, the lack of a road between Antón Lizardo and the

---

[17] 1825 CG 8; "Review of the Real del Monte Mining Association: Annual Meeting, February 25, 1825," *QMR*, no. 4 (January 1831), p. 441. Slightly different descriptions of the shipment are given by English (*General Guide*, p. 97) and by Ward (*Mexico in 1827*, II, 89).

[18] 1825 CG 8.

main highway was one of the government's arguments in denying permission to disembark there. The government also noted that Lizardo was not a "habilitated port" (one to which customs and other officials had been assigned), a point that seemed irrelevant to Vetch. The alternative was to land at the open beach of Mocambo, in the immediate vicinity of Veracruz, where, because of the wind and surf, only in May, June, and July (the most unhealthful months of the year) could heavy machinery be discharged. Nor was Mocambo a habilitated port.[19]

In an article written in July 1825, the editors of the official Mexican government newspaper took a position with regard to the ports of Antón Lizardo and Mocambo that was largely in agreement with Vetch's views. Mocambo, they said, could not be given serious consideration as a port, mainly because its anchorage was so close to San Juan de Ulúa that small Spanish warships might harass vessels attempting to discharge cargo on the beach. Antón Lizardo, on the other hand, with its excellent anchorage, fertile surrounding land, and adequate supply of well water was "destined to be the successor of Veracruz." Growth of an important commercial center there awaited only the "habilitation" of the port.[20]

In undertaking repairs to the Veracruz–Real del Monte route, Vetch planned not to rebuild the road but rather to improve it enough to allow the passage of English wagons and carts loaded with heavy machinery. Francisco Vicelli, whom Vetch first appointed to repair the road from Jalapa to the coast, seems to have been at best remiss in reporting on the progress of the work and at worst incompetent. The chief commissioner removed him—"as this is no country for an enterprise to be allowed to be humbugged by pretenders"—and named Samuel Hutton as superintendent of the repairs to the road from Veracruz to the Real. Hutton's instructions were to spare no expense, inasmuch as "true economy will be to get the job done as soon as possible."

With the scheduled arrival of the first vessel only one month away, Hutton turned to the task in earnest. Repairs to the Vera-

[19] *Ibid.*
[20] *Gaceta diaria de México*, 9 July 1825, p. 3.

cruz-Jalapa section were completed by the end of May, and the time spent in unloading the *Melpomene* and transporting its cargo to Jalapa was to allow the fifty-man road force to extend the repairs from Jalapa to Perote. In carrying out his assignment, Hutton died, apparently of yellow fever.[21]

On completion of the Veracruz-Jalapa section, Vetch informed the Mexican minister of foreign and domestic affairs that although repairs so hastily made could not be expected to be permanent, all those who had taken that route had attested to the comfort in which coaches and wagons now traveled; the Mexican people could now enjoy a far better road than in the past. The cost of the improvements had of course been high, but under the circumstances the company asked only that the government exempt its wagons from the highway toll until the end of that year. Because the Anglo-Mexican Mining Association was to defray a part of those expenses, Vetch requested that the same privilege be extended to the other British company. Similar appeals were later addressed to other branches of the Mexican government; they were eventually placed before President Guadalupe Victoria and rejected.[22]

In his efforts to provide sufficient draft and pack animals to meet the four English ships, Vetch was largely frustrated. He was unable to send mules to Tampico mainly because the Mexico City muleteers with whom he dealt were unfamiliar with that part of the country and averse to making the trip in the rainy season. Adequate transportation to the Real was therefore still lacking when the *Courier* put into port on 17 May 1825 after a fifty-six–day voyage from London. The vessel's cargo had to be left in Tampico in care of a small group of company employees, to be forwarded to the mining camp as soon as mules became available. By late August almost no supplies had reached Real del Monte from that port.[23]

---

[21] 1825 CG 8.

[22] *Ibid.* Of the $19,631 spent on the Veracruz road, $6,666, or approximately one third, were paid by Anglo-Mexican and the rest by the Real del Monte Company.

[23] 1825 CG 8; *Gaceta diaria,* 5 June 1825, p. 4.

As to the animals needed for the Veracruz landings, Vetch planned to purchase 100 draft mules himself and contract for another 200. It was not until the end of June that any mules had been sent from the capital, and they numbered 120 rather than the 200 promised by the Mexico City contractor. Although Colquhoun bought horses and mules in the Jalapa area, the shortage of animals lasted through September, when company officials took advantage of the annual fair in Mexico City to obtain 200 horses, half of them for the mines, at about $15 each, and 500 mules, at $25 or $30 apiece.

Toward the Mexico City muleteer with whom he had entered into a contract Vetch felt extreme bitterness. "I cannot but consider . . . [him] the murderer of our people," he wrote Colquhoun, "for he repeatedly promised he would have 200 beasts on the coast in the first week of May."[24] Whether the muleteer was in fact to blame, there is no doubt that Colquhoun's transport party was severely handicapped by the shortage of draft and pack animals.

The problems encountered in discharging the cargoes of the three ships that arrived in the Veracruz area were extremely serious. Having been denied permission to disembark at Antón Lizardo, the vessels were compelled to drop anchor off the open beach of Mocambo—the *Melpomene*, with Colquhoun aboard, on 28 May, the *General Phipps* on 20 June, and the *Harriet* on 28 June. During June and July the three ships were unloaded, the *Harriet* after a nine-day delay at anchor awaiting clearance. Three cylinders and three cases of iron-working gear, without which the steam engines would have been unserviceable, were washed from the boats and recovered only after two or three weeks of hard labor. Whenever the wind raised a surf, operations came to a halt for several days. Even after the goods were finally landed on the beach, the sea spray damaged them further, and it was with much difficulty that they could be stored in a secure place.[25]

During the protracted disembarkation the party had to make

24 1825 CG 8.
25 *Gaceta diaria*, 8 June 1825, p. 3; 30 June 1825, p. 4; 7 July 1825, p. 4; 1825 CG 8.

camp in a spot that was both wet and unhealthful. By early September 15 Europeans had died and the loss of 5 more was expected. The total number of British and Mexicans who perished in the transport operation can only be surmised. In October Vetch informed a Bolaños official that he could not provide him with any workers because Colquhoun had lost 22 persons on the coast. If that was the total number of English dead, the loss was not insignificant, considering that the group which sailed from the home country hardly exceeded 120. Aside from a statement by a member of the transport party that "yellow fever soon made sad havoc with both English and Mexicans," no mention is made of deaths among the native workers. That many of them were employed is suggested by Vetch's reference to the 50–man road-repair crew and by the fact that, while the ships disembarked at Mocambo, Colquhoun was paying $3,000 a week in wages to local labor.[26]

In requesting the British consul general to intercede with the Mexican government on behalf of Real del Monte with regard to the importation and transport of the machinery, Vetch described the "small vexations and delays" daily put in the party's way by the customhouse officers. At Tampico particularly they insisted on opening and examining every package. Consisting chiefly of engines and tools, the packages had been carefully packed in England for mule carriage, and the delay and expense of their inspection were, according to the commissioner, "all the more galling as instead of finding our operations facilitated on account of the value of the objects in benefiting this country we are treated with a harshness which is never extended to sale goods." Moreover, as Vetch had explained to the minister of foreign and domestic affairs, customs officials who had never seen machinery and parts such as those sent from England could not know on looking at them whether they were what Real del Monte officers declared them to be unless they took the company's word. He was grateful to Alamán for having ordered that there be no more delay than necessary, but regretted that those instructions had so little effect.[27]

[26] 1825 CG 8; Buchan, *Report*, p. 39.
[27] 1825 CG 8.

On his arrival Colquhoun was advised by Vetch to take the machinery and equipment brought by the *Melpomene* and the *General Phipps* to Jalapa at once, so as to remove the transport party from the deadly coastal area. He was further advised to make Jalapa, rather than the coast, his headquarters for the landing and transport operations. Whether Colquhoun followed his superior officer's advice is problematical, for he was reported to be present during the discharging of all three vessels that put into port at Mocambo.

The trek inland was slow and arduous. Although the expedition was fully supplied with wagons and harness from the Royal Arsenal at Woolwich, the draft mules sent from the interior of Mexico were unbroken and the natives of the coast unused to handling them. Moreover, the roads of deep sand made the movement of the heavy wagons a most tedious and difficult task. By mid-August the transport party had moved 380 tons of heavy stores and machinery, in some 270 wagon loads, from the landing site to Santa Fe, apparently a hacienda near Jalapa that was used as a depot, and 100 tons of mule transport had been forwarded to Real del Monte. Sickness in the group, the rainy season, and the shortage of draft animals forced Colquhoun to suspend further attempts to carry all the material on to the Real until the end of the wet season, a decision with which Vetch agreed.[28]

Even though information on the exact route followed from the coast to Real del Monte is sketchy, it is possible to pinpoint enough stops along the way to give a general picture. After leaving Jalapa the group passed through Perote, which is also in the present state of Veracruz. From there, crossing a narrow neck of what is today the state of Puebla, it entered the present state of Tlaxcala and passed through the small towns of Piedras Negras, Atlangatepec, and Buenavista. Once in what is now the state of Hidalgo, it went through Apám and Singuilucan before arriving at the Real.[29]

[28] *Ibid.*; Buchan, *Report*, p. 39; "Review of the Real del Monte Mining Association: Special General Meeting, December 19, 1825," *QMR*, no. 4 (January 1831), p. 442.

[29] 1825 CG 8. See Map 5.

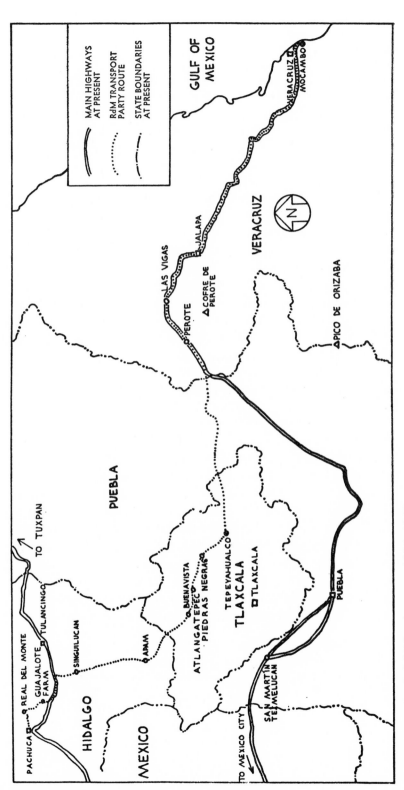

5. Veracruz–Real del Monte route, 1825–1849.

Of the trying experiences undergone by Colquhoun's party in its climb from the coast two are recounted by a company official who was to retrace the route soon afterward: one night, on the plains of Apám, twenty-one mules were swept away and drowned by a sudden rainfall; and in one of the ravines, in a place called the Hacienda of Piedras Negras, a wagon containing thirty-six hundredweight of iron was washed away by the rains, nine mules were drowned, and several men narrowly escaped death.[30]

On 1 November Vetch informed the home office that "Colquhoun & Buchan are here, the former deserving credit for his firmness & perseverance in bringing the equipment from the coast against so many obstructions." The proprietors of the company, meeting in London, voted unanimously to thank Colquhoun and the party under his orders, in transporting the stores toward the mines, "for the great exertions manifested by them, and the zeal with which such services had been performed." Yet the task of carrying the remainder of the machinery and equipment to the Real was to drag on well into the following year. It was not until May 1826 that the engines finally arrived at the mines.[31]

Rehabilitation of the Mines and Mills

Though impressive in extent, the establishment taken over at Real del Monte by the British company was largely in ruin. The state of the property is described in detail in the 1824 inventory of the mines, mills, adits, tools and equipment, buildings, and furniture delivered by the Count of Regla to Commissioner Vetch on 17 July in the presence of officials of the Pachuca Mining Deputation and other witnesses. Of the seventeen shafts on the Vizcaína vein, only six were useful to some degree; of the fifteen on the other Real del Monte veins leased by Pedro Romero de Terreros (Santa Brígida, Acosta, and minor lodes), only one was serviceable. Moreover, of those seven shafts that were not completely caved in or

---

[30] Lyon, *Journal*, II, 161, 166.

[31] 1825 CG 8; "Review of the Real del Monte Mining Association: Special General Meeting, December 19, 1825," *QMR*, no. 4 (January 1831), pp. 441–442; Buchan, *Report*, p. 39.

filled with rubbish, only four were open to depths of more than one hundred yards.[32]

A company official who arrived in the district in November 1824 reported that most of the shafts had fallen in, "leaving their former site only to be detected by the immense craters, overgrown with brushwood at their mouths." Even more serious than the general disrepair of the mine shafts, according to Buchan, was the destruction of the great Morán adit, which, during many years of neglect, had so gone to ruin that it no longer carried off the water, "which consequently rose to a great height in the mines." Two of the four ventilation shafts on that adit were in a serviceable state, but the other two were filled with rubbish. The entrance was impassable.[33]

The seven reduction haciendas received by the company's first officer also showed the ravages of time. Of the minor establishments of San Francisco Javier (La Nueva), San Juan, and Ixtula de Beneficio, to the north and northwest of Real del Monte, little more than the site was left. Sánchez, the principal hacienda in that vicinity and the one closest to the Real, still had a few buildings in working order. The three haciendas to the northeast of the Real, and located on a different stream of water, were the most important in the district. Regla, although it was abandoned and many of its buildings were in need of repair, seems on the whole not to have been too badly damaged; it was the largest mill and the center of milling operations during both the Spanish and British periods of Real del Monte ownership. San Antonio was in far worse condition,

---

[32] Ynventario y entrega formal que hizo el Sr. Conde de Jala y de Regla, á Don Jaime Vetch como director principal de las minas y haciendas de beneficio de metales en los Reales del Monte y Zimapán, las que puso en compañía por viente y un años, con la Sociedad Ynglesa Europea, formada en Londres para este fin, cuyo contrato se formalizó en el mes de julio de 1824 (cited hereafter as Ynventario), in El preliminar, RT, pp. 95–124. Despite its title, the 1824 inventory does not cover the count's property in Zimapán. Generally a mine has but one shaft, which bears the same name as the mine to which it belongs; therefore, unless otherwise stated, the use of a shaft name specifies the mine under discussion. A single shaft was sometimes made to serve several mines in close proximity; in such cases, the mines usually came to be grouped under a single name, that of the shaft.

[33] Buchan, *Report*, p. 38; Ynventario, in El preliminar, RT, p. 106.

its protecting masonry wall being the only part not ruined to some extent. Finally, San Miguel, where the count maintained living quarters, was also badly in need of repair, the walls of some of its interior buildings having fallen in. All the machinery in the mills was gone.[34]

The general state of disrepair that characterized the Regla mines did not extend to Morán, the most important property other than the count's that the English company leased at the outset of its Mexican operations. According to an early survey of the Real del Monte district made by John Rule and other officers of the concern, the two principal shafts, Morán and Santa Bárbara, were in good repair. This mine was expected to be the first in the district to be drained and placed in production.[35]

The task of rehabilitating the mines and mills at Real del Monte, though enormous, must have been undertaken with some enthusiasm. The initial detachment of Englishmen had reason to feel that they represented a company with ample capital and consequently adequate means of "providing suitable establishments for mines." They were confident that the manner in which those mines had been worked in the past would admit of many improvements, the most important being the application of steam engines to the problems of drainage. The lack of fuel, which was to prevent the adoption of this advanced technique in many parts of Mexico, would, they noted with satisfaction, not hamper their efforts at Real del Monte. Besides surveying the district, the group turned at once to clearing adits and shafts; constructing shafthouses, workshops, and storehouses around the principal mines; and building a carriage road between the mines and mills.[36]

---

[34] Ynventario, in El preliminar, RT, pp. 107–120; Buchan, *Report*, p. 38. The mills taken over by the British are shown on Map 2.

[35] "Review of the Real del Monte Mining Association: Annual Meeting, February 28, 1825," *QMR*, no. 4 (January 1831), pp. 438–439. The Morán mine, which was leased to the British by Tomás Murphy in 1824, should not be confused with the Morán adit, which was completed by the first Count of Regla in 1762 and included in the Regla properties turned over to the British company.

[36] 1825 CG 8; "Review of the Real del Monte Mining Association: Annual Meeting, February 28, 1825," *QMR*, no. 4 (January 1831), p. 439; "Special

Among the works intended to bring the Real del Monte mines into a state of ore production, the clearing of the Morán adit held high priority. Capable of draining most of the company's property as far north as (but not including) the Morán mine to a depth of 232 yards, the old drainage tunnel had, by the middle of 1826, been cleared to the Vizcaína vein at the Dolores shaft.[37]

With the gradual recession of the water, the task of clearing out and restoring the main shafts in the district was pressed forward. When the British chargé d'affaires visited the concern in mid-1826, he found that seven of the shafts on the Vizcaína (San Juan, San Francisco, Guadalupe, Santa Teresa, San Cayetano, Dolores, and El Zapatero) and two on the Santa Brígida vein (San José and Sacramento) had been repaired down to the level of the Morán adit.[38]

During this period two of the company's steam engines were put in operation. The first, a small horizontal machine, was placed in the Morán mine, which, by the middle of 1827, was sufficiently free of water to allow some working on its ore. Although a thirty-inch machine at the Dolores shaft was the second of the steam engines to be put in operation, it was the first in importance, for it was intended to begin draining the great Vizcaína vein. Installed sometime before 1 July 1827, this relatively small and unassisted engine surprised company officials by sinking the water slowly below the adit. Looking to the placement of another machine at the San Cayetano shaft, the chief commissioner informed the owner of the Vizcaína that he expected the vein to be dry by the end of that year or the beginning of the next.[39]

General Meeting, December 19, 1825," *QMR*, no. 4 (January 1831), p. 442; Buchan, *Report*, p. 39.

[37] 1825 CG 8; "Review of the Real del Monte Mining Association: Annual General Meeting, February 28, 1826," *QMR*, no. 4 (January 1831) p. 445; "Annual Meeting, February 28, 1827," *QMR*, no. 4 (January 1831), p. 448.

[38] Ward, *Mexico in 1827*, II, 352–353; 1825 CG 8.

[39] Ward, *Mexico in 1827*, II, 353; "Review of the Real del Monte Mining Association: Annual Meeting, February 28, 1827," *QMR*, no. 4 (January 1831) p. 449; "Annual General Meeting, February 28, 1828," *QMR*, no. 4 (January 1831), p. 458; 1827 CG 26.

Though still holding to the necessity of erecting steam engines to drain its mines and bring them into production rapidly, the British company, on 26 May 1825, accepted greater responsibility toward completing the Aviadero adit and eventually draining the entire district without the use of those engines. In a document signed in Mexico City, Captain Vetch and Romero de Terreros agreed to certain modifications in the contract that had been concluded between the count and the company the preceding year. In exchange for the mine owner's granting a seven-year extension of the contract, to 1 July 1852, the company made two concessions: first, it increased the *alimento* payment to $16,000 per year; and, second, it committed itself to begin work immediately on the Aviadero adit and to prosecute that work with all due energy, but with as much economy as possible. [40]

During the first years of the firm's activities in Mexico, development of two outlying mining districts was begun. At Zimapán some ore had been raised by mid-1826 but not yet reduced. At Ozumatlán a drainage adit was completed to the principal vein, and early in 1827 some ore was being extracted from the mines. It was not long, however, before a dispute arose with and between the owners of two Ozumatlán mines (San Pedro de Barreno and La Machorra) over the division of the cost of clearing the adit through those two properties.[41] Commissioner Vetch was unable to settle the matter before his departure, and his successor also failed to bring about the solution to a problem that, in the end, was to play an important part in the company's decision to abandon the Ozumatlán workings.

[40] AN, Manuel García Romero, 1825, fols. 106–108.

[41] "Review of the Real del Monte Mining Association: Annual General Meeting, February 28, 1827," *QMR*, no. 4 (January 1831), 450–451; 1827 CG 26.

4. Management and Finance

Management Problems

THE ADMINISTRATIVE STRUCTURE OF THE BRITISH REAL DEL MONTE Company, praised by a Court of Chancery judge in 1825, was, in fact, the cause of a serious managerial problem that plagued the concern throughout its lifetime. The lack of a proper division of authority in an organization whose headquarters and field operations were separated by several thousand miles of ocean was to make itself felt on numerous occasions.

Under the terms of the company's deed of settlement, the highest authority was vested in the meetings of proprietors, the annual and special general courts of stockholders. In the beginning, the annual meetings were held each February and the special ones were called quite frequently. In 1830 the time for holding the annual general meetings was changed to May or June (they always took place in June), and during most of the company's later years fewer special meetings were convoked. Whether regular or special, the stockholders' meetings rarely did more than ratify the actions of, or approve the proposals put to them by, the Court of Directors and the manager.[1]

The management of the concern was assigned by the deed of settlement to a Court of Directors, initially made up of twelve members but later reduced to nine and then to seven. While the firm's regulations provided that any person holding but one share might serve as a director, membership on the court was at first confined almost entirely to the original founders of the company, who held large numbers of shares, and it changed very little over the years. The court always maintained a direct line of communication with, and exercised authority over, the highest officers in Mexico. From early 1836 on, however, the secretary of the court, John Phillips, began to assume some of its duties, especially as regards communicating with the overseas staff. It was he, not a member of the court, who made the inspection trip to Mexico in 1840, when the directors and the manager felt the need for a firsthand investigation by someone from the London management.[2]

Although the deed of settlement charged the court with the management of the concern, it made provision for an office that was, in practice, to share its administrative authority. The court created the position of manager, apparently to reward John Taylor, who enjoyed a high reputation in English mining circles and who had been instrumental in forming the company. The extent to which final authority was divided between the directors and Taylor, the only person to serve as manager, can be seen in the fact that both submitted reports to the stockholders and both received communications and reports from officers in Mexico. The use of the term

---

[1] "Review of the Real del Monte Mining Association" (various meetings held between 16 April 1825 and 19 August 1829), *QMR*, no. 4 (January 1831), pp. 441–469; "Annual General Meeting, February 15, 1830," *QMR*, no. 4 (January 1831), p. 470. Between the regular meeting of February 1825 and that of February 1830, ten special stockholders' meetings were convened, most of them to approve proposals for increasing the firm's capital.

[2] Henry English, *A General Guide to the Companies Formed for Working Foreign Mines*, p. 53; 1835, 1836 CG 34. Phillips became secretary of the Court of Directors on or about 1 January 1836.

manager to describe Taylor's post is somewhat deceptive. While he occupied what was doubtless the highest single office in the company, he remained in England, never saw the properties in Mexico, and took no personal charge of the mining and milling activities at Real del Monte.

The Real del Monte official directly responsible for the Mexican operations was neither a manager nor a director, but a commissioner who acted on behalf of superior authorities in London.[3] The implication that the first officer in Mexico was but an agent of the real managers of the concern is contained in the original power of attorney given Chief Commissioner James Vetch. In a key passage of that document, Vetch was instructed to do everything "in or about the management of the said Mines in carrying the purpose for which the said Company has been founded into full effect," but, on the other hand, "as we the said Committee of Management could do if personally present."[4] That concept was never lost. All the commissioners in Mexico were aware of a definite limit to their authority—a limit that lay several thousand miles and a long ocean passage away.

The administrative staff at Real del Monte was, at first, quite large. Besides the chief commissioner and, after the arrival of the Colquhoun transport party, a second commissioner, seventeen persons were employed at the mining camp in 1825: a secretary to the chief commissioner, a secretary-assistant to the second commissioner, a mine manager, an assistant mine manager, a principal smelterer and metallurgist, a principal bookkeeper, seven assistant bookkeepers, a surveyor, a draftsman, an engineer, and an assistant engineer. As the fortunes of the company declined, the person-

---

[3] The term *commissioner* lends itself to confusion. Originally three commissioners were sent to Mexico. Only one of them, James Vetch, retained the title, to which *chief* was added. A *second commissioner* was later appointed, James Colquhoun being the only person to hold that title and but for a short time, in 1825 and 1826. Thereafter, the highest-ranking officer at Real del Monte was known as the chief commissioner or the commissioner, and nobody else in the company's employ held that or a similar title.

[4] AN, Manuel García Romero, 1825, doc. 6, following fol. 78 (original English).

nel assigned to the mining camp was reduced. By the late 1830's, a chief commissioner, two mill administrators, a treasurer-cashier, a chief mechanical engineer, and a clerk–mine surveyor were the only administrative staff of an operation that was more extensive than it had been in 1825.

During the quarter-century in which the company worked mines in Mexico, five persons held the position of chief commissioner: James Vetch, from March 1824 to July 1827; Charles Tindal, from July 1827 to July 1832; John Rule, from July 1832 to March 1843; William Rule, from March 1843 to November 1847; and John Buchan, from May 1848 to July 1849. For several months during 1833, while John Rule was back in England, one Roderick Mackensie acted as chief commissioner, and between William Rule's resignation and Buchan's arrival the concern's Mexican operations were under the joint control of two lesser officials named Russell Brenchley and William Woodfield.[5]

The first two commissioners, Vetch and Tindal, were military men, neither of whom had any apparent mining experience before his arrival in Mexico. The Rule brothers were both professional miners from Cornwall. If Buchan was less knowledgeable in mining matters than the Rules before his first trip to Mexico in 1825, he had ample opportunity to gain firsthand experience before he assumed the commissionership in 1848.

An important adjunct of the company's administration in Mexico was a system of representatives in the capital and at the principal Gulf ports. Besides assisting in financial matters, the Real del Monte agents performed numerous other functions, among them aiding in recruitment, procuring mining and milling supplies, and helping to market the silver production. On occasion they even approached the Mexican government on behalf of the concern.

The two most important agencies, those in Mexico City and Veracruz, were established by Captain Vetch almost as soon as

[5] English, *General Guide*, p. 98; 1825–1849 CG *passim*; *Proceedings at the General Courts of Proprietors of the Real del Monte Mining Company* (cited hereafter as RdM *Proceedings*), 1828–1845, *passim*. For information on other English employees at the mining camp, see Chapter 7.

operations were set up at the Real. The Mexico City agency was, as might have been expected, placed in the hands of the Robert Staples Company, whose London partner had negotiated on the Count of Regla's behalf in the formation of the British firm. In Veracruz the company was initially represented by one of its own employees and in Tampico by another.

When Charles Tindal arrived, the Staples Company was still serving as the agent in Mexico City, but before the end of 1827 friction had developed because Staples denied Real del Monte a short-term credit of less than $13,000. Tindal therefore quickly transferred the account to Holdsworth, Fletcher and Company. This firm was to continue on as company agent in the capital throughout the life of the British concern, providing satisfactory service and enjoying cordial relations with each succeeding commissioner.

By the end of 1827 the Real del Monte agencies in Veracruz and Tampico had been assigned to Maurice Voss and Company and to Gordon, Tayes and Company, respectively. In mid-1833 Voss and Company was dissolved and the Real del Monte account transferred to Muñoz and Metfeld. On Metfeld's retirement in 1836, Muñoz entered into partnership with Ernest Schmidt; this house continued as the Real del Monte agent in Veracruz until 1849. The Tampico agency was taken over by a branch of Voss and Company in May 1831. By 1834 it had been transferred to G. A. Papke and Company, where it was to remain until the dissolution of the English mining concern.[6]

An idea of the type of commercial arrangement that existed between company and agent can be gained from an agreement on the payment of commissions concluded in September 1829. Under its terms, the Mexico City agent was to receive 1.5 per cent of the face value of all the Real del Monte bills that it negotiated, brokerage included, provided no endorsements were required; 1.25 per cent of the value of all silver that it sold for Real del Monte, brokerage included; 1 per cent of the value of all Real del Monte silver that

[6] 1825 CG 8; 1827 CG 12, 13; 1828, 1831 CG 12; 1833 CG 28; 1834 CG 33; 1836 CG 35.

it introduced into the Mexico City mint, while the company's production remained "so limited" but subject to revision "when it should have risen"; 2 per cent on the sale of Real del Monte property other than silver and on the purchase of all stores; and .5 per cent on the forwarding of silver bars to England.[7]

Once the company's mining works were under way at Real del Monte and administrative procedures on both sides of the Atlantic established, a regular system of communications between the London management and the mining camp in Mexico was developed. Dispatches from the home office were prepared by the Court of Directors, its secretary, or the manager. Those from the Real were generally written by the chief commissioner, but occasionally by a subordinate officer acting under his instructions. They usually included financial statements drawn up by the treasurer-cashier and reports on the mines and mills prepared by the mine captains and mill administrators. The commissioners' dispatches to the court or to its secretary for the most part dealt with current business; those addressed to Manager John Taylor, a significant portion of them labeled "private," often contained accounts of personnel problems, political news, reports on relations between the company and government officials, and the first officer's views on the progress of the concern. Correspondence was exchanged also between Secretary John Phillips and the treasurer-cashier at the Real, almost entirely on financial matters.

Communications were usually prepared, both in London and Real del Monte, toward the end of each month. They were most frequently carried aboard British packet ships plying between the Mexican Gulf coast and English ports. Copies of the commissioners' letters were sometimes sent to London on other ships, usually British vessels sailing from Mexico to home ports by way of New York. Under normal conditions, six weeks to two months elapsed before a communication prepared in either London or the mining camp reached its destination. Bad weather in the Atlantic or a

[7] 1829 CG 15.

blockade imposed on the port of Veracruz might cause a further delay of from a few days to several weeks.[8]

With so much of the company's administrative responsibility reserved to the London management, and with a time lag of at least three months between the writing of a dispatch and the receipt of an answer, there could not but be considerable inefficiency in the handling of the company's affairs in Mexico. Whenever a misunderstanding arose as to the meaning of orders issued in London or of reports sent from Real del Monte, the difficulties inherent in the communications system were compounded. Proscrastination on the part of headquarters sometimes seriously handicapped operations at the Real. In September 1835, for example, the chief commissioner asked permission to place a small steam engine on one of the ventilation shafts being dug in advance of the Aviadero adit. Having received no clear reply by November 1837—twenty-six months later—he decided on his own account to install the engine.[9]

This episode, or perhaps misadventure, points to an inescapable conclusion: there were in the management of the Real del Monte Company inherent weaknesses that stemmed in part from the long distance between the home office and the mining camp and in part from a reluctance in London to give real authority to the chief commissioner in Mexico. Those weaknesses were, first, a delay in the exchange of communications and in the filling of orders for essential supplies; second, a cumbersome system for arriving at policy decisions, even major ones; and, third, a subtle antagonism between the professional miners and the businessmen in the company.

Though irksome, the lag in communications and supply was not so great an obstacle as to prevent the successful operation of the concern. Far more serious was the dichotomy in the formulation of policy. In the subsequent chapters of this work, numerous ex-

[8] 1825–1848 CG 8, 12, 39, 48.

[9] "Mining Correspondence, Foreign Mines: Real del Monte Mining Company," *MJ*, 1 (12 December 1835), 134; 1837 CG 39.

amples of that problem will appear almost as a matter of course. It might be useful, however, to discuss briefly here one case of a distressingly typical ambivalence that seemed to be built into the divided authority in the running of the company's affairs.

During the commissionership of John Rule, if not before, it became clear that the company must abandon one of its initial concepts: the hope that it could depend indefinitely on occasional strikes of high-grade ore for its financial solvency. In July 1835 Rule began a campaign to convince the London management that such a policy was dangerous and that profits, if they were to come at all, could be derived only from the treatment of large quantities of low-grade ore. It took him nearly a year to win the home office over to his point of view, and even then he met with resistance in carrying out his proposal for solving the problem—fitting out and operating an entirely new mill as a large-scale patio amalgamation plant. After struggling in vain for yet another year to put into practice a plan to which London had agreed in principle, Rule finally gave up and reconciled himself to a halfway measure: at two mills that were already in operation, the capacity for handling low-grade ore was increased. Here, then, is a clear demonstration of administrative inflexibility. Even though officers on both sides of the Atlantic had agreed that conditions that could not be changed—the scarcity of high-grade ore and the relative abundance of low-grade ore—demanded a new course, the concern was simply unable to make a major shift in policy.

This incident also illustrates the subsurface struggle between the miners and the businessmen. John Rule, the first professional miner to head the Mexico operations, insisted for a time on a large patio amalgamation plant because he considered such an establishment essential to the health of the mining camp. The Court of Directors in London was reluctant to permit the rehabilitation of yet another mill because it realized that such an undertaking would be expensive in the short run and because it believed that the outlay of funds for something that its technical leadership considered to be necessary to the very life of the company would violate a business principle the court was trying to establish: the

TABLE 1
Expenditures and Income of the Real del Monte
Company in Mexico, 1824–1849

Year	Expenditure	Income	Profit or Loss
1824–1827	$ 2,159,970	$ 83,432	− $2,076,538
1828	901,070	140,307	− 760,763
1829	633,487	167,849	− 465,638
1830	559,723	170,079	− 389,644
1831	592,384	141,680	− 450,704
1832	378,067	205,245	− 172,822
1833	372,433	276,669	− 95,764
1834	490,392	377,116	− 113,276
1835	542,058	478,039	− 64,019
1836	636,633	530,237	− 106,396
1837	664,157	717,405	+ 53,248
1838	810,599	838,033	+ 27,434
1839	777,042	646,649	− 130,393
1840	774,583	666,972	− 107,611
1841	790,674	724,470	− 66,204
1842	819,518	858,515	+ 38,997
1843	778,989	785,183	+ 6,194
1844	697,047	667,446	− 29,601
1845	633,847	603,642	− 30,205
1846	714,860	764,694	+ 49,834
1847	747,978	633,039	− 114,939
1848–1849	742,979	662,506	− 80,473
Total	$16,218,490	$11,139,207	− $5,079,283

SOURCES: RdM *Proceedings*, 1831–1845, *passim*; Burkart, *AMM*, I (1861), 48 ff.; Buchan, *Report*, p. 41; 1830 CG 26; *Real del Monte Mining Company (Ex-Debt.)*, p. 2.

requirement that the concern in Mexico earn enough money from day-to-day silver production to cover all expenses, including those incurred by new works.

Financial Matters

During the twenty-five years in which the British Real del Monte Company was in existence, it lost some $5 million in its Mexican operations. Table 1 represents the most complete and accurate record of the concern's expenditures, income, and loss in Mexico that I was able to gather. It does not, however, lay claim to exactness, something that would be difficult if not impossible to accomplish because there are small discrepancies within the firm's own papers and differences between the company records available for consultation and those outside sources needed to complete the financial picture.[10]

More important than the discrepancies in the various sets of figures for the amount the English company lost in Mexico is the fact that, upon the firm's dissolution, the financial position was far more disastrous than is reflected by the $5 million deficit incurred through its mining operations overseas. The interest and bonus due on loans that the company secured in 1827 and 1828, a subject to be discussed later in this chapter, should also be considered. According to a brochure published in October 1848, as the stockholders were giving final consent to the company's going out of business, Real del Monte had a debt of $2.25 million, accumulating interest at 4 per cent a year. In February 1850 the *Mining Journal* in London carried a notice that the dissolved company would repay to some of the firm's creditors a small portion of the money due them, the funds to come from the proceeds of the sale of Real del Monte property and from a trust fund set aside in 1843.[11] Whatever the total repayment, the magnitude of the British Real del Monte Company's financial catastrophe must have come closer to $7.2 million than to the $5 million lost in its Mexican mining operations alone. Every penny spent on a share in the firm's ownership was lost; no part of the 1828 loan—principal, interest, or bonus—was repaid; and even the partial repayment of the preferential 1827 loan was but a small percentage of the amount paid in and the interest and bonus promised. Viewed through an accountant's eyes, then, the company's quest for riches among the silver-laden mountains of Mexico was a simple and total failure.

[10] RdM *Proceedings*, AGC 29 June 1835, p. 10; 30 June 1836, p. 9; 29 June 1841, p. 14; 15 June 1842, p. 7; 27 June 1845, p. 5; J[oseph] Burkart, "Memoria sobre explotación de minas de los distritos de Pachuca y Real del Monte de México," *AMM*, 1 (1861), 49, 51–52; John H. Buchan, *Report of the Director, the Real del Monte Mining Company, Mexico, March 1855*, p. 41.

[11] *Real del Monte Company (Ex-Debt)*, p. 1; advertisement, *MJ*, 20 (9 February 1850), 61.

The fortunes of the Real del Monte concern after the initial enormous expenditure of funds led to intermittent pinch-penny financial management, to sharp financial crises on two occasions, to an investigation of the Mexican operations, and to an attempted revolt on the part of a minority of the English stockholders. During the company's first three years in Mexico, when Commissioner James Vetch was cautioning the London management to expect "a long and expensive time before the mines pay a return," a deficit of just over $2 million was incurred. In that period, as a rule, company agents in Mexico were authorized to make massive outlays of funds to put into operation a mining concern that Vetch proudly described as "on a scale never seen in this country." By early 1829, however, the continued delay in silver production and hence income at the Real forced the Court of Directors to impose a monthly ceiling on expenditures overseas, initially set at approximately $16,000 each for February, March, and April.[12] Henceforward, tight financial restrictions were to be frequently and somewhat haphazardly applied, either by direct orders from London or by the financial exigencies in Mexico. Those restrictions were felt in all phases of company operations.

The first financial crisis occurred in the last quarter of 1828 and the first half of 1829. A contributing factor was Commissioner Tindal's inability to reduce appreciably expenditures in Mexico at a time when the Court of Directors in London, in asking the stockholders for additional capital, was assuring them that such cost reductions would be affected. The company's outlay in Mexico for the last two months of 1828 was $69,411 and $49,710 and for the first two months of 1829, $60,775 and $55,470.[13] Political disturbances in Mexico were a second important cause of that initial crisis. In the fall of 1828, Manuel Gómez Pedraza, opposed by Vicente Guerrero, was declared president following an apparently close vote. The results of the election were disputed by the losing

[12] 1825 CG 8; 1829 CG 14; "Review of the Real del Monte Mining Association: Annual General Meeting, February 15, 1830," *QMR*, no. 4 (January 1831), p. 471.
[13] 1828, 1829 CG 13.

party, and turmoil ensued. In the struggle between the Gómez Pedraza and the Guerrero forces (the latter ultimately gaining victory), open fighting broke out in the capital. It was accompanied by general disorder that culminated in the sacking of the Parián, a market place whose shop owners were mostly Spaniards.[14]

On reaching London, the news of the violence and destruction in the Mexican capital undermined the confidence of the Real del Monte stockholders and, for a time, prevented the company's raising badly needed funds. That a relatively common problem—holding down expenses—and a political disturbance that never directly threatened company property should provoke a financial crisis may seem surprising. But it should be noted that these events came after a period of heavy capital investment with very small compensating income. As Table 1 shows, through 1828 the company spent more than $3 million and earned but $220,000 in Mexico. Moreover, the company had only recently dismissed James Vetch, its first chief commissioner in Mexico, for his delay in "bringing forward ores and converting them into money," while a "constant expenditure has exhausted our resources, when we were hoping to reap the fruit of our labors."[15]

While operations on both sides of the Atlantic were temporarily stalled, the blow in Mexico was softened by the directors' authorizing the commissioner to seek help from the Bolaños Company. Tindal turned at once to the sister concern and found the means to weather his financial storm. In April 1829 and again in July of that year, the chief commissioner applied to Bolaños for short-term loans of $17,000 and $20,000–$30,000, respectively, both of which were apparently granted.[16] Real del Monte thus survived its first money crisis and went on.

During the second severe depression at Real del Monte in 1839

[14] Enrique Olavarría y Ferrari, *México independiente, 1821–1855*, vol. 4 of *México a través de los siglos*, pp. 179–183.

[15] 1829 CG 12; "Review of the Real del Monte Mining Association: Annual General Meeting, February 28, 1829," *QMR*, no. 4 (January 1831), p. 464; "Special General Meeting, June 14, 1827," *QMR*, no. 4 (January 1831), p. 453.

[16] 1829 CG 14; 1829 CG 12.

and 1840, the London management decided to appraise the concern in Mexico to determine whether it should be continued. John Phillips, secretary of the court, and F. Schuchardt from Bolaños, Mexico, made the inspection visits.[17] Schuchardt arrived in Real del Monte at the end of October 1839 and spent three weeks looking into all branches of the mining enterprises. In a general sense, the most significant aspect of Schuchardt's report on Real del Monte was that he found so little to criticize. He thought that some of the mines on the Vizcaína vein had been worked lower than the depth at which large bodies of good ore might still be found, but he thought that other areas of the vast mining complex would compensate for the diminishing amount of silver taken from those mines. He approved of the trials and explorations being made on other veins. Schuchardt dismissed the subject of the surface works at Real del Monte by saying that most of their cost had been defrayed and that halting them as a means of cutting expenses would be sheer waste. While the German expert had some technical recommendations to make regarding the reduction plants, he thought that, on the whole, both the Regla and Sánchez haciendas compared favorably with other such mills in the country. Nor could Schuchardt find much fault with labor policy or the size and cost of its European professional staff.

Though not basically different from the opinions of Schuchardt, Phillips's appraisal of the concern placed greater stress on the need for short-term cost reductions in order to allow Real del Monte to survive until steady profit might be made. The secretary of the Court of Directors arrived at the Real in January 1840 and stayed several months. He took part in the campaign of Chief Commissioner John Rule to cut costs, urging him to suspend part of the trials and explorations approved by Schuchardt as the only practicable means to make material reductions in expenses.

17 "Mr. Phillips's Report to the Directors," RdM *Proceedings*, AGC, 29 June 1841, *passim*; 1839 CG 39. Schuchardt's first name is given as "Fernando" in the law granting the German miner Mexican citizenship (Decree of 31 March 1829, *Colección de decretos de los Congresos Constitucionales del Estado de México*, II, 85).

Phillips's report contained an analysis of the expenditures at Real del Monte. He stated that the number of officers assigned to the establishment in Mexico was "barely sufficient for their duties" and that they were by no means overpaid. However, the secretary considered excessive both the *alimentos*, which in 1840 amounted to $25,547, and the direct government duties on silver and related expenses, which totaled $51,880 for that year, but saw no way of reducing those outlays.[18] As for the mining costs, he found tutwork payments somewhat high but, given the adjustments made during his visit, within reasonable bounds. Another heavy charge on the mines was drainage, notwithstanding the fact that fuel was less expensive at the Real than in most other districts of Mexico. Phillips saw hope, however, in the fact that a new and larger steam engine soon to be put in operation would allow a great saving by superseding three of the four then at work. Finally Phillips judged that silver production from the Vizcaína vein alone would cover the costs of the whole Mexican operation and allow the company to make a profit from its other mines.

John Phillips's hopeful report seemed to be prophetic. Profits accrued to Real del Monte in 1842 and 1843; they were small, but they were nonetheless profits. The Court of Directors told the stockholders that "it is gratifying to observe that this great concern, after contending against innumerable difficulties and vicissitudes, has commenced to yield profits."[19] But the road toward steady returns seen by the directors at the June 1843 stockholders' meeting proved to be a mirage. The following year brought another loss, and in early 1845 the financial situation had not improved.

By the spring of 1845 the financial picture had disquieted some of the shareholders; indeed, one of them staged an abortive revolt

18 The combined charges for *alimentos* and taxes on silver ($75,427), both of which Phillips considered excessive, amounted to less than 10 per cent of the total expenditures for 1840 ($774,583); if they had been avoided entirely during that year, the mining company would have nonetheless lost a considerable amount.

19 1839, 1840 CG 39; "Mr. Phillips's Report to the Directors," RdM *Proceedings*, AGC, 29 June 1841, pp. 7–8, 10–11; RdM *Proceedings*, ASGC, 27 June 1843, p. 1.

against the officials who were conducting the company's affairs. In early March Richard Tyrrell, a stockholder in the Real del Monte and Bolaños companies, circulated a letter among the proprietors of the two concerns, making various charges against the management of both. Tyrrell's letter, together with a rebuttal, was published in the *Mining Journal*, and a Special General Court was called. At that meeting, held on 10 March 1845, Tyrrell submitted his circular letter for consideration, claiming that, of the 143 replies he had received, only one had disagreed with his points of view, namely, that the administrations of the Real del Monte and Bolaños companies be merged, that the post of manager be abolished, and that the offices of the two concerns be moved to a more suitable location. The proprietors, he observed, had just heard what was probably the fortieth in a series of contradictory reports from the directors and from Manager Taylor: "at one time prospects of the most unbounded success—at another the tale of disappointment and hopelessness." Thus Real del Monte had gone on paying no dividend to its stockholders, "while it fed its directors at an extravagant rate."

Leading the counterattack, Robert Price, then chairman of Real del Monte's Court of Directors, contended that a merging of the administrations of Real del Monte and Bolaños, which in any event would accomplish no more than a trivial savings, was illegal. Nor were the stockholders permitted by the deed of settlement to dismiss John Taylor from his position of manager and, even if that move could be legally made, Price asserted, it would be short-sighted to remove the incumbent "from a situation which he filled with honour to himself, and advantage to the association." As for the proposal to move the company's headquarters to another location, most of those present agreed with Price's opinion that the concern would be unable to rent three rooms in London's central business district for the amount it was paying in Taylor's residence.

The somewhat cowed Tyrrell made no formal motion for a vote on his charges and suggestions but rather proposed that a decision on the matter be postponed until the next stockholder's meeting, by which time the view of other proprietors might be sought. Seizing his opportunity, Price demanded that any motion that Tyrrell might make, "which was virtually a vote of want of confidence in the directors, ought at once to be put to the question, and decided one way or the other." At the end of the long, vehement discussion, all present, including even Tyrrell, resolved "that the fullest confidence is reposed by the proprietors in the ability and integrity of the board of directors, and is hereby tendered them."[20]

Aside from making its original investment in February 1824, the British Real del Monte Company sought to raise capital twelve times. All of the calls for additional funds were made before the end of 1840 and nine of them before the end of 1831. On all but two occasions the method employed for raising money was the creation of additional shares; in 1827 and 1828, the firm floated loans among its proprietors, acquiring what proved to be a heavy interest-bearing debt that, in the final struggle for survival in 1848–1849, lessened the stockholders' willingness to hold on while a last attempt was being made to save the concern. Table 2 shows the amount of money acquired, along with the method by which it was raised, during the life of the Real del Monte Company.

Inasmuch as the company burdened itself with a debt of approximately $2.25 million, principal and interest, which contributed in no small way to its eventual collapse, some attention is due the firm's two major loans and its failing, almost pathetic, efforts to lighten the load it had assumed. At a special meeting held in June 1827, the directors were authorized by the stockholders to raise a sum not exceeding £50,000 ($250,000), through a loan secured by the effects of the company and to be repaid from capital or profits before any dividend was declared. Each proprietor was asked to pay an amount of not more than £50 for each share he held. For this advance, he was to receive 5 per cent interest each year, plus an annual bonus of £4 for each share on which he paid

[20] "Original Correspondence: Real del Monte and Bolaños Mining Companies," *MJ*, 15 (8 March 1845), 85; "Proceedings of Public Companies: Real del Monte Mining Company," *MJ*, 15 (15 March 1845), 90; RdM *Proceedings*, SGC, 10 March 1845, pp. i–ii.

TABLE 2

Capital Raised by the Real del Monte Company in London, 1824–1849

Date Authorized	Method	Amount Raised
February 1824	Creation of new shares at £400 each	£200,000
January 1826	Creation of new shares at £400 each	200,000
June 1827	Loan from proprietors	46,820
February 1828	Loan from proprietors	88,750
November 1828	Creation of new shares at £150 each	98,100
August 1829	Creation of new half-shares at £30 each	49,620
August 1829	Conversion of loan scrip into shares at £150 each	1,500
March 1830	Creation of new third-shares at £15 each	74,505
February 1831	Creation of new half-shares at £15 each	56,625
December 1831	Creation of new shares at £10 each	55,500
July 1835	Creation of new quarter-shares at £4.5 each	51,732
July 1837	Creation of new quarter-shares at £2.5 each	26,000
July 1840	Creation of new shares at £2.5 each	30,712
Total		£979,864

SOURCES: RdM *Proceedings*, AGC, 27 June 1845, p. 8; "Review of the Real del Monte Mining Association: Special General Meeting, December 19, 1825," *QMR*, no. 4 (January 1831), p. 441; "Special General Meeting, January 3, 1826," *QMR*, no. 4 (January 1831), p. 444; *LJ*, 3 (1825), 69.

NOTE: At the exchange rate of $5 per British pound, the total amount raised was $4,899,320.

the additional £50. As though one millstone were not enough, before a year had passed the directors got permission to attach a second to the concern. In February and March 1828 a loan of £100 per share was asked of the then one thousand proprietors under the same terms that had been established for the 1827 loan.

In August 1829, while creating a new stock issue, the company made the first attempt to rid itself of the burden of paying interest on the two loans. Each proprietor who took up one £150 share of the new stock was entitled to another share of the same face value, provided he surrendered his claim both to the principal of the two above-mentioned loans (of £50 and £100, respectively) and to such interest and bonus as had accrued thereon. The Court of Directors was, moreover, empowered to purchase in the name of the company such loan receipts for £150 as it deemed advantageous to the interests of the concern. By the end of 1833, purchases of loan receipts by the directors and the conversion of scrip into shares had reduced the principal of the debt by only £4,000, leaving an interest-bearing sum of £135,670 on the company's accounts.[21]

During 1833 and 1834 the firm made a second unsuccessful attempt to rid itself of those two interest-bearing loans. Pressed by the now somewhat desperate directors, the stockholders reluctantly approved a series of resolutions designed to eliminate a large and growing debt of approximately £245,810 ($1,229,050), by allowing the note holders to accept shares in lieu of their loan receipts. Real del Monte's management was, of course, simply engaging in a second round of what might be construed as a ruse. Unless the mining company became profitable, neither the loan receipts nor the shares would have much, or perhaps any, value, but at least the creditors had a legal right to collect what they could of the money they had advanced. It should be no surprise, therefore, to learn that the reaction of the company's creditors to the scheme was less than enthusiastic. By the end of 1841 the principal of the debt amounted to £135,570,[22] only £100 less than that shown in the account for 1833.

After the company had entered a brief period of profitable operations in 1842 and 1843, the belief that its fortunes were at last permanently on the rise prompted the management, early in 1843, to make a final effort. But the directors, perhaps chastened but more likely angered by the near-total rejection of their earlier proposals, tried a new and more complicated maneuver. They proposed, and the loan note holders agreed, that the two loans, whose principal, interest, and bonus had swelled to £391,076 ($1,955,380) by 30 June 1842, be capitalized and interest on them paid out of profits at an annual rate of 4 per cent. The Court of Directors was authorized to issue 1,872 red debentures, each worth

21 RdM *Proceedings*, AGC, 27 June 1831, p. 10; "Review of the Real del Monte Mining Association: Special General Meeting, August 5, 1829," *QMR*, no. 4 (January 1831), 469; RdM *Proceedings*, AGC, 25 June 1834, p. 12.

22 RdM *Proceedings*, Adjourned SGC, 12 February 1834, pp. ii–iv; RdM *Proceedings*, AGC, 15 June 1842, p. 10.

approximately £74, and 3,548 black debentures, each worth approximately £71. The red represented the principal, interest, and bonus of the 1827 loan and the black, of the 1828 loan. Beginning on 30 June 1842, both types of debentures were to accrue the annual 4 per cent interest, the holders of the red having a prior call for payment over those holding the black.[23]

It is difficult to determine how many of the loan note holders saw enough merit in this latest scheme and converted their scrip into debentures. Doubtless some did, for both red and black Real del Monte debentures began to appear on the London market. But the company's loan notes continued to be traded. When the Real del Monte Company finally collapsed, it still owed the holders of its varied and multihued certificates of indebtedness $2.25 million.[24]

The unhappy and too-familiar story of Real del Monte's financial plight throughout most of its existence is also reflected in the price its securities commanded on the London stock exchange. Table 3 presents a picture of the company's standard securities, its registered shares, in precipitous and nearly steady decline. The depiction is essentially accurate and self-explanatory, but why the tremendous height from which the plunge began? After all, the initial price of a share of Real del Monte stock was supposed to be only £400. A comment made by the *Quarterly Review* in early 1825 suggests an answer: "To what will not men persuade themselves, when we find that a single share of a certain mine named Real del Monte, on which £70 only had been advanced, rose to a premium of £1,400 a share, or 2,000 per cent!"[25] The rush to amass great fortunes from Mexican silver-mining ventures caused Real del Monte shares to become the object of extreme speculation on the London market, their dramatic rise and fall in price being a part of a general speculative mania and subsequent crash that occurred between 1823 and 1826. A month before the February

23 RdM *Proceedings*, SGC, 7 March, 10 April, 27 April, 27 June 1843, pp. i–iv.

24 "Price of Shares, Foreign Mines," *MJ*, 12 (30 September 1843), 322; *Real del Monte Mining Company* (*Ex-Debt*), p. 1.

25 "Canals and Rail-Roads," *Quarterly Review*, 31 (December 1824, March 1825), 352.

TABLE 3

Representative Prices of Real del Monte Registered
Shares on the London Market, 1824–1848

Date	Price
January 1824	£1,479.00
December 1824	670.00
October 1825	410.00
January 1826	400.00
November 1828	150.00
August 1829	60.00
March 1830	45.00
February 1831	30.00
December 1831	10.00
December 1832	19.00
August 1833	71.00
December 1834	26.00
July 1835	18.00
June 1836	21.00
June 1837	14.00
July 1838	12.00
December 1839	6.00
July 1840	2.50
December 1841	2.13
December 1842	1.25
March 1843	4.00
January 1844	4.25
January 1845	4.00
January 1846	3.50
January 1847	3.50
January 1848	1.88
July 1848	.88
October 1848	.63

SOURCES: RdM *Proceedings*, AGC, SGC, ASGC, 1831–1845, *passim*; "Price of Shares," *QMR*, no. 7 (July 1835), appendix, pp. viii–x; "Price of Shares, Foreign Mines," *MJ*, 2–18 (1836–1848), *passim*.

1824 organizing meeting of the prospective stockholders had formally set a price of £400 on Real del Monte shares, they were being exchanged at nearly four times that value. Although such fantastic inflation could not continue beyond a few months, the artificially high price of Real del Monte stock persisted to the end of the year, when its market fell off. On 21 December the shares were quoted at £740; nine days later their price had dropped to £670. The downward trend continued into the following year; by October 1825 they had been traded for as little as £200 but had climbed up to a price of £410. In January 1826, when a second issue of securities was put on the market, the price was still equal to that set for the original one thousand shares.[26] Thereafter the exchange value of Real del Monte securities began to tumble, and they never again approached their initial price.

[26] Newton R. Gilmore, "British Mining Ventures in Early National Mexico," (Ph.D. dissertation, University of California, 1956), pp. 13–18; *The Morning Chronicle* (London), 21 and 30 December 1824, p. 2; English, *General Guide*, p. 107; "Review of the Real del Monte Mining Association: Special General Meeting, January 3, 1826," *QMR*, no. 4 (January 1831), 444.

5. Mining Operations

L IKE VEINS OF METAL, TWO THEMES RUN THROUGH THE TECHNI-
cal aspects of the British Real del Monte Company's history.
First was the persuasion of nearly every company official who ever
expressed himself that the English could and should carry with
them to Mexico technological improvements for the mining and
milling of silver ore. In mining they had two distinct advantages
over the natives: knowledge and a machine. Company officers
shared with other Europeans searching for silver in the mountains
of Mexico the smug conviction that they simply knew more than
the Mexicans about underground operations, regardless of the metal being mined. Real del Monte officers were equally sure that the
steam engine would both revitalize and revolutionize mining in
Mexico, a country that had as yet barely seen that mechanical
wonder. In milling the British were less sure of themselves. They
had no miraculous engine to apply to the age-old problem of extracting silver from its ore, and they had relatively little experience
in that field. Nonetheless, those of them who knew anything at all

about silver reduction methods, and in particular John Taylor, were aware that the traditional patio amalgamation process of Mexico was woefully inefficient and should be improved. The English adventurers of Real del Monte believed that these advances would permit them to realize a handsome profit for themselves and would contribute significantly to the rehabilitation of a ruined Mexican industry.

Second is the suggestion of an ironic failure: while the British concern collapsed as an economic enterprise, in part because of blunders committed by its leaders in mining and milling, the firm succeeded in making lasting technical advances, particularly in the areas of drainage and the treatment of low-grade silver ore. They lost $5 million, but they aided those who followed them at Real del Monte and helped to rescue the whole industry from the depression into which it had fallen prior to their arrival. The Real del Monte adventurers clung doggedly to the notions that they took with them to Mexico. They never ceased to believe that they could remove water from the mines they took under contract more efficiently and cheaply than the owners had done before, even in the great days of the House of Regla. And they continued to believe that they could devise a method of reducing silver ore better than the one employed for centuries at Real del Monte and throughout colonial Mexico. They were right in both instances, but the company went under while its officers were proving those points. It was left to their successors to profit from the innovations made by the bankrupt English adventurers.

Most of the mining operations, in terms of raising ore, were carried out between the end of 1827, when the preparatory work was completed,[1] and early 1849, when the already-dissolved company sold its Mexican establishment. The income from ore extraction and other sources was, for the years 1824–1827, but a little more than $31,000, while that for the years 1828–1849 exceeded $11 million.[2] During the latter period, by far the greatest effort was

[1] For the location of the principal mines in Real del Monte, see Map 3.

[2] J[oseph] Burkart, "Memoria sobre explotación de minas de los distritos de Pachuca y Real del Monte de México," *AMM*, 1 (1861), table following p. 48.

TABLE 4

Mine Production at Real del Monte, 1824–1844

Property	Expenditure	Income	Loss
Regla mines and mills	$11,244,435	$8,013,235	$3,231,200
Morán mine	827,796	277,200	550,596
Branch mines			
Santa Inés	216,119	166,358	49,761
Valenciana–San Felipe–Cabrera	95,774	9,382	86,392
Gran Compaña	36,861	317	36,544
San Esteban	25,227	707	24,520
Santa Clara	7,558	. . . . . .	7,558
San Nicolás	6,059	. . . . . .	6,059
Tezuantla	2,274	. . . . . .	2,274

SOURCE: RdM *Proceedings*, AGC, 27 June 1845, p. 5.

exerted on the Regla properties at Real del Monte, on the Vizcaína, Santa Brígida, and Acosta veins. The only other area to receive comparable attention was the Morán mine, also located at the Real. Table 4 suggests the relative importance of the properties exploited in that district from the time of its establishment through 1844.[3]

Outside of Real del Monte, the company was engaged in few mining activities. The properties at Ozumatlán and Zimapán were given up by the early 1830's, and those at Pachuca, which was not entered until 1844, were not fully developed by the time the concern went out of business. Finally, during the late 1830's and early 1840's, the company made a protracted but futile attempt to mine quicksilver in the El Doctor district, located in the present state of Querétaro, just west of the Hidalgo border and about fifty miles from Zimapán.[4]

Regla Properties

Between 1827 and 1842, the Real del Monte Company gave highest priority to the discovery and extraction of ore in the Viz-

[3] *Proceedings at the General Courts of Proprietors of the Real del Monte Mining Company* (cited hereafter as RdM *Proceedings*), AGC, 27 June 1845, p. 5.

[4] For a discussion of the company's efforts to supply itself with quicksilver and of the role of the El Doctor mercury mines, see Chapter 8.

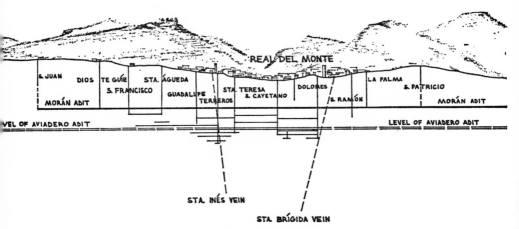

6. Workings on the Vizcaína vein, 1824–1849.

caína vein. (See Map 6.) The initial approach was based on an 1801 report prepared by agents of the third Count of Regla and descriptive of the levels of the Vizcaína mines that had been abandoned because of the prohibitive cost of drainage. Determined to reach and exploit the deepest, but presumably also the richest, part of the count's possessions, the company for several years placed particular emphasis on the 900–yard section of the Vizcaína vein between the Guadalupe shaft on the west and the Dolores shaft on the east. The 1801 document revealed that a level had been dug the entire distance, at a depth of some 65 yards under the Morán adit, and that the productive areas of the vein had been exhausted down to that level and partially worked some distance below. The company's prime interest, therefore, was in what lay beneath the old level.[5]

With a view to completing the drainage of the deep workings of the Vizcaína and providing easy access to the area from which such riches were anticipated, the company set out to sink an entirely new shaft about halfway between the Santa Teresa and Guadalupe

[5] RdM *Proceedings*, SGC, 23 November 1831, pp. 4–5.

mines. Given the politic name of Terreros, the shaft was to be the
English concern's most impressive engineering feat. The digging
was scheduled to begin in January 1830, not only from the surface
but also simultaneously from the intersection of its projected line
of progress with several levels and crosscuts underground; this
plan led the company officers to expect the shaft to be sunk about
320 yards in the short period of twelve months. "The mode of
executing shafts by rising and sinking at the same time in different lifts, as they are called, has been I believe, only practiced to
any extent in Cornwall," Taylor said; "it is unknown to the Mexican miners, and is even now looked upon as almost impossible."[6]

Already several months behind schedule in the spring of 1831,
the Terreros shaft was not finished until three more years had
elapsed. Part of the delay was due to difficulties in obtaining and
shipping to Mexico a new steam engine needed to keep the lower
reaches dry during the final digging. Then, too, minor accidents
retarded the work. The Vizcaína vein was finally reached toward
the close of 1832 and the digging completed, at an unspecified
depth, in January 1834. The total cost as shown in the company
accounts for 1834, and presumably the entire cost of the undertaking, was $242,741.[7]

Since the purpose of the new shaft was to facilitate the raising
of the rich ore thought to lie deep in the Santa Teresa mine, the
barreteros set to work in July 1833, even before the project was
finished, thus beginning what was called the Santa Teresa bonanza.
Its end was nearer than company officials realized. The rather
limited area to which the strike was confined lay between the Santa
Teresa and Terreros shafts, approximately 46 yards along the
Vizcaína vein and about 92 yards below the Morán adit. (This
was an area from which John Taylor, in 1831, had foreseen the
existence of 137 yards of rich ore.) From it, ore worth about

[6] RdM *Proceedings*, SGC, 9 February 1831, pp. 4–5, 8.

[7] RdM *Proceedings*, SGC, 23 November 1831, pp. i, 1; AGC, 11 June 1832, p.
4; 21 June 1833, p. 3; 29 June 1835, p. 9; John H. Buchan, *Report of the Director, the Real del Monte Mining Company, Mexico, March 1855*, p. 40.

$300,000 was extracted between July 1833 and January 1834.[8] The long-anticipated exploitation of the most promising area described in the Count of Regla's 1801 report, then, fell short of being the salvation of the British Real del Monte Company.

Yet the Santa Teresa mine, known by the name of its shaft Terreros, continued to be one of the most important properties leased by the British firm. In September 1843 Commissioner William Rule called it the "principal support" of the mining concern. In less than a year, however, he described it as "rather poor" and saw little prospect of making a significant new ore discovery in its deep workings. On orders from London, he conducted a final test of the lower reaches, but in mid–1845, faced with the need for drastic reductions in expenditures, suspended all activity in the mine.

Next to Santa Teresa, or Terreros, the Vizcaína property that received the most attention was Dolores. Indeed, that mine, which yielded $128,974 during 1831 and $176,310 in the first eight months of 1832, was so promising that, in June 1833, Taylor told the stockholders that "the discovery in Dolores will ensure to a certain extent the success of the concern, and give a pleasing anticipation of further pursuit in depth." Toward the end of 1832, however, ore extraction had been halted to allow the sinking of a diagonal shaft, following the vein downward to the deepest workings in the area. That task was to have been completed by October or November. Taylor's optimistic prediction notwithstanding, the project lagged during the next several years, and it was not until November 1837 that the bottom levels were drained, to a depth of about 150 yards below the adit, and preparations made for the *barreteros* to raise ore.[9]

The frustration of having been so long denied control of the ore ground in the Dolores mine gave way to a kind of indifference on the part of company officials when, on laying open that area, no bonanza was forthcoming. By June 1841 the mine, like Terreros, was

[8] RdM *Proceedings*, SGC, 23 November 1831, pp. 5–6; AGC, 24 June, 1834, p. 3; 1835 CG 35.
[9] 1843, 1844, 1845 CG 48; RdM *Proceedings*, AGC, 21 June 1833, pp. 1, 4–5; 1837 CG 39.

looked upon as a consistent but not spectacular producer, helping to cover the concern's expenses but no more. The mine was, nevertheless, to hold out new hopes and afford yet another disappointment to the company.

In the fall of 1844 an important discovery was made in the San Enrique winze of the Dolores mine, which came to include workings in San Cayetano as well. By the end of April 1845, that winze, sunk beneath the bottom level of the mine, had become the most productive point on the Vizcaína vein, yielding large quantities of both *azogue* and smelting ore. At about the same time, the company started sinking a second winze, San Pablo, a short distance east of San Enrique.

The workings in the San Enrique and San Pablo winzes of the Dolores mine came to rank among the two or three most important sources of ore in the entire Real del Monte mining complex. By April 1847, however, the high-grade ore in Dolores had begun to decrease both in quantity and quality. In sinking the San Pablo winze, the miners had encountered two slides that had interrupted and fractured the vein, which no longer had the appearance of a fine silver lode but was filled with clay.

Even when the miners succeeded in digging beyond the slide, the vein was found to be productive only of *azogue* ore in quantity, but contained little smelting ore. The company collapsed while the last chief commissioner, John Buchan, was struggling to reduce expenditures and to find salvation in a productive Vizcaína reached through the San Pablo winze of the Dolores mine.[10]

Despite the importance given the Terreros and Dolores mines, other sections of the long Vizcaína vein were not overlooked. Extending the Morán adit eastward in the direction of the mines of San Ramón and La Palma began at the end of 1833. Work progressed slowly, and it was not until the spring of 1838 that the adit was cleared as far as San Ramón. Some trials and explorations

[10] RdM *Proceedings*, AGC, 27 June 1838, p. 4; 29 June 1841, p. 4; 15 June 1842, p. 1; 1844, 1845, 1847, 1848 CG 48; "Mining Correspondence, Foreign Mines: Real del Monte Mines," *MJ*, 18 (29 July 1848), 356, (26 August 1848), 399, (30 September 1848), 457, (28 October 1848), 504.

were carried out during the next few years, but without encouraging results. In late 1843 company officials considered San Ramón not sufficiently promising to warrant the expense of any work other than that necessary to keep the shaft open, should a further trial on the eastern end of the Vizcaína be attempted. The firm's downfall ended all work in San Ramón before any ore discovery was made.

The company was at first more fortunate in its explorations at the western end of the Vizcaína, where by 1838 work began in the San Francisco and Dios Te Guíe mines. Before the end of 1841, San Francisco was being looked into as a source of income. Three years later, William Rule regretfully notified the home office that San Francisco had thus far yielded so little ore that, in order to reduce expenditures, he had halted the principal trials in that mine. All work was soon suspended and, like San Ramón at the other end of the Vizcaína, San Francisco ceased to occupy the attention of the English company.[11]

The most important area worked by the British Real del Monte Company, aside from the Vizcaína, were the Regla properties on the Santa Brígida and Acosta veins. (See map 7.) Neither lode produced a large amount of ore before 1840, but together they held out the possibility of compensating the company for the repeated disappointments it had experienced in working the Vizcaína. The Santa Brígida mines took on considerable importance during the last stages of the British adventure; indeed, the vein as a whole rivaled the Vizcaína for first place among the properties worked by the concern. Some ore was taken from the southern end of the Santa Brígida lode, near its intersection with the Vizcaína. A second and more productive area was centered around the Sacra-

11 RdM *Proceedings*, AGC, 25 June 1834, p. 4; 27 June 1838, pp. 5, 7; "Mr. Phillips's Report to the Directors," RdM *Proceedings*, AGC, 29 June 1841, p. 10; 1841, 1842 CG 39; 1843, 1845 CG 48; "Mining Correspondence, Foreign Mines: Real del Monte Mining Company," *MJ*, 11 (11 December 1841), 394. One of the most important strikes made in the Real del Monte district in the early 1850's by the Mexican successor to the British mining concern was precisely in the untouched ground in the San Ramón mine (Buchan, *Report*, pp. 43–44).

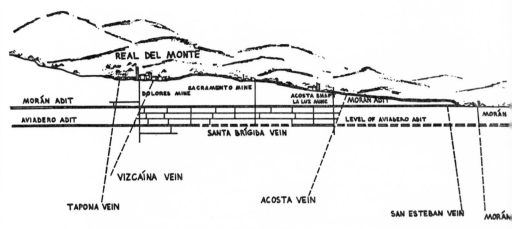

7. Workings on the Santa Brígida and Acosta veins, 1824–1849.

mento mine, which, though not at first counted among the sources of rich or abundant ore, after 1845 yielded a steady, if not spectacular, amount of *azogues*. It was, in fact, still producing when the British firm went out of business.

Not until 1838 was the concern able to begin large-scale explorations on the Acosta vein. At that time the drainage of the northern part of the Real del Monte district permitted work through the old Acosta shaft. In mid-1839, Commissioner John Rule was so encouraged by the mine's increasing production that he had a thirty-inch steam engine no longer needed on the Dolores shaft moved to Acosta. His decision seemed justified by a discovery of ore that yielded some $120,000 in the eight months beginning in August 1841.

The Acosta mine was one of the company's principal sources of ore supply in 1842. Early the next year, however, the lower workings became flooded and production began to fall off. It was not long before the entire Acosta vein appeared to be failing. Between 1845 and 1848, the ore raised from that lode contributed relatively little to the company's income. Early in 1848, when the company was beginning to collapse, a fair amount of both smelting and *azogue* ores was discovered. It was then observed, not without some irony, that, while the *barreteros* were able to raise ore from above the level of the water, they were not permitted to descend two or three levels lower, where indications pointed to enough ore to make the concern profitable.[12]

Morán

During the early years of the company's mining operations, the Morán mine, on the vein of the same name, proved to be troublesome, promising, and finally disappointing. (See Map 8.) Just as it was being brought into production in 1827, it was the scene of two short, violent skirmishes between the English company and the Mexican *barreteros*. The labor dispute was more than compensated for, however, by the growing conviction that Morán, though not extensive, was extremely fruitful. The mine continued to inspire optimism through 1828, 1829, and 1830. When it failed completely as a productive mine in 1831, Morán dealt the English concern one of the harshest blows it had received thus far.[13]

Resigned to the fact that a profit would not be gained from its once richest mine, the company sought to make the best of a bad situation by revising its contract with Tomás Murphy. The most important change in the terms was a reduction in the *alimento* payment from $20,000 to $10,000 a year. Not until two years before it went out of existence did the British concern attempt to resume a large-scale exploitation of Morán, which, after the 1831 failure, had been worked sporadically and only to the extent required by Mexican law for retaining possession.[14]

Before the company could try once more to make a profit from Morán, it was compelled to engage in a difficult negotiation in order to extend the agreement under which it possessed and worked

[12] 1839, 1841 CG 39; 1845–1848 CG 48; RdM *Proceedings*, AGC, 27 June 1838, p. 8; 15 June 1842, p. 1; "Mining Correspondence, Foreign Mines: Real del Monte Mines," *MJ*, 18 (1 April 1848), 156.

[13] RdM *Proceedings*, SGC, 9 February 1831, p. 2; AGC, 26 June 1831, p. 4; 11 June 1832, p. 8.

[14] RdM *Proceedings*, AGC, 11 June 1832, pp. 2, 8, 9, 12; 21 June 1833, pp. 9, 12; 27 June 1845, p. 5.

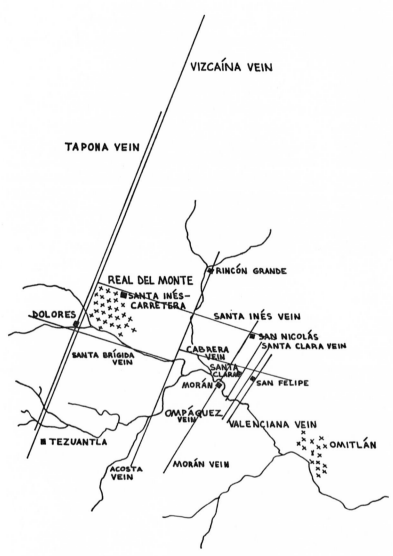

8. Morán and the branch mines, 1824–1849.

the mine. Real del Monte officials in London and Mexico became involved in a two-year dispute with the mine owner—regarding whose identity there was some doubt—and with agents of different members of the Murphy family claiming to represent the true proprietor. (It will be recalled that in March 1824 John Taylor, on behalf of Real del Monte, signed a contract with John Murphy, acting for his brother Tomás, for the lease of the mine for twenty-one years, that agreement being ratified in Mexico in July of the same year.) Only after a protracted series of talks, complicated by a struggle within the Murphy family, was the Real del Monte Company able to conclude an agreement for taking a second lease on the Morán mine. The new contract, made in both London and Mexico in early 1848, assured the British firm the right to reimbursement of a recognized debt of $670,000 against the mine. *Alimentos* were reduced to $1,000 a year, and the company reserved the right to abandon the mine, without penalty, any time after seven years from the effective date of the agreement, September 1846.

Work in the Morán mine was conducted for but a few months after the conclusion of the negotiations for re-leasing the property. By May 1848, just as John Buchan was arriving at Real del Monte to make a desperate attempt to save the concern, the amount of smelting ore yielded by the mine was beginning to fall off. In June the last chief commissioner noted that Morán was still capable of helping the company; yet, as a part of the general economy measures he was obliged to take, he suspended all explorations and ore extraction in the mine.[15]

Pachuca

Since accounts of the Real del Monte Company's mining efforts on other properties at its principal camp, known collectively by the disparaging name "branch mines," are quite similar to those already treated—a little good luck and a lot of bad, work largely de-

---

[15] Acta de los socios del Real del Monte, 1° de junio de 1840, RdM, Account-file IV-C-1, pp. 9, 11–12; 1848 CG 48; "Mining Correspondence, Foreign Mines: Real del Monte Mines," *MJ*, 15 (29 July 1848), 356.

termined by the extent to which the mines could be drained, and prospects fluctuating between promising and discouraging—to relate them would contribute little to this work. Nor is much to be gained from looking into the company's much-troubled operations at El Doctor, Ozumatlán, and Zimapán. Their stories would also sound too familiar. Pachuca, one district away from the Real at which the concern carried on some mining, remains and definitely deserves attention. There the British Real del Monte Company sat in the most direct sense squarely atop a fabulously rich mine, which it was too weak financially and technologically to exploit fully. Doubtless the Rosario mine could have saved the English adventurers; it made their successors rich.

Twenty years after undertaking its Mexican operations, and only five years before its dissolution, the British concern turned its attention to the Pachuca mining district. It did so after a series of experiments with an ore treatment method new to the whole Real del Monte–Pachuca region (the barrel, or Freiburg, amalgamation process) had furnished convincing evidence that hitherto refractory ore could be treated profitably by that method. Noting in February 1844 that the company's success in reducing what were called "colorado and black tierras" had caused a "great sensation in the neighborhood," William Rule made a trip to Pachuca, where there were said to be numerous long-abandoned mines capable of yielding great quantities of those types of ore. In that nearby camp he made an agreement for the company's leasing the Rosario mine, located on two veins (Santa Rita and Jacal) and reputed to have been productive in the distant past.[16]

Full exploitation of the Rosario mine was subject to two difficulties. First, ore from the new property had to be carried laboriously by pack mule over a mountainous trail to the reducing mills at Real del Monte and Huasca. Second, Rosario ore could be handled efficiently only in the slowly developing barrel amalgamation plant

[16] 1844 CG 48. For the location of Pachuca and its veins worked by the British mining concern, see Maps 2 and 3.

at the Sánchez hacienda. Although for those reasons work in Rosario did begin slowly in 1844 and was even partially suspended in the latter half of 1845, in April of the following year the mine temporarily became the company's most productive property in terms of the quantity of ore raised. Of that month's total production of 435 tons, the Pachuca mines accounted for 135. In June 1847 the raising of *azogues* from Rosario was halted for a practical reason; the barrels then in operation at the Sánchez mill could be fully supplied from the Santa Brígida vein and, until more barrels could be put to work, Rosario's ore could not be reduced. Despite the fact that a small amount of smelting ore was extracted the next year, Rosario, which in the 1850's was to yield one of the most spectacular bonanzas in the history of the Real del Monte–Pachuca district,[17] was considered a liability to the British company.

Through its subsidiary, the Pachuca Mining Company, the Real del Monte Company made a second penetration into the Pachuca camp in 1844. The new firm began operations in two mines, La Esperanza and La Rejona, both of which had the advantage of being located on the side of a high mountain above the town and could thus be drained, should that prove necessary, by means of adits rather than expensive steam engines. Eventually, three other mines were worked to some extent. Despite the "advantage" of mountainside mines and experienced personnel on loan from the parent concern, the branch company did not prove to be a profitable venture. On ordering a Real del Monte–Pachuca officer to suspend all operation of the Pachuca Mining Company in the spring of 1848, the secretary of the Court of Directors sounded a plaintive note that adumbrated the death knell of the parent firm: "To your-

[17] 1845–1848 CG 48. An 1859 report on the Mexican mining company had this to say of Rosario: "This mine, although it has now yielded the very large quantity of 702,659 *cargas* of ore (94,106 tons, 2 cwts., 36 lbs.), leaving a profit of $3,898,659, presents no appearance of falling off. A large reserve ground is in sight and the vein improving in depth . . . The probability is that a continued production for many years is to be relied on" (Thomas B. Auld, [*Report of the Director, the Real del Monte Mining Company April 1859*], p. 7).

self . . . and to others who have rendered assistance in this unfortunate adventure, I can only return my personal thanks and express my regret that the want of success prevents them from being properly remunerated."[18]

Drainage Problem at Real del Monte

The best place to evaluate the extent to which blunders in mining committed by its leaders, or simple bad luck, contributed to the failure of the English mining company is not in Pachuca or one of the more distant outcamps but back at Real del Monte. And the best subject to follow in examining the themes stated at the beginning of this chapter is mine drainage. The pride of John Taylor and his lieutenants demanded that the English apply their superior knowledge and the steam engine to the ancient problem of keeping underground water from hampering ore-raising operations. Just how well, or poorly, did the English do in draining the Real del Monte mines?

The Real del Monte Company began its mining activities in Mexico by committing two errors that doubtless helped bring about its downfall. The first was Commissioner James Vetch's determination to construct a large, permanent plant, a course of action that Manager John Taylor supported for three years. The cost of that undertaking was so great that the firm's initial capital was quickly exhausted and the Court of Directors was forced to begin a disheartening series of calls for additional funds. In an effort to correct this first mistake in judgment, the company adopted a policy of retrenchment in 1827. Though by no means halted immediately, the heavy outlays were gradually curbed. The calls on capital were nonetheless continued, and only an extraordinarily willing body of stockholders enabled the concern to go on in the face of steady losses. As the discussion of the company's financial management

18 "Pachuca Mining Company," *MJ*, 14 (24 August 1844), 285; "Proceedings of Public Companies: Pachuca Mining Company," *MJ*, 15 (31 May 1845), 218; "Mining Correspondence, Foreign Mines: Pachuca Mining Company," *MJ*, 16 (4 July 1846), 248; "Mining Notabilia (Extracts from our Correspondence): Pachuca Mining Company," *MJ*, 17 (5 June 1847), 261; 1848 CG 45.

has shown, Real del Monte never did fully recover from the damage done by the first of its two fundamental errors in strategy.

The second error was the original decision taken in London to drain the lowest levels of the Vizcaína vein by steam power and to exploit a large body of rich ore supposedly left standing by the third Count of Regla in 1801, when he suspended the deep drainage of that lode. It was not until the end of 1833 that the magnitude of the second mistake became apparent. By that time the long-sought rich ore deep in the Vizcaína vein had been found but had proven to be a disappointment. From an area in which Taylor, basing his calculation on the above-mentioned 1801 report, foresaw the existence of 137 yards of rich ore, only 46 yards were encountered. They were exhausted after yielding merely $300,000 worth of silver by the beginning of 1834. The entirely new shaft, Terreros, had by then been required, and its cost, approximately $243,000, was nearly equal to the value of the ore it had been dug to reveal. Moreover, the company had already accumulated about 86 per cent of the amount it would ultimately lose in its Mexican operations. The financial results of the decision to drain the deepest levels of the Vizcaína vein in hopes of finding the bonanza that company officials had been encouraged to believe awaited them were, then, as disastrous as those of Vetch's decision to construct expensive surface works before going after silver ore. There is, however, another and perhaps more important dimension to the results of the Vizcaína drainage decision.

When the company adopted as its first order of business the finding and working of ore in the deep levels of the Vizcaína, it committed itself also to the steam drainage of all the ground below the Morán adit. In doing so, the British concern was to take on one of the most vexing and persistent problems it would encounter in Mexico. In another sense, however, drainage was one of the areas in which the English made a far-reaching change in Mexican mining techniques: essentially the replacing of the long out-dated *malacate* with the steam engine. In accordance with a deliberate plan to effect that technological advance, the company began its operations with several small steam-powered machines. As the problem of lowering the water level became more difficult, the company had to send larger and larger engines to Real del Monte. The attempts at steam-engine drainage were never entirely successful, and, from time to time, completion of the Aviadero adit was regarded as a necessary supplementary measure. By 1848 the company had made tremendous advances over the drainage system of its predecessor and a significant contribution to a technological revolution in Mexican mining, but it desperately needed a new and larger engine to carry on.

At no time did the British concern make a really strenuous effort to complete the Aviadero adit, which had been begun by the third Count of Regla in 1816. It was most energetic in pursuing the project when prodded by the count or when successful at the mines. Until the Santa Teresa bonanza of 1833, Romero de Terreros' insistence was responsible for most of the work, which consisted of driving in the adit from its mouth, at a very slow pace, through hard rock. The expansion of the company's operations as a result of the Santa Teresa strike included plans for sinking two adit shafts in advance of the proposed line of driving, in order to provide ventilation and to allow for the digging of the Aviadero from more than one point. In giving its authorization to proceed with those shafts, the London management acknowledged that its contract with the Count of Regla called for the energetic pursuit of work on the Aviadero.[19]

Its contractual arrangements with the Count of Regla notwithstanding, the English concern made little uniform effort to include the Aviadero adit in its overall drainage plans for the Real del Monte district. Only one of the advance shafts was completed. In the fall of 1835 Commissioner John Rule reported that the first adit shaft, named La Virgen, was deep enough to require artificial drainage to carry it down to the Aviadero level, where a second face could be commenced in the digging of the adit itself. Two years later, when his request for permission to place a small steam

19 RdM *Proceedings*, AGC, 21 June 1833, p. 4; 25 June, 1834, p. 5.

engine on the shaft to facilitate its completion and hence to speed up the driving of the main tunnel had apparently been ignored in London, Rule decided on his own to install a pressure steam machine at La Virgen. Another two years were to elapse before the Aviadero was completed to the adit shaft, although by that time a level that would become a part of the main tunnel had been pressed some distance south from that shaft, in the direction of the Vizcaína vein.

During the company's remaining years in Mexico, little was done to carry the Aviadero southward from its mouth toward the Vizcaína vein. A September 1842 report showed not much advance in the tunnel beyond the Virgen shaft; indeed, most of the ninety yards driven from that point had been covered between 1837 and 1839. Almost no reference is made to further work in this area. In the spring of 1848, just before the firm ceased to operate the Real del Monte mines, six Mexican *barreteros* were engaged in driving the Aviadero south from La Virgen; their progress through very hard rock was painfully slow, about two feet a week. Approximately nine hundred yards had been dug from the opening, with some three thousand to go before the adit would reach the Vizcaína.

The original prospectus of the British company cast doubt on the usefulness of the Aviadero adit, especially in view of plans to send steam engines to Mexico for the drainage of the Real del Monte mines. The company seems to have adopted an attitude of indifference toward the great tunnel and toward the obligation it had assumed, in its contracts with the third Count of Regla, to pursue the driving of the Aviadero with all due energy. Its disdain was well expressed by a man who became probably the concern's chief spokesman during the final decade of its life, John Phillips, secretary of the Court of Directors. Writing in the *Mining Journal* in 1845, Phillips discussed the widespread use of drainage tunnels in Mexican mining and noted that the Real del Monte district afforded the best example of them. To illustrate his point, he described the old Morán adit in some detail. His only reference to the Aviadero shaft was almost offhanded when he said that "an adit of much greater depth is now in progress in the same district, but it cannot be completed for a long time to come."[20]

The initial efforts to introduce steam-engine drainage at Real del Monte were, for the most part, concentrated on the Vizcaína vein. Captain Vetch installed one small, thirty-inch engine on the Dolores shaft, and Tindal placed another on the San Cayetano shaft. As if to call attention to the change it was bringing about, the English firm arranged for an elaborate ceremony, attended by government officials and diplomatic representatives of Great Britain and the Netherlands, along with an agent of the indisposed Count of Regla, to mark the starting of the second machine on 9 November 1828. By the end of 1829 the English had drained the mines of the Vizcaína to a depth of 108 yards below the Morán adit, the level at which their deep workings had been suspended by the second Count of Regla in 1801. Those steam engines, which pumped water at the rate of 600 gallons per minute, were operated at a cost of approximately $30,000 a year. That expenditure was in marked contrast to the $250,000 spent by the second count in using 28 *malacates* to maintain the drainage to the same level.[21]

In 1830 company officials had to admit that two small steam engines were not adequate for a deeper drainage of the central Vizcaína, and a decision was made to dig an entirely new shaft (Terreros) for a third. Both Commissioner Tindal and his mine manager, John Rule, strongly urged the directors in London to send

[20] 1835 CG 35; 1837, 1842 CG 39; "Mining Correspondence, Foreign Mines: Real del Monte Mining Company," *MJ*, 1 (12 December 1835), p. 134; 12 (10 November 1839), p. 367; 18 (27 May 1848), 252; RdM *Proceedings*, AGC, 30 June 1836, p. 5; *Real del Monte Mining Company* (*Ex-Debt.*), p. 1; "Descriptive Notice of the Silver Mines and Amalgamation Process of Mexico— No. II," *MJ*, 15 (22 February 1845), 59. Phillips was right in saying that completion of the Aviadero was a long way off, for that adit was not finished until 7 November 1868, twenty years after the demise of the British firm (Socabón del Aviadero, in Informe de la negociación minera del Real del Monte y Pachuca por 1868, marzo 1 de 1869, RdM, miscellaneous package no. 1).

[21] 1828 CG 12; "Review of the Real del Monte Mining Association: Annual General Meeting, February 28, 1829," *QMR*, no. 4 (January 1831), 465; Buchan, *Report*, p. 40.

out a new and larger machine for the Terreros shaft. After some delay the home office consented. The Terreros engine, therefore, was considerably superior to those taken originally to Mexico. It had a fifty-four–inch cylinder and was believed to incorporate "the recent improvements . . . sanctioned by use in the English mines." It was shipped from Falmouth in November 1830 and finally put in operation thirteen months later.[22] With the installation of the Terreros machine, the British company had begun the second phase of its campaign to improve on colonial drainage methods: the importation of larger and larger steam engines into Mexico.

For the remainder of the 1830's, when most of the mining activity was confined to the central portion of the Vizcaína vein, the company successfully stemmed the underground water with three steam engines. At the close of the decade, however, the question of effective drainage at the Real again claimed the attention of company officials. The London management accepted Commissioner John Rule's arguments for sending him yet another new and larger steam engine. He reasoned that a single seventy-five–inch machine could, by itself and less expensively, provide drainage power equal to that of the three engines in operation. Then, too, if the decision were taken to pursue the Vizcaína vein deeper, the new machine and the fifty-four–inch engine would be adequate.

In November 1840 Manager Taylor personally inspected the engine and shipped it to Mexico, but twenty-seven months were to pass before it was set in motion on the Dolores shaft. On its arrival at Veracruz in March 1841, the enormous machine presented company officials with a difficult transport problem. The cylinder alone weighed nearly eight tons and was described as "the heaviest piece of any kind that has passed over Mexican roads." The large parts of the engine were conveyed in company wagons, one equipped with special wide-rimmed wheels. The smaller parts were transported on pack mules by private carriers; all arrived at the Real in May. The removal of the thirty-inch engine from the Dolores shaft

[22] 1836 CG 35; RdM *Proceedings*, SGC, 9 February 1831, pp. ii, 9.

and the preparations for the installation of its giant successor caused an even longer delay. It was not until March 1843 that the seventy-five–inch steam engine was put to work.

When, early in the 1840's, the company shifted much of its mining activity from the Vizcaína in the south to the Santa Brígida and Acosta veins, the need for a steam engine on one of the northern mines naturally arose. In 1841 the first engine to be operated on any but a Vizcaína mine since 1829 was placed on the San Pedro shaft of the Acosta lode. The installation of this thirty-inch machine, which had formerly been worked on the Dolores shaft, "excited great interest" in the mining camp. At the inaugural ceremony held in November, Commissioner John Rule entertained fifty-five of the community's officials and principal citizens, who witnessed the blessing of the engine by clergymen from Real del Monte, Huasca, and Pachuca.[23] That celebration is of more than casual interest; it marks the beginning of a third phase in the British company's campaign to effect a basic change in the techniques of mine drainage in Mexico. With steam engines providing the majority of the drainage power, the British would now proceed to unwater an entire mining district.

During the next five years, the company placed another small steam engine in the northern part of the mining camp (at the Acosta shaft) and replaced the first one with the fifty-four–inch machine from the then abandoned Terreros shaft. With those two machines in the north, with their seventy-five–inch companion in the south, and with such help as the retarded Aviadero adit could provide, the company had accomplished the general drainage of its whole mining complex and indeed of virtually the whole district by 1847. The deep workings of the Vizcaína, Santa Brígida, and Acosta veins, all of which were connected underground, were 230 yards under the Morán adit, or 122 yards below the level at which mining had been abandoned by the second Count of Regla. The three engines at work on Acosta and Dolores, discharging some

[23] 1840, 1841, 1843 CG 39; RdM *Proceedings*, AGC, 29 June 1841, pp. 4, 5; 27 June 1843, p. 1.

2,700 gallons per minute, were just controlling the water in the mines. The cost of drainage, moreover, had risen to $90,000 a year.[24]

Although the English concern in 1847 could claim a major technological advance through the use of its steam engines, it was nonetheless unable to control the flow of underground water in Real del Monte enough to allow deeper mining in those three veins on which it was concentrating its effort. Company officers in Mexico, therefore, made another plea to London for a larger machine, the third such appeal since 1830. The plan this time was to continue draining the whole mining complex, but to add more steam power to that task. An eighty-five–inch engine would be imported for the northern part of the mining district, and the next two larger machines, those with seventy-five–inch and fifty-four–inch cylinders, would be operated on the Vizcaína vein in the south. As the first step in a strenuous, but futile, attempt to provide that eighty-five–inch engine, the Court of Directors resolved to apply a portion of the 1846 profit to its purchase rather than to an interest payment on the firm's indebtedness. In Mexico, Commissioner William Rule began making preparations for the receipt and installation of the new giant. That work, however, was soon interrupted by the news that the directors were detaining the steam engine in England until they learned that the United States blockade of Mexico's Gulf Coast had been lifted. To the disappointed commissioner, this action meant that his desperately needed machine would probably not reach camp until 1848—and that he was in difficulty.[25]

By the time the London management considered that political conditions in Mexico would permit the shipment of the steam en-

---

[24] 1846 CG 48; Buchan, *Report*, pp. 40–41. Buchan found that expense comparatively low. According to his judgment, "English energy and enterprise" had effected a drainage that, under the old system, would have required at least 180 *malacates*, employing 7,000 horses and upwards of 2,000 men, and would have cost approximately $2,000,000 a year.

[25] 1846, 1847 CG 48; "Mining Correspondence, Foreign Mines: Real del Monte Mines, Report from the Directors," *MJ*, 17 (27 March 1847), 137.

gine, the company was deep into its final financial crisis. The mining establishment in Mexico was advised that, owing to the lack of funds in England, the directors could send out the machine only when notified that the mines themselves might produce enough profit to cover the cost of transportation. The gloomy answer was that they could not, even if they had only to pay for moving the engine from the coast to Real del Monte.[26] The British company was dissolved with no further attempt to furnish the concern in Mexico with the new machine.

[26] 1847 CG 48.

6. Milling Operations

THE BRITISH REAL DEL MONTE COMPANY ENTERED MEXICO WITH the preconceived notion that it must improve on that country's traditional ore-reduction method, the patio amalgamation process. As in the case of mine drainage, the English concern eventually succeeded in putting its fixed idea into practice but at the same time failed to reap the full economic benefit from having done so. The company struggled desperately and, from the point of view of its own life as a business venture, vainly with a basic problem: how to extract silver from all the ore available from the mines, particularly that of low grade and "rebellious" nature, at a cost low enough to leave a profit in the operation. The company failed to find a solution, but at the same time—and this is another irony in the technical aspects of its history—it laid the foundations for the highly successful milling operations of its successor, and it definitely improved on Mexico's traditional ore-reduction method.

In its milling operations, the English concern went through three stages, roughly contiguous in time: smelting, patio amalgamation, and barrel amalgamation. Cutting across those three stages was a long and for the most part fruitless struggle with a problem referred to as "hacienda power" (a milling plant large enough to handle all the ore available from the mines, regardless of the reduction method tried).

Smelting

Inasmuch as John Taylor was named manager of the Real del Monte Company largely because he was regarded as one of the foremost mining experts in England, his views on the reduction of silver ore are important. Taylor set forth some of those views in the introduction he prepared for a book of selections from the writings of Alexander von Humboldt dealing with Mexico, a work published in London in 1824. While acknowledging that a shortage of fuel and Mexican prejudice in favor of amalgamation might prevent the English from effecting a basic change in ore reduction methods, Taylor argued that wherever possible the attempt should be made. He said that if fuel could be acquired in sufficient amounts and success had in the dressing of silver ore before reducing it, then smelting could take the place of the patio amalgamation process. He stressed the need for great skill in ore dressing, whether it be by heating or by washing, and he emphasized the fact that the abandonment of amalgamation would free the Mexican mining industry from its dependence on a steady and reasonably cheap supply of quicksilver. Great advantage was seen in smelting, advantage both to the English mining companies and to the Mexican nation.[1]

At the outset in Mexico, company agents tried to follow Taylor's guidelines for successful milling operations. They would dress and smelt ore that Mexicans had for centuries been amalgamating. They began with the knowledge that the Real del Monte district was well supplied with fuel in the form of extensive forests and woods. After a survey conducted by John Rule, two stamping mills

[1] John Taylor, *Selections from the Works of the Baron de* [sic] *Humboldt, Relating to the Climate, Inhabitants, Productions, and Mines of Mexico*, pp. xiv, xxi–xxv.

were built, one at the Vizcaína vein and the other in the valley near the Morán mine. The plan was to pulverize and wash the ore in the manner of dressing practiced widely in Cornwall. By the middle of 1827, however, the company officials admitted the defeat of their attempt to impose the English method of ore preparation. In announcing the abandonment of the experiment, the London management pointed to the too-speedy effort to introduce a new system into Mexico, given the small and untried labor force that would be called upon to put it into practice. There is some evidence, however, that a lack of surface water in the Real del Monte district was a more important reason for the failure. Just as the trial of the Cornish dressing system was getting under way, Commissioner James Vetch severely criticized John Rule for having recommended stamping mills without being certain that there was enough water both to operate a wheel steadily at Morán and to wash the ore in both mills.[2] As Vetch pointed out, there was little or no water in the stream bed running through Real del Monte throughout the long dry season.

Once it was clear to officials on both sides of the Atlantic that they could not make a rapid and dramatic change from amalgamation to smelting as the sole method of ore reduction at Real del Monte, the English concern settled into a kind of compromise. It would operate patio amalgamation plants at both the Regla and Sánchez haciendas. But at the same time, it would not give up smelting, so dear to the heart of the most powerful man in the London administration. The early blow to their illusions notwithstanding, company officials therefore pressed ahead with efforts to construct a superior smelting establishment at the Regla mill. In the eyes of the not disinterested John Taylor, they succeeded. Reporting to the June 1831 stockholders' meeting on steps taken at Real del Monte to improve ore-reduction methods, he said of smelting: "I believe that this important branch of economy is more advanced [at the Regla mill] than in any other part of Mexico." The

[2] 1825 CG 8; "Review of the Real del Monte Mining Association: Annual Meeting, February 28, 1825," *QMR*, no. 4 (January 1831), p. 440; "Special General Meeting, June 14, 1827," *QMR*, no. 4 (January 1831), pp. 453, 454.

value of the smelting ore raised from the bottom of the Dolores mine had been more than four times that of the *azogue* ore in the first six months of 1832, and company officials concluded that the "obvious means" of availing themselves of their produce was to enlarge the concern's smelting capabilities. Accordingly, blast machinery, intended to put more smelting furnaces into operation at the Regla mill, was purchased in England and dispatched to the Mexican mining camp.[3]

A plan of operations based on the anticipation of a steady supply of smelting ore seemed even more justified in 1833, when the Santa Teresa bonanza was at its height. The ore produced the following year, however, so fell off in quality as to cast doubt on the wisdom of placing that much emphasis on smelting. Whereas in 1833 the average grade of ore raised in Real del Monte had been 11.75 ounces of silver per quintal, in 1834 it dropped to an average of 7.5 ounces.[4] The company would soon be compelled to change its basic policy toward the reduction mills.

In July 1835 Commissioner John Rule advised London that the prospects with regard to smelting ore were not very good, but he saw compensation in the discovery of a large amount of *azogue* ore. He predicted that, although their value could not be realized so easily, it was the *azogues* on which the company's prosperity was likely to be based. For that reason he requested authorization to increase the concern's capacity to treat the low-grade ore. Rule's communication signaled the beginning of both a shift in emphasis from smelting to patio amalgamation and a campaign to enlarge the milling establishment at Real del Monte by rehabilitating another of the ruined reduction haciendas acquired from the Count of Regla. The commissioner suggested constructing a patio plant at the San Antonio hacienda, which had numerous advantages, the chief ones being an ample water supply for motive power and the fact that its retaining walls and a few buildings were still standing.

[3] *Proceedings at the General Courts of Proprietors of the Real del Monte Mining Company* (cited hereafter as RdM *Proceedings*), AGC, 27 June 1831, pp. 4–5; 21 June 1833, pp. 4–5; 25 June 1834, p. 5.

[4] *Ibid.*, 29 June 1835, p. 6.

Although the cost of repairs to the hacienda was estimated to be only $30,000, the directors in London decided that, however desirable the project might be from a technical standpoint, it was too costly an undertaking until "by the acquisition of positive profits, the expenditure may be met without difficulty or inconvenience."[5]

If the home office was reluctant to authorize an outlay that seems trivial in view of the sums already expended in the first decade of operations in Mexico, it was nonetheless well aware that it must eventually deal with the problem of fluctuations in the grade and uncertain supplies of ore. In the manager's June 1836 report to the stockholders, in which he announced the directors' decision to delay the rehabilitation of San Antonio, Taylor acknowledged that the poorer ore was more plentiful at Real del Monte and, echoing the opinion expressed by his deputy at Real del Monte, suggested that "thus it may prove, as in all the other great mines of Mexico, that the greatest resource will be found in the *azogue* rather than the smelting ores." That being the case, he said, Commissioner Rule had been authorized to increase the number of *arrastres* at the Regla hacienda as one means of expanding the patio operations at the Real, and had already been sent equipment for that purpose.[6]

Until the middle of 1837 John Rule held to his argument that the company needed to rehabilitate the San Antonio hacienda in order to cope with the problem of sufficient "hacienda power" to deal with the ample low-grade ore raised from the mines. During that time, production of smelting ore dropped. The decline was alarming to the officers in Mexico, first, because of their desire for company earnings, and, second, because they had counted on income from the smelting ore to pay for the renovation of the San Antonio mill. The failure to make a steady profit was due to a lack not of ore but of the means to produce it. Real del Monte faced a kind of dilemma, which Rule summed up as follows: "until the necessary hacienda power is obtained, we must experience the burthen of

[5] "Mining Correspondence, Foreign Mines: Real del Monte Mining Company," *MJ*, 1 (19 September 1835), 29; RdM *Proceedings*, AGC, 30 June 1836, p. 6.

[6] RdM *Proceedings*, AGC, 30 June 1836, p. 6.

costs of its creation on the one side, and the want of its produce on the other."

A general improvement in conditions at the Real led the commissioner, paradoxically, to defer rather than press his plan for opening a new reduction hacienda. When, in July 1837, rains furnished the water power necessary to operate new *arrastres* at both the Regla and Sánchez mills, Rule concluded that the additional grinding capacity thus gained would allow the concern to postpone the rehabilitation of the San Antonio mill. The question of plant capacity was set aside for the next six years in a policy decision that probably played a role in the company's eventual failure, if it can be assumed that the larger the patio amalgamation plant the lower the unit cost of ore reduction. As to smelting, that would-be European improvement on the traditional Mexican method of ore reduction was never again to be considered a panacea for the Real del Monte Company, but it continued to be regarded fondly by the British. Indeed, it received a favorable judgment from the two investigations made of the mining establishment at Real del Monte. In 1839 F. Schuchardt, experienced in Mexican mining matters, stated that smelting at Regla yielded results as good as those of any other mill in Mexico working under similar conditions. And John Phillips found that for the year 1840 the cost of smelting was only 34 per cent of the value of silver produced, while that of patio amalgamation was 46.25 per cent.[7]

Patio Amalgamation Process

In seeking the best means of treating all the ore that could be raised from its mines, the Real del Monte Company tried again and again to perfect the patio amalgamation carried out at Sánchez and Regla. Those company officials who had to cope with the larger problem of extracting silver from ore in an economical manner were never comfortable with the patio process. They found it to be slow and increasingly expensive (owing largely to the rising cost of quicksilver) when dealing with common types of low-grade ore

[7] 1837, 1839 CG 39; "Mr. Phillips's Report to the Directors," RdM *Proceedings*, AGC, 29 June 1841, p. 9.

—and almost entirely useless when dealing with those types that were called "rebellious." It cannot be argued that the concern wasted all the effort it put into "improving" patio amalgamation at Real del Monte, for it did treat a large and probably the greater part of its ore by that method. But, in a sense, the English expended huge amounts of time, energy, and money in a fruitless effort to learn a Mexican trick they did not even like.

It was mainly during the late 1830's and the 1840's that the company made its most serious attempts to profit from ore amalgamated in the patio, but the struggle began even while smelting was uppermost in the minds of officials in Mexico and in London. As early as 1832, company agents recognized that the manner in which they employed the traditional Mexican system of treating silver ore was less than perfect, and they therefore invited the Count of Regla to lend his assistance. Romero de Terreros sent a technician to Regla to test a variation in the patio method, and the company's commissioner agreed to defray the cost of the experiment. Tindal eventually remarked, however, that, like every self-styled amalgamation expert who went to the mill, this technician had new ideas but showed no results.[8] The comment is interesting because it indicates that the count's man was not the first to give advice to the British firm. Moreover, the comment well expresses a frustration that company officers were to experience in numerous "improvements" suggested by others in the years to come.

Not all of the experimentation in the company's reduction mills was so fruitless. In 1835, after tests had been conducted by several Mexican *azogueros*, Commissioner John Rule modified the practice of amalgamation at Regla and Sánchez. The most important innovation was the adoption of the "Guanajuato method" of combining quicksilver and other ingredients, mainly salt and copper pyrites, with the crushed ore. The usual practice at the Real had been to cover the patio with roofing and to have men mix the amalgam by walking about in the patio. Occasionally the mass was warmed in ovens. The new method was to keep the patio uncovered

[8] 1832 CG 12.

and exposed to the sun and air, to discontinue the use of warming ovens, and to substitute mules for men in the mixing. Rule himself considered that these experiments had definitely "improved our patio process," for they increased the production of silver and reduced the consumption of principal materials.

There is some evidence that, with the adoption of the "Guanajuato method," the company had gone as far as it could go with the patio amalgamation process. The main support for this view is Schuchardt's report on general operations at the Real submitted to London in November 1839. He stated that, in view of the grade of ore supplied the mills and the high cost of materials, especially quicksilver, Regla and Sánchez compared favorably with haciendas in other parts of Mexico, except for those at Guanajuato; in the mills of this district, the handling of the patio process had, because the ore was especially suited to that mode of reduction, reached the "highest state of perfection." The Bolaños official found Real del Monte's grinding equipment to be good, the quality of material used excellent, and the superintendence of the process conducted by intelligent men. The weather at the Real, which was cloudy much of the year and cold during another long period, proved an unfortunate factor; like the location of the haciendas in deep valleys where the sun rose late and set early, nothing could be done. Schuchardt did, however, note a high, and increasing, rate of quicksilver loss at both Regla and Sánchez, for which there appeared to be no adequate explanation.

When John Phillips found in 1840 that the cost of amalgamation, relative to the value of the silver produced, was significantly higher than the cost of smelting, he gave as reasons for the sharp difference the low grade of ore being supplied the haciendas and its "refractory nature." These unfavorable attributes of the ore were, he said, causing a large consumption of materials, especially quicksilver, "the enormous price of which has affected mining in Mexico very seriously." Phillips estimated that the increase in the price of mercury between 1827 and 1840 had been so drastic that the cost of amalgamation in the company's mills was some $40,000 higher in 1840 than it would have been had the price of mercury remained at the 1827 level.[9]

The treatment of certain types of ore that were characterized as rebellious or refractory was also a matter of concern and had been for a number of years. In 1836, for example, the chief commissioner had advised London that attempts to reduce "manganese ores" from the Santa Inés vein by the patio method had proved fruitless. Of considerably more importance is John Rule's statement that success in amalgamating rebellious ore had never been anticipated. Again in 1838 the subject of treating refractory ore arose. On that occasion, Rule had been compelled to store some of the low-grade ore from the Dolores mine because it had been found to be "stubborn in the amalgamation" process. He had then attempted a preamalgamation treatment known as calcination, whereby the crushed ore was heated and mixed with a salt solution.

During the period of the Schuchardt and Phillips surveys, the English concern turned its attention increasingly to the problem of reducing the rebellious, or refractory, ore. Real del Monte officials invited the inventors of procedures for improving patio amalgamation, or their agents, to test their projects at Regla and Sánchez. Early in 1840 trials were begun on three new processes. After about a year's experimentation, the company decided on the large-scale application of a system discovered by a Mr. Spangenberg at Bolaños, where it seems to have been used successfully, agreeing to pay the inventor 1 per cent of the value of all the silver produced through the use of his patent. The newness of Spangenberg's method, however, is somewhat questionable, for it did not basically change the patio process but merely provided for adding to the amalgam sulfate of copper calcined with salt. Nonetheless, the outcome of the experiments and the adoption of the "new" system were well received in London. The Court of Directors, relying on a standard businessman's criterion, noted that the

[9] 1835 CG 35; 1839 CG 39; "Mr. Phillips's Report to the Directors," RdM *Proceedings*, AGC, 29 June 1841, pp. 9–10.

concern's haciendas had made a considerably better financial showing in 1841 than in the previous year.

At the mining camp in Mexico the question of finding a wholly adequate method of reducing the low-grade and rebellious ores economically was by no means settled by that contest. As early as October 1842, company officials were again showing disappointment with the patio results, and the Sánchez hacienda administrator tried unsuccessfully to improve on Spangenberg's method. Commissioner John Rule echoed the frustration expressed by his predecessor a decade earlier when he informed London that it was "very discouraging" to conclude, after the numerous trials of new techniques in the patio, "that little if any advantage has been derived from any of them, above the common process, when that latter is carefully conducted." Although further experiments with would-be methods to perfect the patio process were carried out both in Mexico and in England through the next few years,[10] John Rule's condemning letter might be considered as a demand that the company stop trying to improve its manner of handling the patio method and search for a substitute.

Barrel Amalgamation Process

During its last five years of life, the Real del Monte Company made the most sustained effort to supplant altogether the traditional Mexican method of treating silver ore. The English launched a two-pronged attack on the problem. First, they tried to move the chemical mystery of amalgamation from the patio, where it was slow and destructive of precious quicksilver, to barrels, where it was quick and less destructive of that costly commodity. Second, they tried to master a process, called the flotation method, that would require no quicksilver at all. They conducted a serious, if not quite successful, offensive in the first prong of the attack, but

[10] 1836–1838, 1841, 1842 CG 39; 1843 CG 48; RdM *Proceedings,* AGC, 29 June 1841, p. 5; 15 June 1842, p. 2; "Mining Correspondence, Foreign Mines: Real del Monte Mining Company," *MJ,* 10 (2 May, 3 October 1840), 142, 315; "Real del Monte Mines, Report of the Directors, March 25th," 16 (4 April 1846), 143.

they seem to have used the second as no more than a diversionary move.

Amalgamation in revolving barrels was not new to Mexico when the English first arrived, and it had at least been suggested at Real del Monte long before the 1840's. Between 1788 and 1798 Friedrich Sonneschmidt, a German mining expert who accompanied Fausto de Elhuyar to Mexico when the latter was named director-general of the Tribunal of the Mining Guild, made a sustained but failing effort to introduce into the then Spanish colony a substitute for patio amalgamation. Among his attempted innovations was a kind of barrel amalgamation process that had been developed in Hungary by Baron von Born and with which both Sonneschmidt and Elhuyar had become familiar before leaving Europe.[11] In 1825 Commissioner James Vetch mentioned the possibility of using the barrel, or Freiburg, process of amalgamation at Real del Monte. But Vetch never pressed the matter beyond a recommendation to London. Finally, when in 1839 Schuchardt filed his report, he considered the feasibility of adopting the barrel process but thought that obstacles to the plan, especially the high cost of salt and the lack of pyrites, could not be easily overcome.

Barrel amalgamation was introduced at Real del Monte by a "gentleman named Meinecke," who in August 1843 approached Commissioner William Rule with a proposal that he be allowed to experiment with the Freiburg method in reducing *azogues*, especially those which had proved to be rebellious in the patio. Meinecke, who had had previous experience in Zacatecas with the barrel method, asked no remuneration unless he obtained a result satisfactory to the company; William Rule was therefore willing to consent to the test. By the end of the year, Meinecke had concluded his experiments at the Sánchez mill and fully convinced the commissioner that the barrel process was the best method for treating the low-grade ore that proved refractory in the patio. Rule was particularly impressed by the fact that the cost of the process had

[11] Clement G. Motten, *Mexican Silver and the Enlightenment*, pp. 10–11, 47–48, 52–53; Walter Howe, *The Mining Guild of New Spain and Its Tribunal General, 1770–1821*, p. 313.

been about 20 per cent of the value of the silver extracted, notably less than that of any patio variation thus far tried at the Real.[12]

A succinct description of the Freiburg process, which the firm was about to look upon as its salvation, is given by John Buchan:

The ore, after being ground and sifted, is roasted in furnaces with 5 *per cent.* of salt (chloride of sodium), by which the silver is separated from its original mineral state of sulphurets, and converted into chlorides of silver. The ore thus prepared is next made into a stiff paste by revolving in large barrels (containing each 25 cwt. of ore) with water, and then, after the addition of iron and quicksilver, the first ingredient by superior affinity again separates the chlorine from the silver, which is collected by the quicksilver, and converted into an amalgam; when, by the subsequent process of washing, the amalgam is first separated from the refuse mud, and then, by distillation, the silver from the quicksilver.[13]

During the period of Meinecke's tests, the London management looked upon their apparent success in one light, and the mining camp in another. The directors at the home office foresaw "early profits" in adopting the new method. But the commissioner at Real del Monte considered such an optimistic prediction an underestimation of the true scope of the amalgamation problem. The barrel process did appear to hold out the greatest promise of any method yet tried, but serious study and further trials would have to be conducted on those low-grade ores. William Rule cautioned that the firm must be willing to submit to a long period of expensive development before it would perceive any profits.

Behind William Rule's impatience with what he must have considered a misunderstanding of the initially successful, but still only preliminary, barrel tests lay a question that he had already raised:

[12] 1825 CG 8; 1839 CG 39; 1843 CG 48. Zacatecas was not the only mining district in Mexico that had tried the Freiburg barrel process by 1843. As early as 1839, the Mexican Company in Oaxaca described it as "the best method hitherto adopted at the company's haciendas for the reduction of silver ores" ("Proceedings of Public Companies: Mexican Company," *MJ*, 10 [9 May 1840], 147).

[13] John H. Buchan, *Report of the Director, the Real del Monte Mining Company, Mexico, March 1855*, p. 10.

hacienda power. Shortly after assuming the direction of the concern in Mexico, he had called Manager Taylor's attention to the
subject, which had been broached, pressed for a time, and then
dropped by his brother some years earlier. The commissioner
argued that the mining camp was so lacking in plant space to
handle low-grade ore, regardless of the amalgamation process used,
that it was still too dependent on the quality and quantity of smelting ore. When Meinecke's initial tests had shown promise, Rule
again brought up the question of hacienda power. He favored the
rehabilitation of the San Antonio mill for a large-scale barrel plant,
and he mentioned the hacienda's retaining walls, the buildings still
standing, and its steady supply of water for motive power.[14] Those
were, of course, the same advantages that John Rule had cited in
1836 and 1837.

From early 1844 through 1847, the company attempted to com-
bine two themes in its milling operations: the use of barrel amalgamation to handle rebellious ore and the building of sufficient
hacienda power to make a profit out of the barrels. At the same
time, the English concern became temporarily excited over the
flotation method of silver ore reduction, something that proved to
be only a short flirtation. The first step was a campaign waged by
William Rule to convince the London management to authorize
construction of a large-scale barrel amalgamation plant. Rule's
plan was to abandon the Sánchez hacienda and to prepare San
Antonio, which he estimated could handle from 120 to 135 tons
of ore a week. With Regla capable of treating some 115 tons a
week, both by patio and smelting, the company would still be able
to confine its reduction operations to two mills. The commissioner's
efforts at persuasion were effective. At the June 1845 stockholders'
meeting, the Court of Directors reported that they had already begun to ship to Mexico machinery necessary for use in connection
with the barrels to be erected in the rehabilitated San Antonio. In
view of the possibilities held out by the new amalgamation process
and of the ore ground that had been revealed by explorations in the

[14] 1843 CG 48.

mines of the Santa Brígida and Santa Inés veins of Real del Monte
and in the Rosario mine of Pachuca, the management expressed
the cautiously optimistic opinion that "there is reason to expect
that the undertaking will yet become permanently profitable."

Preparations for the building of a forty-eight–barrel plant at the
San Antonio hacienda were hardly under way in late 1844, when
a sudden drop in the supply of smelting ore left the company in a
precarious financial situation and brought activity to a halt. There
being no improvement in the firm's economic position by the middle of the following year, Commissioner Rule suggested that plans
for San Antonio be temporarily set aside and that the small barrel
plant at Sánchez be expanded to twenty-four units. The more
modest project, he estimated, would require but four months' time
and cost only $10,000. Once completed, the concern could then re-
duce the large stock of low-grade ore on hand and apply the profit
thus obtained to completing the larger establishment that had been
authorized by London. Despite Rule's determination to return to
San Antonio, the British Real del Monte never built the large-scale
Freiburg mill at that hacienda, which, owing to its superior water
supply, seemed to hold out so much promise.

The less ambitious project at Sánchez itself proved to be extremely difficult to complete. The twenty-four–barrel plant, which
was to have been quickly and cheaply erected as a temporary expedient, was not finished until late 1847. Its first eight units cost
$7,000 more than William Rule estimated for the entire project.
There are several reasons for the long delay and high cost of putting up the twenty-four barrels at Sánchez, the only Freiburg establishment that the English company was ever to construct at
Real del Monte. First, the disastrous financial results of 1845 and
1847 severely curtailed the funds available in Mexico for extra
works. Second, the London management decided to apply most of
the 1846 profit to the purchase of yet another huge drainage engine
rather than to the construction of a really large barrel plant. Third,
in 1846 the supply line from England was interrupted by a blockade imposed by the United States on the Mexican Gulf ports, im-

peding the shipment of such milling equipment and quicksilver as the London management was willing to send to Real del Monte.[15]

While the company was striving to install and operate enough barrels to treat profitably the low-grade and recalcitrant ore so readily available from its mines, its officials flirted with an ore reduction method that required no mercury at all and that for a few exciting months seemed capable of revolutionizing the mining industry of Mexico. Sometime during 1845, Spangenberg, the former Bolaños officer who had sold his "improvement" of the patio process to Real del Monte in 1841, informed the Court of Directors in London that a metallurgist named Ziervogel, of Hettstadt, Germany, had discovered a method of separating silver from copper ore that appeared applicable to the reduction of silver ore; this simple process did not call for the use of quicksilver. Though understandably skeptical, the directors eventually agreed to consider purchasing the rights to the invention and to send Spangenberg to Mexico for the purpose of conducting trials on the new process.

Spangenberg began his experiments at Real del Monte in early February 1846; after a few months of consistently good results he had made a strong impression on the concern's chief commissioner. In his enthusiasm, William Rule said that "a great number of people in the neighborhood have anxiously watched these trials; and I believe nearly all parties are of the opinion that it will very soon supersede all other methods of reducing silver ores in this country." By the end of November 1846, Spangenberg's trials had indicated that the Ziervogel method of silver ore reduction was cheaper than the barrel process and that he could achieve success even with the extremely rebellious ore from the Rosario mine in Pachuca. Commissioner Rule was convinced at that time that the company ought to adopt the new mode of ore treatment on a large scale.

In just thirty days, however, William Rule changed his mind

[15] 1844–1847 CG 48; RdM *Proceedings*, AGC, 27 June 1845, pp. 1–2, 4; "Mining Correspondence, Foreign Mines: Real del Monte Mines, Report from the Directors," *MJ*, 17 (27 March 1847), 137.

and his recommendation to London. He was most impressed by the fact, somehow earlier overlooked, that Spangenberg's flotation process had lost approximately 25 per cent of the silver shown by assay to be present in the ore, while the barrel method generally lost only 10 per cent. "The process is very pretty," lamented the commissioner, "and I should not like to see it abandoned, but at the same time I do not consider it so superior to the barrels, that the Directors should be induced to spend much money to perfect it."[16] A full year's experimentation with a process of ore treatment that at one time was thought capable of replacing all others in Mexico thus came to very little.

The British Real del Monte Company began its operations in Mexico with attempts to improve on the traditional Mexican patio amalgamation system of reducing silver ore by smelting, but failed. It ended these operations by again trying to introduce a substitute for the patio process. The momentary stir caused by the flotation method notwithstanding, the most serious contender was the barrel process. From the point of view of profit-making, the company was again unsuccessful. Its failure, though, was not due to shortcomings in the new ore reduction method but to the fact that the company was unable to develop a large enough barrel amalgamation plant before its resources for technical improvements were exhausted.

Although barrel amalgamation did not prove to be a panacea for the British Real del Monte Company, it did prove eventually to be an effective substitute for the patio process in the treatment of the rebellious ore so prevalent in the Real del Monte–Pachuca district. According to some company officials, the barrel method was just as expensive as the patio process; moreover, it placed an additional strain on the supply of fuel at the Real.[17] But the British concern was compelled, especially during its final days, to deal with extremely rebellious ore that simply could not be reduced

16 1845, 1846, 1848 CG 48; "Mining Correspondence, Foreign Mines: Real del Monte Mines, Report from the Directors," *MJ*, 17 (27 March 1847), 137; "Real del Montes Mines, Report of the Directors, March 25th," 16 (4 April 1846), 143.
17 1848 CG 48.

profitably in the patio. Several years of trials seemed to indicate that, if a large-scale barrel plant could be constructed, the company would become profitable through the use of the plentiful ore from the relatively unexploited Santa Brígida and Santa Inés veins in Real del Monte and the Rosario mine in the neighboring Pachuca. That the trials were pointing in the right direction is shown by the experience of the Mexican company that succeeded the British firm. During the first period of its operations, it reduced the major part of its ore by the barrel process—at a handsome profit—and it continued to find the method useful up to the time it sold its assets to a United States firm in 1906.[18]

[18] In the decade 1849 through 1858, the Mexican Real del Monte reduced approximately 210,000 tons of ore by the barrel process, but only 42,000 tons by the patio process. During that period, the concern made a profit of $6,079,730 in working its mines. In 1870 the company was still reducing about half of its weekly production of 1,125 tons of ore in three mills that used the barrel method and half in two patio mills (Buchan, *Report*, pp. 8, 26–31; Thomas R. Auld, [Report of the Director, the Real del Monte Mining Company, April, 1859], table following p. 8, pp. 10–17; Julián Mello [director, Mexican company] to Board of Directors, 5 December 1870, RdM, Dirección a Junta Directiva, Vol. 11).

By 1873 the Mexican concern was reducing more ore by patio than in barrels. Although the patio method continued to dominate the milling practices of the Mexican firm until its sale early in the twentieth century, some barrel amalgamation was carried on. Its importance is illustrated by the fact that, in 1898, when the company considered confining all of its milling activities to the Loreto hacienda in Pachuca, the director suggested preparing that plant for the reduction of five hundred tons a week by the patio process and five hundred tons in barrels. In the end, both the patio and the barrels were abandoned. Beginning in 1907, the United States company rebuilt Loreto as a cyanide process plant and constructed a new mill, called Guerrero, in Real del Monte, to use the cyanide process system (José de Landero y Cos [director, Mexican company] to Board of Directors, 7 April 1873, RdM, Dirección a Junta Directiva, vol. 14; Actas de la Junta Directiva de la Compañía de Real del Monte y Pachuca, 10 August 1898, p. 379; Marvin D. Bernstein, *The Mexican Mining Industry, 1890–1950: A Study of the Interaction of Politics, Economics, and Technology*, p. 46).

7. Labor

To say that the british real del monte company had labor troubles in Mexico would be an understatement. To say that those troubles contributed both to the company's downfall and to a change in mine-labor practices at Real del Monte would be no overstatement. The British adventurers went into an area that was virtually depopulated and so had to recruit workers. Those brought from Europe, and in particular the Cornishmen, proved to be disorderly. Native workers gathered in various mining camps and in the capital city of Mexico fought pitched battles with the British concern. The main issue between the company and the European labor force was discipline. Distrusting the Mexicans to handle their imported machines, particularly the steam-driven pumping equipment, company officials demanded absolute reliability from the Europeans. They did not always get it. The main issue between the company and the Mexican labor force—the same one that had, during the time of the first Count of Regla, led to a violent and prolonged strike—was the *partido*. As though compelled to carry on the tradition of labor turbulence of the Real del Monte–Pachuca district, Mexican mine and mill hands revived that cause and defeated their new bosses in several struggles over it. Although the English lost each successive contest involving the *partido*, they all but eliminated the practice from the mines they operated.

European Labor Force

Among the assumptions that the British leaders took with them to Mexico was the view that only Europeans might be trusted with the operation and maintenance of steam engines. Company officials came in time to distrust native labor to the point that they were reluctant to allow Mexicans to hold most jobs requiring mechanical skill or the supervision of other employees. There were, of course, exceptions to this general rule. Perhaps the most notable one was the *azoguero*, a highly specialized Mexican who not only handled the application of quicksilver but was largely responsible for the entire complex patio amalgamation process. Then, too, on one occasion the company replaced English sumpmen with Mexicans. But the company officials' assumptions and prejudices led them to keep on hand a European, in fact very largely English, labor force. Its size and composition was determined at any given time by the scope of mining and milling activities and by the short-run financial condition of the concern at Real del Monte.

Though on the whole less troublesome than the Mexican workers, the European laborers and salaried personnel were by no means uniformly tranquil and dependable. Indeed, the company was immediately faced with personnel problems. Owing to "excesses" committed by the first two English parties that arrived at the mining camp, a "spirit of insubordination" prevailed for a time. Commissioner Vetch reported, however, that he had been able to bring the establishment "under pretty good discipline & I hope that we may go on quietly & creditably to the English character."

A year after his arrival at Real del Monte, Vetch made a series of recommendations on personnel policy. He believed that the company would do well to offer a form of piecework, by which a miner might earn as much as $2.00 a day at a time when the average daily wage was approximately $.50. Recalling that the Cornishmen already at the camp were difficult to manage, he suggested that the London office not send workers from that part of Great Britain, particularly "on salary, for they would not exert themselves." Rather, quarrymen, coal miners, and "such other men as from their circumstances would be inclined to emigrate" might be recruited in Ireland and in the border region between England and Scotland. Finally, he proposed the appointment of ten or fifteen trustworthy men, possibly former noncommissioned army officers, as clerks to keep records of the ore taken from the mines and introduced into the haciendas. Vetch's recommendations led to the sending of eleven Cornish miners to be employed on piecework, and, those men having proved satisfactory, twenty-five others were dispatched before the end of 1827.[1]

In mid-1833, when news that the Bolaños Company needed workers reached the Real, some European employees, under the threat of joining that firm, demanded higher pay. Contending that men who had accepted salaries of $63 per month were, in fact, earning nearly $90 through piecework arrangements, Commissioner John Rule was able to convince the foreigners to stay on without a wage increase. For future protection he concluded a no-raiding agreement with Bolaños, according to which neither concern would accept a worker from the other unless a "certificate of license" were issued.[2]

The status of the European workers at the Real was some years later to be discussed at length in reports to the Court of Directors. F. Schuchardt held out little hope of significantly reducing the outlay for the laborers and professional staff. Admitting that the number of non-Mexican agents and artisans was high, he said that such a large force was made necessary by the fact that "the Real del Monte mining concern is the most extensive perhaps in the

[1] 1825 CG 8; "Review of the Real del Monte Mining Association: Annual General Meeting, February 28, 1828," *QMR*, no. 4 (January 1831), 457–458.
[2] 1833 CG 14.

whole Mexican Republic as regards the number of mines and engine power which is necessary for working them." Its five steam engines could not be operated, he thought, with less than the twenty Englishmen employed. Nor did he find the number of blacksmiths, founders, fitters-up, masons, carpenters, roofers, brickmakers, and others excessive, especially since their work was directly or indirectly connected with the upkeep of the steam engines. As to the underground mine captains and the superintendents of surface ore yards, he observed that none was idle or superfluous. The European personnel at the reduction mills had already been cut as much as possible; the office staff at the Real was small; and the salaries of the officers and artisans were none too high.[3]

In 1841 Secretary John Phillips gave careful consideration to the number and salaries of the workers at the Real. Acknowledging that the wages paid to company miners and artisans were high, Phillips believed that the only way to lower them was by encouraging more English workers to go to Real del Monte "and thus producing competition." He suggested, however, that the company exercise caution in urging his countrymen to go to Mexico, for it might be forced to employ more men than absolutely needed. The secretary noted another circumstance tending to frustrate company attempts to reduce the scale of wages paid European workers: the "higher rate paid in nearly all the other mining districts, and in the various establishments in the city of Mexico and elsewhere." Many of its best men had sought and found higher wages at other firms, he said.

All things considered, the secretary found the average scale of wages paid Europeans at Real del Monte "not exorbitant." The drainage engines, the steam whim for extracting ore and refuse, a water pressure engine, and blast machinery at the Regla hacienda required the "attendance of steady and experienced Englishmen, because the Mexicans cannot yet be trusted with the management of such complicated machinery." Phillips added that during 1840 there had been twenty-two *malacates* in use at the Real, all of

[3] 1839 CG 39.

TABLE 5
Salary Scale at Real del Monte,
1830–1849

Position	Monthly Salary
Blacksmith	$80–90
Carpenter	65–80
Engineman	53–58
Hacienda employee	80–90
Miner	58–70
Pitman	70
Storekeeper	60–70
Sumpman	69
Timberman	60
Underground mine captain	85–100
Wagon driver	54–68
Wheelwright	90

SOURCE: 1830–1849 CG *passim*.

which, along with the stamps and *arrastres* at the haciendas, were operated by Mexicans. In that year, some eighty Europeans had been employed, at an average fixed wage of about $65 per month. They sometimes worked overtime and were paid accordingly; in cases of tutwork or contract arrangements their wages were suspended.[4]

Requests submitted to Mexican government officials for residence permits or for permission to carry firearms show the number of Europeans employed by the English concern to have been eighty-two in 1835, ninety-three in 1838, and eighty-five in 1839. The scattered available data (see Table 5) do not give a complete picture of the salary scale or permit a thorough analysis of Phillips' statement that the average fixed wage was approximately $65 per month. They do, however, shed light on the subject.[5]

[4] "Mr. Phillips's Report to the Directors," *Proceedings at the General Courts of Proprietors of the Real del Monte Mining Company* (cited hereafter as RdM *Proceedings*), AGC, 29 June 1841, pp. 8–9.

[5] Those Europeans who could be called company officials received considerably higher salaries. The Regla mill superintendent, for instance, earned between $167 and $250 per month; the Sánchez superintendent from $133 to $167; the surgeon between $135 and $146; the treasurer-cashier between $100 and

In the middle of 1841, some of the English workers at the Real staged a semistrike, which led to a change in the company policy of employing Europeans in areas where steam engines were located. For some time the chief commissioner and other company officials had tried to convince the *barreteros* to work regularly on Sundays, Mondays, and Monday nights. Rule decided to press the natives a little by assigning English miners, sumpmen, and other workers to the task of breaking ore when the Mexicans were reluctant to do the job. During a day and a night in early May, a party of nineteen Englishmen therefore worked on the ore ground of the Santa Teresa–Terreros mine.

Two weeks later Rule assembled another crew of English workers to break ore in the San Cayetano mine. Out of fear that the native *barreteros* would do them injury, the Europeans objected to going underground. The chief commissioner, informed of their hesitancy, went to the pit head and tried to assure them that their fear was unjustified and that the measure was merely a temporary expedient designed to teach the Mexican *barreteros* a lesson. When the first officer learned that the entire ten-man work crew had agreed in advance to stand together in the face of being compelled to work, he concluded that the European laborers needed a lesson more than did the natives. Besides discharging four sumpmen and sending them back to Europe, he laid off the other six men for a week and cut their salaries by amounts varying from $2 to $5 per month.

Having deliberately reduced his staff of "trustworthy" sumpmen, Rule decided on an experiment: he would deepen the Terreros shaft "exclusively with Mexicans, with only occasional English superintendence." When that trial proved successful, he adopted a policy of substituting Mexican sumpmen for Europeans whenever possible in the sinking of the engine shafts. "This is something we have been discussing," he reported to London, "and not been able

---

$250; and the chief mechanical engineer from $222 to $292. Chief Commissioner John Rule received about $485 per month in 1834 and $1,040 in 1838 (1830–1849 CG *passim*).

to carry into effect until forced to do so." The commissioner did not fail to note the saving that would accrue to the company in labor costs by virtue of the generally lower scale of wages paid to native workmen.[6]

During the late stages of operations in Mexico, many of the European salaried workers suffered pay cuts and even dismissals, and some of them left the company for better opportunities elsewhere. The first layoffs occurred in the spring of 1843 and involved six artisans and enginemen "whose services were no longer required." Not long afterward, another six Europeans were removed from the company's service, but for quite a different reason. Those men, employed in the Acosta mine and nearby yard, were caught stealing rich ore and selling it to independent smelters in the Real del Monte district. All were turned over to the Mexican authorities for punishment, which the chief commissioner hoped would "be a good lesson to deter others." The six apparently received prison sentences of several years.

During 1844 a basic but selective salary reduction among European workers was put into effect. The wages of miners who had been receiving $63 per month were cut to $55; those of enginemen, from $70 to $60; those of blacksmiths from $90 to $70; those of landers (men stationed at the pit heads to receive the ore or rubbish as it was hoisted from the mines), from $58 to $50. In all, the salaries of eighteen were reduced from $1,165 per month to $1,030, a savings of a mere $135. The general wage-cut policy proved to be less than a financial coup.

In its final years in Mexico the British concern was caught between its desire to hold down all expenditures, including those for payment to its foreign labor force, and its need for key workers it thought it could trust. By May 1845 company officials at Real del Monte were urgently requesting London to replace their two principal blacksmiths, who had recently jumped to the apparently more affluent El Oro Mining Company (located in the present state of Mexico, near the border of Michoacán), and two of their carpen-

6 1841 CG 39.

ters who had also left. Doubtless to avoid a further flight of European workers, Chief Commissioner William Rule decided to terminate the policy of basic salary reductions at the end of the following month. Thereafter, he would restore the wages of his skilled foreigners to their former level. Later that year, under strong pressure to cut expenditures any way possible, Rule was forced to dismiss more of his European workers.[7] The company apparently retained to its end the policy of holding down the number of its preferred non-Mexican employees while maintaining their pay scale at a level sufficient to prevent their departure for more lucrative jobs outside the company's service.

If the foreign company operating in Mexico was sometimes less than generous with its European workers, upon whom it depended for those tasks not trusted to the natives, the imported laborers were also less than appreciative of their employer's intermittent stinginess. Additional evidence of labor difficulties is found in an incident that occurred while John Phillips was investigating the firm's operations in 1840. While at the mining camp, he was informed that several English employees were engaged in dishonest practices. He passed this intelligence on to the chief commissioner, who decided that the three men be tried. Before a group made up of Phillips, Commissioner John Rule, the treasurer-cashier, the chief mechanical engineer, and one of the mine captains, charges against each of them were read and their statements taken. The allegations included the employment of Mexican peons on personal property and billing the company for their wages; the building of a house with wood belonging to the firm; the forcing of peons to trade in a shop run by one of the accused; the use of iron belonging to the company for working a privately operated mine; and the sale of a carriage built at company expense. The committee concluded that some of the charges were unfounded, others borne out by the evidence taken. In view of the doubt cast on some of the accusations, Phillips accepted the three men's explanations on all counts and pursued the matter no further.[8]

[7] 1844 CG 37; 1843 CG 39; 1843, 1845 CG 48.
[8] 1840 CG 39.

Mexican Labor Force

Few of the problems that confronted the British firm during its twenty-five–year history exceeded in importance that of its relations with the Mexican mine and mill workers. Those relations were seldom easy, frequently strained, and sometimes characterized by violent strife. Interestingly, the company had first to create a native labor force at the Real before it could begin to fight with it.

The first British detachment to arrive at Real del Monte encountered not only widespread ruin but a dispersal of the district's working population. A month after Captain Vetch and his party entered the town, the Pachuca Mining Deputation was prompted to request a Mexico City newspaper to announce that, in view of the fact that the English concern had leased the Count of Regla's mines and was undertaking their rehabilitation, workers who had left the Real to seek a living elsewhere might return with the assurance that they would find jobs. A year was to pass before the company itself took steps to deal with the labor shortage. During that time, the chief commissioner believed that the solution lay in the large-scale importation of English or other European miners, provided that friction with the Mexicans was avoided by making gradual the introduction of so many foreigners into the country.[9]

Despite the fact that some Cornish miners were sent to the Real in response to Vetch's suggestion, the company did not follow the manpower policy recommended by its first chief commissioner. Indeed, once the first significant opportunity to produce silver ore arose, the English concern moved in quite the opposite direction. It began and carried out a policy of recruiting Mexicans to serve as the basic work force, that is, as the first-class miners and helpers in the pits and as the general laborers in the mills. The company thus restored a mining population to the once-deserted camp. In doing so, the foreign company also helped to prepare the way for a return of labor strife to an area of Mexico that had known it well in the past.

[9] *El sol*, 10 August 1824, pp. 227–228; 1825 CG 8.

The first stage of the recruitment campaign was an effort to put as many Mexican miners as possible on the task of breaking away and raising ore from Morán, the company's first producing mine. During one week in late 1827, $5,000 worth of ore was taken from that property. Reporting that happy event to London, Chief Commissioner Charles Tindal claimed that only an average of nineteen men had been employed, day and night, on pitches on which at least a hundred could have worked. Immediate attention was, therefore, turned to the need for workers in Morán. Tindal's initial step was the construction of a few small huts near the camp's producing mine, to be assigned to those *barreteros* who would agree to work steadily. The first time one of them refused to go underground he was to be ejected and his living quarters given to another. The second measure, taken also at Morán, called for the establishment of a store where miners might satisfy their "daily wants" by purchasing on credit against their weekly pay. These two inducements would, the commissioner believed, attract a permanent labor force. He was mistaken.

Forced to expand his recruitment program, Tindal requested the governor of the state of Mexico, who had demonstrated interest in the success of the mines, to issue circulars to the local authorities as a means of inducing the unemployed population to go to the Real. In January 1828 he informed Governor Lorenzo de Zavala that the concern's most serious problem was the "lack of hands"; despite the efforts made, "we do not have one fifth of the number we need." As soon as the Vizcaína vein was laid dry, he would be able to employ thousands of workers, he said, explaining that he called the situation to the governor's attention because "this negotiation is so important to the State of Mexico." The commissioner's plea was apparently answered. Some months later Tindal thanked the prefect of Tulancingo, as well as "our common friend, Lorenzo de Zavala," for their help in sending workers to the Real.[10]

Tindal also sought to increase his labor force by sending one of the company's Mexican employees into the Zimapán district for

[10] 1827, 1828 CG 12.

recruits. The first attempt attracted some sixteen miners to work in Morán. On the first Saturday after they arrived, however, they were threatened by a group of Real del Monte *barreteros* and most of them fled that night. Angered by the episode, Tindal acted to prevent a recurrence and again looked to Zimapán for more miners.[11]

In its quest for mine workers the company was aided by its Mexico City agent, Holdsworth, Fletcher and Company, which circulated handbills announcing job opportunities in the nearby mining district and placed advertisements in the city's newspapers. One such announcement, carried in *El Sol*, stated that the English company that was exploiting the Vizcaína vein, the Morán mine, and "other rich mines" needed many types of workers, including *barreteros*, timbermen, carpenters, and peons. Morán was described as drained and producing ore, and the Vizcaína vein was expected shortly to be placed in the same condition. Finally, the advertisement noted, the English firm was paying the *partido* in all of its properties, in addition to a daily salary of four reals.[12]

Not stopping with the announcement of job openings at Real del Monte, Holdsworth and Fletcher gathered candidates in wagons and packed them off to the mining camp. By mid-January 1828 it had dispatched three wagonloads of workers, including a Russian carpenter, and was preparing to fill five more vehicles sent by Tindal. Later that month Holdsworth and Fletcher was instructed by a Real del Monte official to advertise in the Guanajuato newspapers for *barreteros* and timbermen, the two classes of mine workers most needed. Encouraged by the fact that some Guanajuato miners had gone to the Real unsolicited, the commissioner wished to hold out no monetary inducement but, instead, the promise that all who made the trip would find "plenty of work and good accommodations."

---

[11] 1827 CG 12. This was not the first time that Real del Monte *barreteros* greeted mine workers from other districts with jealous wrath. A similar, though somewhat more serious, incident occurred in the days of the first Count of Regla.

[12] 1828 CG 12; *El sol*, 5 January 1828, p. 3848. The advertisement was re-run on 11, 16, 20, 27 January 1828, pp. 3872, 3892, 3907, and 3936, respectively.

Carrying his campaign even further afield, Tindal, in his capacity as commissioner of the Bolaños Company, attempted to enlist the aid of the chief officer of the Zacatecas branch. He asked that the *barreteros* in that mining district be told that Real del Monte could employ any of them who wished to make the long trip. He said the pay was one-eighth *partido* and four reals a day, adding that he would be willing to defray the worker's travel expenses, as he had already done for a group from Zimapán.

The number of people transported, or induced to go, to Real del Monte is uncertain, but it must have been high. At the end of March 1828, Tindal advised the prefect of Tulancingo that the population, including *barreteros*, was "daily increasing"; that many volunteers were arriving; and that one hundred miners and their families were momentarily expected from Guanajuato. The company's recruitment program in Guanajuato was, in fact, so successful that it drew a protest from the director of the Anglo-Mexican Mining Association, of that city. Tindal rejected the complaint, contending that he was justified in offering immediate work to unemployed miners when Anglo-Mexican could do no more than hold out a promise for the future.[13]

Disputes with Mexican Workers

In several respects, the pattern of labor relations between the British company and its Mexican workers was set by the time the British took the first silver out of Real del Monte. Their attitude of mistrust toward the Mexicans was quickly expressed by Captain Vetch when he asserted that the "natives" could not be assigned positions of trust. Then, too, he appealed to the British chargé d'affaires in the capital to persuade the Mexican government to abandon its plan of putting some two hundred men in the district into a civil militia. He complained: "To put arms into the hands of these miners would require 2 companies of the best regular troops of Spain to keep the peace here."[14] Nevertheless, the Real del Monte concern soon decided to recruit a large body of Mexican

[13] 1827, 1828 CG 12.
[14] 1825 CG 8.

workers rather than import Europeans on a major scale. No sooner had a significant ore strike been made at Real del Monte than the Mexican miners brought in to work it raised the specter of the *partido*—the main cause of conflict between the Mexicans and their English employers. Finally, from the outset the native workers were willing to use violence or the threat of violence, and the foreign company was willing to use military force provided it by the state or national government. The pattern of labor relations at Real del Monte, then, was to be characterized by mutual hostility between the Mexicans and the British, considerable strife, and a long contest between workers and their employers on the basic issue of wages.

Strike of 1827. Between the end of 1826 and September 1827 the company was engaged in its first serious controversy with the Mexican laborers. Late in 1826, when the concern was about to begin ore extraction, the chief commissioner proposed the *carga*, or weight, system that was rejected by the *barreteros*. Under this plan each worker would be compensated in money in accordance with the weight of the ore he broke away and raised during a day's shift. Maintaining that this method of payment, not the *partido*, was the one generally employed in the district during the eleven years in which the Regla properties had been abandoned and mining carried out on a limited scale, Vetch contended that it held out advantages to the workers. However, if it was completely unacceptable to the *barreteros*, he would be willing to discuss the matter. Though not unalterably opposed to the gradual introduction of a modified *partido*, the company was not inclined, he said, either to accept the *partido* immediately or to accept it at any time in the form demanded by the workers. The *barreteros* refuted Vetch's arguments, insisted on the *partido* as it had been traditionally paid in the Regla mines, and asked the third Count of Regla to prevail on the British concern to accede to their demands.[15] (As practiced in the past at Real del Monte, the *partido* provided that each *barretero* be paid four reals, or about fifty cents, a day for a specified amount of ore

[15] 1827 CG 26.

production, plus one eighth of all the ore he was able to extract over and above that daily quota.)

The argument over the system of payment continued until the British company began extracting rich ore from the Morán mine in early June 1827. Then the *barreteros* struck, demanding that the *partido*, to which, they claimed, all miners in the district were "accustomed," be paid at once. Commissioner Vetch promptly requested the mayor of Real del Monte to call for troops to protect the company's property. Addressing a similar appeal to the British representative in Mexico City, he explained that he was fearful that the town official would not act until it was too late and the *barreteros* had carried out their threat to "raze to the ground" the company's headquarters (Casa Grande) at the Real. "We are prepared with 40 or 50 English to resist any attack," Vetch wrote, "but should we be able to resist it, the shedding of blood cannot but set off an eternal feud between these two nations." Within a few days, detachments of soldiers, both infantrymen and cavalrymen, arrived from Tulancingo and Texcoco. It is worth noting that, in urgently requesting military assistance from the prefect of Tulancingo, a Pachuca government official said that the workers in the neighboring town were beginning to show signs of violence reminiscent of the occurrences of 1766 and that the authorities could not handle the situation with the militia, part of which was made up of "interested workers."[16]

With the troops maintaining order at the Real, Vetch felt his position to be strong enough to demand the arrest of six *barreteros* whom he named as the leaders of the strike. Mayor Ignacio Bars consented to the detention of four of the accused. On the following day, 12 June, an agreement was worked out among company officials, representatives of the *barreteros*, and the Pachuca Mining Deputation whereby the miners would return to the pits for a month on the company's terms. During that time, discussion of

[16] *Ibid.*; Vicente Paez (deputy prefect of Pachuca) to prefect of Tulancingo, 7 June 1827, AEM, expediente concerning 1827 strike at Real del Monte (cited hereafter as expediente 1827), doc. 9; Vetch to Ignacio Bars (mayor of Real del Monte), 6 June 1827, AEM, expediente 1827, doc. 10.

the wage issue was to continue, with the understanding that at the end of a definite period the *partido* would be granted in some form. Agreement was, however, nearly blocked by Vetch's insistence that the ringleaders of the strike be arrested. The *barreteros* refused to work until those men were released. Realizing that they would be unable to produce sufficient evidence to convict the prisoners, the company officials decided to "make a virtue of necessity" and asked the mayor of the Real to set them free.

After a brief resumption of work, the *barreteros* again struck in the first week of July. Angry groups of them roamed the streets of Real del Monte and prevented other workers from traveling to the Morán mine. Vetch attributed the new outbreak to "no possible cause that I can assign except that of being instigated by a few malicious and designing persons." He singled out as one of the agitators an Augustinian monk named José Reyes, who "has rendered himself notorious from his habits of drunkenness & from the low company he keeps & I believe it can be proved that he has been seen drinking with the miners & exciting them against the Company."[17]

When Charles Tindal assumed the commissionership of the Mexican concern in late July, the *barreteros* not only were refusing to work but also were using threats of violence to prevent the English miners from extracting ore and the Mexican peons from helping them before the *partido* was established. Owing to the presence of soldiers in the Real, the *barreteros* did not succeed in bringing mining operations to a complete halt; each evening, however, they thrashed those peons who in the morning had been driven underground by the troops. Still the company delayed, and the strike dragged on. The *barreteros* applied further pressure by attacking the English miners at Morán, an action that led Tindal to complain to the governor of the state of Mexico. The commissioner charged that he had met determined opposition not only from the *barreteros* but also from government officials and members of the Pachuca Mining Deputation. Although the English assigned to the

[17] Bars to Paez, 12 June 1827, AEM, expediente 1827, doc. 11; Paez to prefect of Tulancingo, 7 July 1827, AEM, expediente 1827, doc 23; 1827 CG 26.

Morán mine would defend themselves against the threat to their lives, Tindal was afraid that the pumping machinery in the mines would be damaged, and the huge investment already made—some $2 million—would be lost. Serious trouble might well lie ahead, he noted, because troops stationed at the Real had made it clear that in the event of a showdown with the English they would side with the Mexican workers.[18]

On 29 August Tindal made an offer to the *barreteros* in which the Cornish tutwork, or incentive, system would be combined with the traditional Mexican *partido*. According to his plan, the workings within the various mines would be periodically surveyed and classified in terms of their extent and the quality of the ore they contained. Each Saturday those workings would be, so to speak, auctioned to gangs of *barreteros*. A gang bidding on a given piece of ground would state how much ore it wished as a *partido* for each thirty-quintal bag it extracted for the company. The mine administrator was at liberty to accept the bid that seemed most advantageous to the concern. In addition to the *partido*, the miners would receive the usual four-real daily salary. They were, however, to furnish their own tools, blasting powder, candles, and other equipment. Though reported to be acceptable to the majority of the *barreteros*, the offer was rejected. Tindal was compelled to make a second suggestion.[19]

José Rodrigo de Castelazo read the company's new proposal to the *barreteros* on 1 September. With its unanimous acceptance, the three-month strike came to an end.[20] Tindal's second offer, which

[18] 1827 CG 12; Tindal to Lorenzo de Zavala, 26 August 1827, AEM, expediente 1827, doc. 42.

[19] Modificación de las propuestas ofrecidas a los barreteros del Mineral del Monte, 29 de agosto de 1827, AEM, expediente 1827, doc. 49-A; Tindal to Zavala, 2 September 1827, AEM, expediente 1827, doc. 51.

[20] Paez to Zavala, 2 September 1827, AEM, expediente 1827, doc. 46; 1827 CG 12. Governor Zavala praised "Sr. diputado D. José Rodrigo Castelazo" for his role in settling the strike—without mentioning that Castelazo was both the mining agent of the Count of Regla and in the employ of the English company (*Memoria en que el gobierno del Estado libre de México da cuenta al primer Congreso Constitucional, de todos los ramos que han sido a su cargo . . . desde 26 de octubre de 1826, hasta 15 de igual mes de 1827*, p. 15 [hereafter the annual

was to serve as a formal labor contract between the British concern and its Mexican labor force throughout the company's existence, differed from his earlier one in two important respects. First, the Cornish tribute system was discarded and a simple *partido* system established. Each *barretero* was to be assigned to a specific section of a mine; for his normal tour of duty, day or night, he was to receive four reals and one eighth of all the ore he extracted, whether smelting or *azogue*. Second, the *barreteros* were not hired in gangs on a contract basis, but as individuals paid direct by the company in cash and ore. The concern supplied their tools, powder, candles, and other equipment as well.[21]

Uprising of 1828. The 1827 strike, of course, was only the beginning. Despite the Mexicans' success in forcing the English to sign an agreement that recognized the *partido*, the issue of the form in which wages were to be paid had only been introduced by the strike.

The next skirmish occurred in the latter part of 1828, when the Morán mine *barreteros*, insisting that they, not the company officials, were entitled to name the administrator of the works, refused to go underground. At the commissioner's request, the state government sent a detachment of troops to the Real, and thereby prevented an uprising for a time. After the soldiers were ordered to leave in mid-September, the *barreteros* engaged in a slowdown.

It was not until late November that the troops actually left, and by then the company and workers had apparently come to an understanding, for nothing more was heard of the problem of naming an administrator for the mine. Before they departed, however, the soldiers clashed with about two hundred Morán *barreteros*. A sergeant provoked the *barreteros* into stoning his fellow soldiers, who

---

reports of the government of the state of Mexico, which usually cover the year prior to the presentation date, will be referred to as *Estado de México 1826–1827*, etc.]).

21 Reglamento que la Compañía Inglesa del Mineral del Monte ha formado para el laborío de las minas que trabaja, con respecto al partido y obligaciones de los operarios, AEM, expediente 1827, doc. 50. An English translation of the 1827 labor contract appears as Appendix B of this study.

in turn retaliated by firing into the crowd gathered at the pit head to receive their pay one Saturday. The captain of the dragoons, one militiaman, and two workers were wounded, the latter seriously. The incident led Governor Zavala to accede to one of the company's persistent requests: that he use his influence to convince the federal government to station troops permanently in Real del Monte to maintain order. In appealing to Mexico City for such a detachment, Zavala used the argument that a civilian militia could not be expected to keep the peace, since it would be largely made up of the very miners who took part in the uprisings. By December 1828, as the result of orders issued in the capital, forty infantrymen of the Mexican army were stationed full time at the Real.[22]

Skirmish of 1833. For the next five years the company had no trouble with its Mexican working force, and peaceful labor relations led to the removal of federal troops from the Real. In the meantime, officials succeeded in persuading many of the *barreteros* to accept the Cornish tutwork system both for development work in the mines and for ore extraction. The company was, in fact, returning to a position its chief commissioner had taken during the 1827 strike: a wish to "improve" on a Mexican practice. In the spring of 1833, just as the Santa Teresa bonanza was about to begin, a delegation of native workers prevailed upon Commissioner John Rule to cease violating the 1827 labor contract by assigning men who had accepted tutwork arrangements to ore ground. Rule refused, and for a time the delegates seemed to accept his position.

In the first week of May, however, work in the Santa Teresa mine was suspended. Rule charged that a gang of forty or fifty militant *barreteros* was guilty of criminal activity and succeeded in so convincing the mayor of the Real. The latter said he could not move against the offenders, who Rule alleged were "leagued to-

---

[22] 1828 CG 12; Tindal to Zavala, 6 September 1827, AEM, expediente 1827, doc. 52; Bars to Zavala, 21 September 1827, AEM, expediente 1827, doc. 56; Bars to Paez, 9 November 1828, AEM, expediente 1828, doc 1; Zavala to minister of foreign and domestic affairs, n.d., expediente 1828, doc. 4; minister of foreign and domestic affairs to Zavala, 11 December 1828, AEM, expediente 1828, doc. 5; *Estado de México 1827–1828*, p. 16.

gether by a kind of Free Masonry," until a military force was stationed at the Real. Thereupon the commissioner requested troops from the governor of the state and suggested to his Mexico City agent that a remonstrance to the federal government might also be in order.

Before any soldiers entered Real del Monte, the dispute was apparently settled by the company's agreeing to re-establish the *partido* in accordance with the 1827 contract; in any case, the *barreteros* were working by mid-May, even though they continued to show a "turbulent disposition." Shortly afterward, the arrival of a detachment of thirty cavalrymen from Toluca, the capital of the state of Mexico, quieted the situation at the Real.[23]

Dispute of 1840–1841. The British company remained at peace with its Mexican workers until late 1840, when, within a year of his cautioning the London management that any attempt to change the *partido* at Real del Monte would be both impracticable and dangerous, John Rule made such an attempt. In so doing, he provoked the most complex labor dispute of the company's existence. The conflict spread from the mining camp to the capital and came to involve a lawyer assisting the Mexican workers, a diplomatic representative aiding the English company officers, and Mexican government officials attempting to act as mediators.

Before treating the contest itself, it should be useful to discuss the status of the *partido* issue at the beginning of the 1840's. The Real del Monte Company had by that time made it a practice to avoid strict adherence to the September 1827 labor contract, which required the company to accept a wage system that included the peculiarly Mexican profit-sharing plan, by introducing the Cornish tutwork system. Company officers had pressed the application of this incentive-pay plan as long as they were not directly challenged by the Mexican *barreteros*. Whenever they were directly confronted by the workers, the British officers retreated. As a result, by about 1840 both the Cornish tutwork system and the Mexican

[23] 1833 CG 15.

partido system were part of the wage-paying practices at Real del Monte.

Before the 1840–1841 labor dispute broke out, both adversaries had exhibited some ambivalence as to exactly what they wanted. On the one hand, the Mexican laborers demanded and won full adherence to the *partido* system only in 1826–1827, when they thought the Morán mine was about to produce large quantities of rich ore, and in 1833, when they thought Santa Teresa was in bonanza. In both instances they saw large profit in sharing the anticipated rich ore with their employers. Otherwise they had been willing to accept the lower but more sure income from tutwork contracts for the sinking of shafts, the driving of crosscuts, the exploring for silver-bearing rock, and even for the raising of low-grade ore. On the other hand, the English company had come to realize that the difference between tutwork and *partido* was subtle rather than basic and that acceptance of the latter was not always against their own best interests.

Shortly before the Real del Monte Company embarked on its most strenuous attempt to reduce the *partido*, in 1840 and 1841, three reports that defended the system in principle were sent to the London management. In October 1839 Commissioner John Rule furnished John Taylor with a description of the *partido* as employed in the company's mines at the Real. Rule made three major points. First, once the company had concluded an agreement covering the *partido*, which was "held by the common people as a sacred compact," attempts openly to modify the established method of payment had always caused serious disturbances. Indeed, he said, the same thing had happened elsewhere in Mexico. Second, the commissioner thought the *partido* was not incompatible with "a high state of prosperity." He evoked the example of the fortune made by the Regla family despite the necessity to pay the *partido*. He also demonstrated with figures how the company was economically better off in the wage category by paying the *partido* than was the Bolaños Company at Zacatecas, where the *carga* system was practiced. Third, Rule admitted that in an absolute as opposed to comparative sense, company wages were too high and ought if possible to be cut. However, he warned, the time was not ripe to do so, especially as the British would be looked upon as foreigners tampering with a time-honored native custom.

John Phillips also submitted a pro-*partido* report to London; he described the *partido* as being "as well adapted to the peculiar character of the Real del Monte mines" as were the systems employed in other mining districts. A third report, compiled by the seldom-critical Bolaños official Schuchardt, blamed the allegedly short-sighted Spaniards for allowing the *partido* to become so entrenched in Mexico and cautioned the London officials that any precipitous attempt to do away with that firmly established practice was fraught with danger. He warned in particular against the possibility of a general uprising among the Mexican workers, who, "even should they fail in killing the European officers and workmen of the company, they certainly would never be prevented from destroying the buildings and Engines constructed on the mines."[24]

Now to the most interesting of the several fights between the English company and its Mexican workers over the *partido*. It should be noted at the outset that the company tried to reduce the amount of ore it gave to the *barreteros*, not to do away with the profit-sharing plan altogether. Faced with a difficult financial situation in the fall of 1840, Commissioner John Rule opened negotiations with representatives of the *barreteros* in the hope of inducing them to accept a cut in the share of ore they received through the *partido* from one eighth to one tenth, or even to one twelfth. The company's proposition met with firm opposition, which stiffened still more when a Mexico City lawyer named Sierra y Rosso was given power of attorney by the mine workers to negotiate with the company officials. Anticipating delaying tactics on the part of the lawyer, or his outright refusal to accept the company's proposal, Rule took steps to "dictate to the *barreteros*," should that become necessary. He prevailed on the mayor of Real del Monte to request

[24] 1839 CG 39; "Mr. Phillips's Report to the Directors," RdM *Proceedings*, AGC, 29 June 1841, p. 8.

a detachment of fifty infantrymen from the government of the department of Mexico and asked the British representative to support the mayor's petition.[25]

The next round in the struggle took place in Mexico City. On learning that, "for some unexplained reason," no troops would be sent to the Real and that the *barreteros*' lawyer was "representing to the Government to the Company's prejudice," the chief commissioner hastened to the capital. There he found that the governor of the department was sympathetic toward the company but nonetheless persuaded that it was not necessary to send troops to the Real. Favoring mediation, the governor called several meetings of company representatives (Rule, Castelazo, and the company lawyer) and Sierra y Rosso, acting for the *barreteros*. The sessions were attended also by the British minister and "several leading persons connected with the government."

While those conversations were under way, a six-man delegation representing the Real del Monte *barreteros* arrived in the capital. On 16 November the company's first officer, accompanied by the British representative, met with the workers' spokesmen and with Sierra y Rosso. Having obtained Rule's consent, the governor, acting as mediator, offered the *barreteros* a one-tenth *partido* in all the firm's mines for ten years. He then requested the six delegates to carry that proposal back to the Real to discuss it with the main body of *barreteros* and to return to Mexico City as soon as possible with a reply.

The mine workers were not to be moved by persuasion. In late November and early December, the company Treasurer-Cashier Russell Brenchley, at the mining camp, advised Rule, who was still in Mexico City, that the *barreteros* were as unyielding as ever. "Vigorous action" on the part of the governor was essential, he thought, if anything was to be done with them. Perhaps expressing an ever-stronger feeling on the part of the management, Brenchley said with some bitterness that he expected the commissioner to

---

[25] 1840 CG 39. Under the 1836 centralist constitution, the territorial units known as states within the terms of the 1824 federalist constitution were stripped of most of their autonomy and called departments.

have no success with the *partido* or any other issue, "the Mexicans, as I have said before, appearing to think that we came here for no other purpose than to be pillaged."

On 7 December the workers' delegates presented the governor with a letter from their lawyer and a paper containing their views, namely, that they strongly objected to any alteration in the one-eighth *partido*. The company's commissioner decided to let the matter rest for a time and, while observing the general feeling at the Real, to make preparations for compelling the Mexican workers to accept the company's terms. At the same time he notified London that the matter would have long since been settled satisfactorily had it not been for the "unfortunate and accidental circumstance" of Sierra y Rosso's arrival at Real del Monte at the critical moment when the first meeting on the subject was to be held.[26]

The troublesome lawyer had encouraged the workers to resist the company's proposals for a moderate reduction in the *partido*. The chief commissioner's description of his adversary contains some interesting observations on Mexican politics:

In common circumstances this Mr. Sierra y Rosso would be considered a very ordinary person, as neither his talents nor his acquirements are such as would command much attention. But it unfortunately happens that, while he possesses a certain boldness and energy of character without much prudence, he has acquired a degree of importance and influence here from his connection with the celebrated Santa Anna, who patronizes and protects him . . . and although Sta. Anna is not ostensibly in Power, such is the general belief that he will very soon play an important part in the affairs of this Country, that he and the principals of his party, of which Sierra y Rosso may be considered as one, even now have very great influence.[27]

Early in 1841 Rule was ready to make a definite move. He was

---

[26] 1840 CG 39; 1840 CG 46.

[27] 1840 CG 39. At an elaborate, and somewhat macabre, ceremony held in Mexico City in September 1842, a Licenciado Ignacio Sierra y Rosso delivered a funeral oration over President Santa Anna's foot, shot off at Veracruz three years earlier during the "Pastry War" between French and Mexican forces. (Enrique Olavarría y Ferrari, *México independiente, 1821–1855*, vol. 4 of *México a través de los siglos*, p. 488.)

convinced that the company had either to dictate to the *barreteros* or abandon its effort to reduce the *partido*. To counter Sierra y Rosso's charge that, once having agreed to pay the workers a one-eighth share, the company was bound for all time to maintain that rule, the commissioner secured a ruling from local mining officials to the effect that such a change in the firm's circumstances had taken place that the *barreteros* were "in a situation to receive the Partido which the Company offers." He also asked the British representative and the governor of the department to use their influence in persuading the federal government to dispatch a military force of from sixty to eighty men to the Real. Ready to proceed, Rule awaited only the arrival of the soldiers.

For the next six weeks Rule watched for the troops to back his plan for forcing a reduction in the *partido*. They never arrived. Late in February, Rule was told that the government could not afford to maintain a detachment of infantrymen at Real del Monte and the cavalry troop regularly stationed at Pachuca. The company was caught in a dilemma: to lower the *partido* the English firm would need the Pachuca cavalry to protect its property from retaliation by the *barreteros*; yet, unless those same men could be sent to and from the capital to escort silver bars and cash, the works would have to be shut down. Commissioner Rule chose inaction as a way out of that trap:

Considering the great danger if we proceeded, and considering that the risk has now been increased, and that the question is now complicated by the intervention of Sierra y Rosso and considering the difficulties and inconveniences of keeping pending a long time a question of this sort; we have decided for the present to suspend all proceedings in the matter.[28]

Clash of 1845. The last serious dispute between the Mexican *barreteros* and their employers occurred in August 1845. It had, in fact, begun two months earlier, when discussions were held between the workers' representatives and company officers in the presence of the Pachuca Mining Deputation. At that time the chief

[28] 1841 CG 39.

commissioner was certain that he had parried the miners' demand that all ore extraction be done on the basis of the *partido*. The *barreteros*, however, once again turned to Sierra y Rosso for assistance. From the moment of the lawyer's arrival at the Real on 6 August, most of the underground work was suspended. On the several occasions on which Rule met with the workers and their lawyer, "they pertinaciously clung to the agreement entered into between Mr. Tindal and themselves in the year 1827, by which they became entitled to a *partido* of one eighth of the ores."

The commissioner contended that, for some time, only Terreros had been worked on the *partido* and, upon that mine's suspension, none of the company property had employed that system. But the *barreteros*, encouraged by the discovery of rich ore in the Dolores mine, pressed for the resumption of the *partido*. Rule noted somewhat wryly that, whereas in 1827 "it was hoped and indeed expected that the mines on being drained would be a profitable concern," quite the reverse had occurred. The $70,000 loss during 1844 and up to the end of July 1845 had threatened the very existence of the company. Sierra y Rosso appeared to see the company's side of the case and approved the following proposition put to him: that the *barreteros* be paid one dollar per day, *golpeadores* (strikers in hand-drilling) seventy-five cents, and peons thirty-eight cents.

The company's proposal was discussed at length among the workers, some of whom seemed willing to accept it, but others, either in the majority or more militant, remained firmly opposed to anything less than the *partido*. During those tense days, "large assemblages of people bearing a menacing attitude frequently occurred." The company officials, as they had often done before, requested the Mexican government to dispatch troops to the mining camp. On receiving some assurance that fifty soldiers would be sent to the Real, the chief commissioner decided to take a strong stand against the *barreteros*' demands and, in the event of a full-scale strike, to close down the concern. On the night of 14 August after it had become evident to Rule (and probably to the *barreteros* as well) that no troops would arrive, about one thousand workers gathered in the plaza of Real del Monte and around the Casa Grande, threatening to burn all of the company's property to the ground unless the *partido* were reinstated. Rule capitulated, but he was able to convince Sierra y Rosso, and through him the *barreteros*, that the share of ore granted under the *partido* be set at one tenth, until one third of the firm's investment had been repaid, and one eighth thereafter.[29]

In its final years, the company was spared further strife with its native labor force, but the six clashes between 1827 and 1845 had taken their toll. Company officials complained all through that period, indeed to the bitter end, that wages paid at Real del Monte were too high. On the other hand, the same officials sometimes candidly admitted that the pay of the Mexican workers was no higher than that of similar workers in similar mining camps in other parts of the country. Whatever the relative level of wages paid at the Real, one point can be made: the English concern was unable to offset its declining ability to earn enough to make ends meet by cutting the wages paid to the main body of mine and mill hands. Therefore, the militant Mexican workers' resistance to pay slashes must be considered a part of the reason for the company's economic failure. Moreover, the energy that the English officers exerted trying to coerce, or only to outmaneuver, the native laborers must have been enervating to the company as a whole.

One final point remains—the fate of the *partido*. On the question of whether the Real del Monte Company would retain the kind of profit sharing implied in the *partido* system, the British in Mexico seem to have lost the battles but won the war. It will be recalled that in 1845 the *barreteros* once again forced the company to reinstate the *partido* as the only means of paying for ore extraction. Yet, within a few weeks of their victory, the Mexican laborers seemed to lose interest in their prize. Those working in La Luz, which together with the San Enrique section of Dolores was the source of most of the company's ore production, found that the in-

29 1845 CG 36, 48.

dependent smelters did not care to purchase the colorado ore prevalent in that mine. Many of the *barreteros* showed a willingness to return to tutwork and to leave all the ore to the company.

This new indifference toward the *partido* persisted. By mid-1847, the *barreteros* were taking their share solely from the smelting ore, leaving the *azogues* to the concern. From the three most productive areas of Real del Monte, only about 30 tons of smelting ore were raised each month, whereas the yield of *azogue* ore was approximately 540 tons. This situation, together with the fact that the Rosario mine in Pachuca was worked under the *carga* system, led to the *partido*'s ceasing to be the general method of wage payments for ore extracted by the British concern.[30] In the final analysis, whenever the company attacked the *partido* it met with defeat, but when it acted with more subtlety it was able to replace the *partido* with tutwork. In successfully combatting the *partido* in the mines it controlled, the British company definitely altered the labor practices at Real del Monte.

[30] 1845, 1847 CG 48. The *partido* was to be in and out of favor with both the *barreteros* and the management during the remainder of the nineteenth century. In August 1852, following a short strike similar to that of 1827, John Buchan, the first director of the Mexican company, was compelled not only to reinstate the *partido* for the Real del Monte *barreteros* but also to extend the system to Pachuca, where it had not hitherto been employed and where the Rosario mine was coming into bonanza (Buchan to Nicanor Béistegui and Manuel Escandón, 12 August 1852, RdM, Dirección a Junta Directiva, vol. 1). In September 1874 the Real del Monte *barreteros* presented a deposition to the Board of Directors, explaining that they were on strike because company officials had made a major cutback in the labor force rather than seek new productive areas on which to employ all the miners. They also urged the concern to establish the *partido* as a means of stimulating ore production (*Manifestación comedida que hace la comisión de barreteros del Real del Monte a la Compañía Aviadora de Minas de aquel distrito*). In the late 1880's and early 1890's, the management itself reintroduced the *partido* on occasion, as an incentive to the workers (meetings of Board of Directors, 23 October 1889, RdM, Actas de la Junta Directiva, vol. 1888–1891, p. 207; 7 December 1892, vol. 1891–1894, p. 229).

8. Supplies

SUPPLYING COMMODITIES ESSENTIAL TO THE REAL DEL MONTE
Company's mining and milling operations and cash for its payrolls was a complex undertaking. The concern in Mexico depended
on the home country for much of its equipment and for nearly all
of its vital machinery. Indeed, the invoices and other records of
stores shipments found among company papers list almost everything imaginable, from the gigantic boiler for a seventy-five–inch
steam engine to pen holders, quills, and ink powders used in writing. The company's heavy dependence on its London office for such
a variety of goods, especially manufactures, suggests something at
the same time obvious and instructive. The English firm erected in
Mexico an establishment that demanded far more material than
that used by mine operators of New Spain from the sixteenth
through the eighteenth centuries. And it did so in a country that
in its colonial period and well beyond may be described as pre-
industrial. New Spain's economy was largely based on agriculture,

grazing, and mining. It was tied to an imperial system that required, even if it did not effectively enforce, a continuous reliance on the metropolis for manufactured goods. As a result, except for the making of coarse textiles, colonial Mexico was virtually without industry at the turn of the nineteenth century.

For about half a century after gaining its independence in 1821, Mexico retained the "colonial" and pre-industrial type of economy. One reason might be described as a habit of looking to the land, either in terms of agriculture and grazing or in terms of mining, as the basic source of wealth. Perhaps a more important reason was the political turmoil so characteristic of Mexico until the late 1870's. There are, of course, exceptions to this generalization. Two significant ones are seen in the attempts to construct a modern cotton textile industry and to build a railroad between Veracruz and Mexico City.[1] Nonetheless, it remains true that the British Real del Monte Company, like all other foreign mining ventures in early nineteenth-century Mexico, had to set up and maintain operations in a country from which few manufactured products could be obtained.

The following discussion of the company's supply system illustrates the problems that any foreign enterprise encountered in providing for its needs in an economic setting not keyed to industrial production. It also serves as a basis for assessing the extent to which those problems contributed to the English company's failure.

Supplies from Mexico

Many products native to Mexico were acquired direct from producers and merchants, both in the Real del Monte–Pachuca area and in places as far distant as Guanajuato and Veracruz. Some of the same items, and others from within and without Mexico, were made available to the company through its agents in Mexico City, Veracruz, and Tampico. After an abortive attempt to raise food-

[1] For discussions of those two early attempts to promote Mexican industry, see Robert A. Potash, *El Banco de Avío de México: El fomento de la industria, 1821–1846*, and David M. Pletcher, "The Building of the Mexican Railway," *Hispanic American Historical Review*, 30 (1950), 26–62.

stuffs for both men and animals on company-controlled farms, the English elected to purchase staples from nearby private haciendas. Wood was also found close to the mining camp. The company went further afield for things like salt, litharge, and copper pyrites, all used in the patio amalgamation process; it thereby generally had an opportunity to buy from competing producers or merchants. But for the source of one of its most urgent mining necessities, blasting powder, the concern could turn to just one legal producer. The Mexican government had a technical monopoly over the manufacture and distribution of explosives.

Without knowing the exact quantity and monetary value of every Mexican product consumed by the British company, data that are not precisely calculable from the records found in the company's papers, it is impossible to say for certain which native commodity was the most used and which was most dear. The lack of quantitative information is not so serious, however, for the purpose of this discussion of supply problems is better served by knowing which products obtained in Mexico caused the English firm the most concern. Judged by that criterion, wood for fuel and timbering, the ingredients of the amalgamation recipe, and food for men and mules must rank relatively high. But they do not approach the importance of blasting powder and cash for the payrolls. Therefore, those two commodities will receive the most attention. The company's problems in supplying itself with each had their own peculiarities.

As early as 1828, Commissioner Charles Tindal complained to the governor of the state of Mexico that "once again" the mining camp was threatened with a shortage of explosives. He urged Zavala to instruct the Pachuca distribution center of the federal government monopoly to send powder to the Real immediately and to provide a steadier supply in the future.[2] Besides revealing that this was not the first time the company was faced with a scarcity of explosives, Tindal's letter calls attention to a peculiar and important aspect of the blasting-powder problem: the fact that the Mexi-

[2] 1828 CG 12.

can government was the sole legal supplier to the mining companies.

The government's monopoly of the production and distribution of explosives was a colonial inheritance. By 1571 local officials of the viceregal administration of New Spain were regulating powder production. In 1590 the Spanish government leased the monopoly to private individuals, in whose hands it remained until 1766, when the crown once again assumed responsibility for producing and distributing explosives both for military and mining purposes. Soon after the turn of the nineteenth century, the government fixed the price of powder furnished to miners at four reals ($.50) per pound. In encouraging the rehabilitation of the mining industry, the first government of independent Mexico continued the policy of providing powder to miners at a low cost. Regulations for the equitable distribution of this commodity were issued in November 1824. They called for the appointment of commissioners to determine the needs of the various areas of the country. The distribution of powder manufactured in two factories, one at Santa Fé (near San Luis Potosí) and the other at Zacatecas, was to be carried out through local agencies of the monopoly, on the basis of the commissioners' recommendations.[3]

The high level of production achieved by the government monopoly toward the end of the colonial period was not maintained. Between 1795 and 1799, for example, powder sales amounted to approximately $670,000 annually. In the first full year after independence, 1822, they dropped to some $167,000. From then until 1830, production remained low, varying between $165,000 and $178,000 a year.[4]

It is therefore not surprising that the Real del Monte Company

---

[3] *Memoria sobre el estado de la hacienda pública, leída en la cámara de diputados y en la de senadores, por el ministro del ramo, 4 de enero de 1825* (hereafter annual reports of this ministry, which usually cover the year prior to the presentation date, will be referred to as *Hacienda 1825*, etc.), p. 7; Real orden de 27 de abril de 1801, "Ordenanzas de minería y colección de leyes y órdenes," (cited hereafter as "Ordenanzas, leyes y órdenes"), in *GDM*, p. 59; *Hacienda 1826*, p. 21.

[4] *Hacienda 1825*, p. 7; *Hacienda 1833*, p. 4.

was short of powder in 1828. In answer to pleas addressed to the Pachuca distributor for the national monopoly, the company learned only that no supplies could be expected from that source. In August Tindal asked his Mexico City agent to make a representation to the governor of the state of Mexico, on the company's behalf. "If the administration of powder does not improve," the commissioner said, "we will have to choose between buying it contraband or close down the mines."

During an acute shortage of mine explosives in late 1832, Chief Commissioner John Rule chose the first alternative. Unable to obtain powder through normal channels, Rule requested José Noeggerath, to whom the company had leased its Zimapán operations, to procure from 150 to 200 pounds—if necessary from a contraband source. He even suggested that the shipment be sent to the Real by back roads and at night. The apparently desperate situation that had led him to propose the illegal purchase of powder did not end with that single delivery from Zimapán; in less than a month he placed another order, this one for from 250 to 300 pounds.

On at least one other occasion during the 1830's the threat of a powder shortage arose. In June 1837 the Mexico City agent informed Rule that work in one of the government's factories had been suspended for several weeks, and consequently only small amounts of powder were available in the capital. Asking the British chargé d'affaires to petition the Mexican authorities to reopen the factory, the commissioner said that, inasmuch as the government had a monopoly of the production of powder, which it sold "at a price well above what would be the market price," the mining concern was forced either to acquire its supply from only one source or suspend operations.[5]

The fact that the subject is not mentioned again in the company records suggests that the factory resumed its powder output in time to prevent serious damage to the English concern. It is difficult to test Rule's contention that the Mexican government monopoly

[5] 1828 CG 12; 1832 CG 16; 1837 CG 35.

drove the price to an artifically high level. Company documents show only that the price of powder used for underground blasting was 4.5 reals ($.56) per pound between 1834 and 1838, and 4.1 reals ($.52) in 1839. During the same period, according to government records, the factory at Zacatecas made most of the explosives used in mining and the one at Santa Fé most of the powder for military purposes. The unit cost at Santa Fé is not given, but at Zacatecas powder cost approximately 3.5 reals ($.44) per pound. If transportation expenses are taken into account, it would seem that the company was being charged no more than the Mexican government paid to manufacture and distribute explosives. Possibly John Rule was comparing the price fixed by the state monopoly with that of powder available through contraband. As early as 1832, owing to the government's having freed the production of saltpeter and sulfur—the principal ingredients of blasting powder —a significant portion of the explosives consumed in the country came from contraband sources.[6]

The long-standing complaint that the Mexican government's monopoly of blasting powder maintained that commodity at an artificially high price was, for a time, put to rest. In early 1844 the price dropped from approximately fifty-six to thirty-one cents a pound. The benefit was, however, short-lived. In the summer of 1846, the Mexico City agent reported that there was no blasting powder in the capital. Rule saw as the only alternative buying military powder at one dollar a pound. Even that was in short supply, and the company was thus once again forced to consider closing down its entire mining operations.

Seeing no end of the shortage in sight and having had to halt nearly all digging in one of the mines, Rule sent an agent to the capital to appeal to the government for help in a situation that was becoming desperate. Officials in Mexico City acknowledged the injury that the scarcity of powder was causing the mining industry in general, and the British firm in particular, and promised to study the matter. A few days later, on 3 September 1846, Acting

[6] 1834–1839 CG 28, 34, 38, 40, 65; *Hacienda 1837*, Table 15; *Hacienda 1838*, Table 12; *Hacienda 1834*, p. 9.

President José Mariano Salas decreed an end to the government's monopoly of the manufacture and sale of explosives.

The Mexican government's action meant that the company was permitted to purchase blasting powder where it could be procured most cheaply, or even to manufacture powder itself. After September 1846 the company papers do not mention either a difficulty in obtaining powder or an exorbitant price placed on that commodity. This omission is somewhat surprising, especially since the war between Mexico and the United States doubtless curtailed the source of supply. A clue to the apparent self-sufficiency of the company may be contained in Commissioner Rule's remark that the government decision to allow private concerns to manufacture blasting powder was welcome news. The company, he claimed, could produce it at a cost of about nineteen cents a pound and was already "putting up a small establishment" to do so.[7]

It seems safe to say that the need for money generally causes anxiety. So it was for the English at Real del Monte. But there is a curious irony about their problems in supplying themselves with adequate amounts of cash for day-to-day operations. The Real produced silver, but the company could not pay its local bills, including most of its wages, with uncoined silver. Therefore the company had to ship bulk silver to Mexico City and carry silver coins back to the Real. On both legs of the journey company carriers were subject to attack, but the cash was far more attractive as a target for bandits than were the heavy silver bars. Money supply problems, then, were primarily concerned with transporting coins safely from the capital to the mining camp. Often when unsafe conditions on the road caused an interruption in the flow of money to Real del Monte (interruptions were frequent after about 1827), the British company found it necessary to withhold wage payments or make short-term loans to meet a money shortage. The former expedient was first used in 1829, the latter in 1832. Several times the

[7] 1846 CG 36; 1844, 1846 CG 48; Decreto del Gobierno, septiembre 3 de 1846, in Manuel Dublán and José María Lozano, comps., *Legislación mexicana ó colección completa de las disposiciones legislativas expedidas desde la independencia de la República*, V, 158–159.

concern was compelled to take dramatic steps to transport payroll money. In late 1832, for example, two shipments of cash were secreted into the Real, one hidden under the saddles of pack mules and the other ($8,400) under the seats of a coach carrying a Pachuca Mining Deputation official and William Rule. In 1843 the stagecoach method again succeeded in slipping $15,000 past would-be robbers and into the strong room at company headquarters.[8]

Only once was a shipment of cash intercepted and robbed. On 28 January 1831 Commissioner Tindal was shocked to learn that one of the money wagons bound for the Real had, that very day, been sacked near Tizayuca, a town a little more than halfway between Mexico City and Pachuca. He immediately reported the incident to Holdsworth and Fletcher and to the British minister, asking them to request the Mexican government to intervene in the matter. Tindal gave the following account of the disaster: With an escort of six English and nine Mexican company employees, the wagon had left Mexico City on 27 January and traveled to a point close to Tizayuca, where the party spent the night. On approaching town early the following morning, the company group was informed that a large band of robbers was waiting in ambush. Reinforced by a lieutenant and nine militiamen from Tizayuca, the party had gone beyond the town about five miles when it was assaulted by from eighty to one hundred armed and mounted men. In the ensuing fight, from which all the Tizayuca reinforcements except the officer fled, two company employees, one English and the other Mexican, and the Tizayuca lieutenant were killed and the others in the original escort wounded, some seriously. Three of the bandits were killed and several wounded, and the rest carried off $14,200, five carbines, seven horses and saddles, and miscellaneous stores. The leader of the robbers, who was shot to death by the English company officer commanding the escort, was described as "mounted on a fine black horse, rather a handsome man, young with florid complexion & had a military appearance."[9]

Prodded by the British minister, the Mexican government cap-

[8] 1829 CG 12; 1832 CG 15; 1843 CG 36.
[9] 1831 CG 15; 1831 CG 26.

tured some of the bandits but apparently did not recover any of the stolen money. (It was assisted to some extent by the company, which contributed $59 to cover the expenses of an officer and fifteen men who searched for the robbers.) At about the time the Court of Directors in London was telling the stockholders of the incident and commenting that it was "due to the Mexican authorities to add that they have evinced great vigilance in the apprehension of the parties concerned in this outrage," Minister Richard Pakenham was informing the British Foreign Office that some of the culprits had been captured and dealt with. "Four of the persons who robbed the Real del Monte waggon have been executed," he reported, "a fifth has been sent to California for eight years, and a sixth sentenced to serve in a condemned regiment at San Blas."[10]

To say that blasting powder and money caused the worst supply headaches is not to imply that the myriad of other products sought within Mexico left the firm free from worry. The company's officers had to be constantly on the alert both to take advantage of favorable purchasing opportunities and to avoid the disadvantage of being forced by temporary shortages to buy in an unfavorable market. In short, company leaders in Mexico, who wanted above all to be producers of silver for export to England, had also to be local businessmen.

The price of Mexican products was naturally a matter of importance to the company's well-being. The cost of some commodities seems to have remained fairly constant and to have elicited little complaint from officials. Copper pyrites, essential to patio amalgamation, were supplied mainly by Mead and Company of Guanajuato, and the price varied only between $14.00 and $16.00 per *carga*. Mules cost about the same in 1825 when James Vetch bought a herd in Mexico City for $25.00 to $30.00 a head as they did in 1838 when the treasurer-cashier recorded a purchase of

[10] 1831 CG 26; *Proceedings at the General Courts of Proprietors of the Real del Monte Mining Company*, AGC, 27 June 1831, p. vi; Pakenham to Lord Palmerston, 3 June 1831, Public Records Office, London, Foreign Office 50, Vol. 66, cited in Newton R. Gilmore, "British Mining Ventures in Early National Mexico" (Ph.D. dissertation, University of California, 1956), p. 165.

seventy-two animals at $24.00 to $28.00 a head. Salt, on the other hand, fluctuated considerably in price. It reached Real del Monte from Campeche by way of the Gulf ports of Veracruz and Tampico or overland from the west-coast state of Colima. For the most part its cost at the mining camp ranged between $1.06 and $1.63 per arroba, but in August 1835 the company was forced to pay nearly $2.50 per arroba for a shipment of Yucatán salt. Company officials occasionally found means to acquire a necessity at a favorable price by buying in a glutted market. Tallow, important because it was used both for illumination in the mines and for lubrication, provides a good example. Tallow purchases were usually made late in the year, after the general slaughter of goats throughout Mexico. As a result, the company paid only $4.50 per arroba, whereas the price at other times of the year was $5.50, or even more if the tallow producers sold to speculators in Mexico City.[11]

In the struggle to keep the mining concern stocked with two of the locally obtained necessities, the English at Real del Monte tried to be their own producers. With one—wood for fuel and timbering—they were for many years successful. With the other—food staples—they failed early and turned to Mexican farmers.

At the outset, the company felt it had a rare advantage with regard to the acquisition of wood in a country known to be deficient in timber. Whereas Manager John Taylor had warned all English mining adventurers who planned to introduce steam power and smelting into Mexico that they might face a severe fuel shortage, his own company was specially blessed. The first party to arrive at Real del Monte in June 1824 noted the large wooded areas, some of them included in the nonmining property leased from the Count of Regla, which would assure the company of a good supply of fuel.

That optimism was not entirely unfounded, for it was not until shortly before the English concern went out of business that it faced a really critical shortage of fuel and timbers. To be sure, the ever-increasing demand for wood caused some problems. In 1831

---

[11] 1825 CG 8; 1829 CG 15; 1834 CG 28; 1835 CG 34; 1835–1838 CG 35; 1837 CG 38; 1838 CG 39, 40. Company mules were branded with the sign of crossed miners' picks.

the company petitioned the Real del Monte town council for permission to supplement the supply of wood taken from its own forests by doing some cutting on town-controlled land. By 1836 the company had to purchase additional timber land, approximately 3,750 acres near the town of Huascazaloya. After cutting wood in the vicinity of the mines and mills for seventeen years, the company learned in 1842 that it had used all of the largest and best pieces. Commissioner John Rule therefore turned farther afield and obtained a contract with a timberland owner near Singuilucan for the right to cut wood on his property. This new source was about twenty miles from Real del Monte, but the forest lay near the carriage road between the Real and Veracruz, making the transport of timbers and fuel to the mining camp no insurmountable task.

The very serious wood shortage that confronted the firm just before it collapsed is another of those ironies that are so common in the company's history. The mere fact that company officers had to cope with the problem at a time when they were desperately trying to keep the concern afloat was bad enough. Even more galling was the fact that the main cause of the shortage was the increased fuel consumption brought about by the adoption of the barrel amalgamation process, an improvement in ore reduction methods thought capable of saving the firm. In January 1848 the three steam drainage engines then operating on the mines were burning 2,600 *cargas* of wood each month. The Sánchez hacienda alone consumed an additional 1,200 *cargas*, most of it in the preamalgamation treatment of ore destined for the barrels. From January until the last chief commissioner was ordered to close operations, the company was just barely able to keep both its steam engines and calcining furnaces in fuel. At the end of August 1848, John Buchan estimated that he had enough wood to operate the drainage machines and mills for about two weeks.[12] The supply of fuel, deemed

---

[12] John Taylor, ed., *Selections from the Works of the Baron de* [*sic*] *Humboldt, Relating to the Climate, Inhabitants, Productions, and Mines of Mexico*, p. xxi; "Review of the Real del Monte Mining Association: Annual Meeting, February 28, 1825," *QMR*, no. 4 (January 1831), 439; 1831 CG 12; 1836, 1842 CG 39; 1848 CG 48; "Mining Correspondence, Foreign Mines: Real del Monte Mines,"

no obstacle to success at the beginning of the British operation in Mexico, was a critical problem at the end.

Early in its operations in Mexico when optimism was still the rule, the company tried its hand at farming. The objective was to produce food for the men (particularly the English) and for the animals employed at the mining camp. The experiment began on four large agricultural properties—Ixtula, Tepezala, San José, and Guajalote—all near the reduction haciendas and all including tillable fields.[13] After some initial doubts as to whether the farms should be used exclusively for pasturage or for the cultivation of grains, cultivation was partially attempted. In 1826 George F. Lyon, a Bolaños–Real del Monte official, found some two thousand acres under cultivation "upon the English plan." Up to 1830 as many as five Englishmen and thirteen Mexicans worked regularly on the agricultural experiment. Thirty to forty temporary native hands were hired as the season warranted.

In the early 1830's the company ceased its attempt to become a producer of its own foodstuffs, and the four original estates were leased out for something more than $1,000 a year. They remained under the British company's control, however, and were eventually turned over to its successor. In 1849 the nonmining properties were described as useful to the concern for their woods only. For the grains, straw, and other agricultural products that it needed, the company turned to native growers. Apparently there were enough Mexican farmers in the region of the mining camp to assure the

---

MJ, 18 (28 October 1848), 504. For the general location of the company's timber lands, see Maps 2 and 5.

13 Ynventario y entrega que hizo el Señor Conde de Jala y de Regla de sus haciendas de campo nombradas Yxtula, Tepetzala, San José y el Guajalote, a D. Jaime Vetch, director principal de la Sociedad Ynglesa Europa, con quien formó compañía por viente y un años para el avío de las minas, de que también es dueño, en los Reales de Monte y Zimapán, cuyo contrato se formalizó en el mes de julio de 1824, in Libro en que se hallan, el preliminar con que la Sociedad de Aventureros formada en Londres convino celebrar una compañía . . . con el S. D. Pedro Terreros Conde de Jala y de Regla . . . ; la escritura pública con que se afianzó el contrato, y los ynventarios judiciales, RT, pp. 127–135. For the location of the farms, see Map 2.

company a competitive market in which to buy. For example, between 1835 and 1838 the price of barley remained at about $3.00 per *carga*, while the price of corn declined from $5.25 per *carga* to $3.50.[14]

Supplies from Abroad

Along with steam engines and the various pieces of equipment necessary to their erection and maintenance, quicksilver was the most important article obtained from England. The ordeals of transporting steam engines across the Atlantic, landing them, and carrying them up Mexico's eastern cordillera from the Gulf coast to Real del Monte were matched by the difficulties the British concern encountered in supplying its reduction haciendas with mercury. Attention must also be paid to the supply line established between the London office and the mining camp, in particular to interruptions in that line that halted or retarded the flow of goods from England to Real del Monte.

Even if only steam engines and mercury are considered, it could be argued that the company's mining operations in Mexico depended heavily on the London headquarters for supplies. But that dependence went further. The company imported an extraordinarily wide variety of articles from England. In April 1839, for example, the Court of Directors dispatched a shipment, consigned to the Real through Muñoz and Company of Veracruz, which included the following items:[15]

iron cut in H-pieces	shoe thread
working barrels	whitewash brushes
crusher rollers	clasp knives
miners' shovels	spike nail gimlets

[14] 1825 CG 8; 1830 CG 13; 1835 CG 34; 1836 CG 35; 1835 CG 37; 1838 CG 40; 1839 CG 44; 1840 CG 46; G. F. Lyon, *Journal of a Residence and Tour in the Republic of Mexico in the Year 1826, and with Some Account of the Mines of That Country*, II 151–152; "Proceedings of Public Companies, Real del Monte Mining Company; At the Annual General Court, Held 25th June, 1834," *QMR*, no. 7 (July 1835), p. 170; Acta de los socios del Real del Monte, 1° de junio de 1849, RdM, Accounting file IV-C-1, p. 8.

[15] 1839 CG 65.

screws	marking brushes
folio paper	payroll books
India rubber	safety fuses
record books	files
ink powders	dressed hemp
red lead	trace rope
copying paper	leather knives
one pole case	millwright chisels
pumps	carpenters' ploughs
iron piston caps	black lead
steeled shovels	desk locks
white yarn	foolscap
chalk lines	memorandum books
socket gouges	ground white lead
broad nail gimlets	cash journals
scratch brushes	spices
India ink	saws
pen holders	medicines
quills	

The goods sent from England consisted mostly of necessities, as the above list shows. The sole requisition for luxury items found among the company papers was for "a quarter cask each of good brandy, madeira, and port" requested by the treasurer-cashier of the mining camp in October 1842.[16]

Although mercury was seldom in short supply, its exorbitant price eventually caused the English company much concern and, in the long run, did it real damage. An inflated price, the result of both Spanish government policy and the difficulty of transporting

---

[16] 1842 CG 47. Such austerity on the part of the British officials who continued on at Real del Monte was not to persist during the period of greater affluence under Mexican ownership of the concern. In March 1852, for example, John Phillips, then the London agent of the Mexican company, sent John Buchan forty-five dozen bottles of a highly recommended claret (Phillips to Buchan, 30 March 1852, RdM, Phillips Londres, vol. 1). Some years later, the third British director of the Mexican firm, Stewart Auld, requested Phillips to place an order with "Crosse & Blackwell" for a long list of stores, including kippered salmon, lobsters, oysters, dried herrings, jams, salad oil, mustard, and preserved partridges (1865 CG 60).

quicksilver to the mines and mills of New Spain, had also been an ancient problem for colonial Mexican miners during all but the final decades of the Spanish Empire in America. In the last stages of its imperial hold on the mainlands of the Western Hemisphere, the Spanish government tried to lower and regularize the price of mercury. At the end of the eighteenth century, quicksilver prices, which had been high when the supply was short and low when the supply was adequate, were fixed at approximately $41 a quintal if the shipment to America was from Almadén, Spain, and $63 a quintal if the shipment came from Austria. While the first government of newly independent Mexico made no attempt to continue pegging the price of a commodity whose supply it did not control, it did issue a decree exempting all imported quicksilver, regardless of origin, from customs duties.[17]

From its establishment until the end of 1831, the British company was seldom bothered by a high price for the mercury it needed. It paid between $50 and $55 for a quintal of that vital product on the east coast of Mexico and some $8 more at the site of its mines (see Table 6). Besides the precedent of a low quicksilver price, two other conditions seem to account for the English firm's initial good luck. First, although general importations from Spain were prohibited in 1824, mercury was still allowed to enter the country.[18] Second, a reduced demand for the product on the part of an industry seriously damaged during the 1810–1821 political activity and only beginning to recover in the first decade after independence may well have prevented a significant early price rise.

An event that took place in Europe in 1831 completely altered the supply-demand relationship that had thus far governed the quicksilver market. During that year, the London branch of the House of Rothschild gained from the Spanish crown, as security against the repayment of a loan, control of the distribution of mercury from Spain's Almadén mines. The Vienna branch having at

[17] Decreto de la Junta Provisional, 20 de febrero de 1822, "Ordenanzas, leyes y órdenes," in *ODM*, p. 66.

[18] Ley del 13 de febrero de 1824, Guía de la Hacienda de la República Mexicana, p. 36, cited in Potash, *Banco de Avío*, p. 35.

TABLE 6

*Price of Quicksilver Paid by the Real del
Monte Company, 1825–1848*

Year	Lowest Price per Quintal	Highest Price per Quintal
1825	$ 50.00**	$ 50.00**
1826	51.00**	51.00**
1827–1832	53.00**	55.00**
1833	79.00	89.00
1834	80.00	90.00
1835	95.00	115.00
1836	100.00	122.00
1837	104.00	135.00
1838	105.00	112.50
1839	105.25	139.00*
1840	125.00	134.00*
1841	115.00	126.00*
1842	108.50**	128.00*
1843	102.00**	121.00**
1844	113.00**	117.00**
1845	117.00**	149.00*
1846	118.00**	154.00*
1847	119.00**	140.00
1848	120.00**	144.00**

SOURCES: The RdM Papers contain no information on the price of quicksilver
for 1825 and 1826; data for those years were taken from *Balanza general del
comercio marítimo por los puertos de la República Mexicana*, I (1825), 111; II
(1826), 152. The rest of the data was drawn from correspondence, lists of supplies entering the Regla and Sánchez mills, and invoices of goods shipped to the
company by Holdsworth and Fletcher and by Muñoz and Company, 1828–1846
CG *passim*.

NOTE: Unless followed by asterisks, the figures refer to the price of a quintal
of mercury at Real del Monte. A single asterisk (*) denotes the price quoted in
Mexico City, to which $4 have been added for handling and for shipping to the
Real. A double asterisk (**) indicates the price quoted at Veracruz or Tampico,
to which $8 have been added to cover those costs.

the same time obtained a lease of Austria's Idria mines, the Rothschilds exercised a world monopoly of quicksilver.[19] The result was
a significant increase in the price that miners in Mexico had to pay
for mercury.

[19] John Reeves, *The Rothschilds, the Financial Rulers of Nations*, pp. 180–181;
Frederic Morton, *The Rothschilds, a Family Portrait*, p. 79.

The first company reference to the higher cost appears in a letter dated 17 September 1833, in which the chief commissioner asked his Mexico City agent to send him a supply of mercury, acknowledging that the price was $80 per quintal. In December John Rule again placed an order with Holdsworth and Fletcher; the price had risen to $85. That was only the beginning. For the next fifteen years the British Real del Monte Company, together with the other mining concerns in Mexico, was to cope the best it could with quicksilver prices maintained at an artificially high level by the European financial house.[20]

Although the company was trapped by the quicksilver monopoly, officials were unwilling to accept confinement without a struggle. They tried two sets of tactics: to mitigate the effects of the monopoly by importing mercury through company channels and to escape entirely from dependence on quicksilver from abroad by producing that metal themselves in Mexico. They were at least partially successful in the first effort, but they failed entirely in the second.

By the mid-1830's, the company had begun to buy mercury in London and ship it direct to the mining camp in Mexico. If the mining company could not in any way circumvent the Rothschild monopoly, it could at least avoid the charges of middlemen in Mexico. There is little doubt that the practice afforded some relief from the high and increasing price that the company had to pay for the most important single product used in its milling operations. In 1837, for example, John Rule notified the home office that he had been obliged to buy some eighty-three quintals of quicksilver in Mexico City at $130 per quintal. Considering the comparative freight costs, he estimated that the price was 25 per cent higher than it would have been had the quicksilver been received on the company's account in England. Then again, in early 1844, at a time when a Rothschild agent had fixed the price of mercury in Mexico City at $145 per quintal, the company imported 150 quin-

---

[20] 1833 CG 15. A close friend of Nathan Rothschild, who headed the London branch of that family, was T. F. Buxton, the first chairman of the Real de Monte Mining Company Court of Directors (Morton, *The Rothschilds*, p. 61).

tals direct from its London office at a price of $113, paid in Real del Monte. Unfortunately, the company was not able to make consistent use of that money-saving tactic. Owing to a shortage of disposable funds in England with which to purchase and ship more than a fraction of the mercury needed in the mills between 1838 and 1841, the commissioner at Real del Monte was compelled to obtain the bulk of his supply in Mexico, at an estimated loss to the company of from $20,000 to $30,000.[21]

By making a concerted effort to develop its own source of quicksilver supply within Mexico, the company tried to bypass the Rothschild monopoly entirely. The effort began in the spring of 1837, when John Rule learned of the existence of an allegedly promising mercury mine near the town of El Doctor, in the department of Querétaro. By the fall of that year the commissioner had gotten London's approval to contract for the mine. Real del Monte was thereby committed to a long, intensely disappointing quest for native quicksilver that became, in a sense, an unsuccessful six-year program to shift from a monopoly-clogged overseas source of supply to a self-controlled domestic one.

To relate in detail the dreary story of the firm's attempt to develop a paying mercury mine at El Doctor would contribute little to this work. It is only too similar to the several other accounts that might be given of unsuccessful endeavors to develop paying silver mines at Real del Monte: high initial hopes, very strenuous early efforts, cutbacks because no income offset costs, and finally a reluctant admission that the whole undertaking was futile. One part of the El Doctor venture is, however, both interesting and instructive.

---

[21] 1837, 1841 CG 39; 1844 CG 48, 65. Real del Monte was not, of course, the only British company working mines in Mexico that sought to offset the effects of the artificially high price of quicksilver by purchasing it in England and shipping it to the camp. The United-Mexican Mining Association, for example, began that practice in the 1830's and developed it into a system of regular monthly shipments from the home office to the site of operations in Mexico ("Proceedings of Public Companies: United-Mexican Mining Association," *MJ*, 5 [29 July 1837], 38; "Mining Correspondence, Foreign Mines: United-Mexican Mining Association," *MJ*, 13 [8 April 1843], 123; "Mining Correspondence, Foreign Mines: United-Mexican Mines," *MJ*, 18 [30 December 1848], 613).

Through the good offices of the British chargé d'affaires, who met with the Mexican ministers of finance and foreign affairs to assure a favorable reception, the company submitted a formal representation to the government asking for aid in the exploitation of its mercury mines. This document stressed the high price of quicksilver in Mexico, the result of the Spanish monopoly; the fact that the company was about to begin an expensive search for a Mexican source of mercury; the heavy losses that the English had already suffered in uplifting the Real del Monte mining district from its "crushed and ruinous state"; and the alleged training it had afforded "natives" in the operation of machinery.

Commissioner John Rule made three specific proposals, none of which was ever acted upon. He asked: (1) that, for a period of fifteen years, the Mexican government grant a "Bounty or premium" of $7 per quintal for all quicksilver produced from mines worked in Mexico; (2) that, in lieu of making an outright payment to the company, the government permit the company to deduct the production bonus from the taxes paid on its silver output; and (3) that all European machinery, tools, iron, steel, and other goods required for the working of the quicksilver mines be imported into Mexico free of duty. The request faced strong competition in the French fleet then blockading the port of Veracruz. In late November 1838, the British chargé informed Rule that, owing to Manuel Eduardo de Gorostiza's retirement as minister of finance, to a conference of ministers at Jalapa with the French admiral, and to "the great question now pending of war or peace with France," he had been unable to press for favorable government consideration of the appeal. Rule, in turn, advised London that "the very important events taking place in this country, between the French and the Mexicans," had apparently prevented action on the representation.[22] That there is no further mention of the subject in company records suggests either that the company dropped its plea for assistance, which seems unlikely, or that the government rejected or simply forgot about the request, which probably was the case.

[22] 1837–1839 CG 39.

Ironically, at the time the British company was failing, developments were in progress that were eventually to lower significantly the price of quicksilver in Mexico. Throughout 1847 that commodity sold in London for approximately $112.50 per quintal; in April 1848 it was selling for $100.00; and in June of that year, for $87.50. As Table 6 shows, however, the lowering of the price in England was not immediately reflected in the price paid by the company at its mining camp in Mexico. During the late 1840's, events were taking place in California that perhaps accounted for the sudden fall in the price of quicksilver on the London market and eventually forced the value of that product down in Mexico. In June 1846 the English firm of Barron and Forbes, located at Tepic, Mexico, entered into a contract with a Mexican cavalry officer who had claimed the New Almadén mine near San José, California, for its quicksilver content. Under Barron and Forbes, this mine began, by the end of 1850, to supply mercury to the Mexican mining industry at $90.00 per quintal; in time, it broke the Rothschild monopoly.[23]

Certain dispatches sent by officials from the Real del Monte mining camp to company headquarters in London, along with some published remarks of officials in England, give the impression that one of the major causes for failure were halts in the flow of needed supplies from England to Mexico. A careful investigation of the overseas supply line and of the interruptions in it tends to belie the cries of strangulation uttered by company officials but, at the same time, to confirm the fact that the English mining establishment did indeed rely very heavily on goods sent it from the home country. The link with England was, therefore, vitally important. Breaking it completely for any length of time could have done great harm to operations in Mexico. Interruptions did occur and they were annoying, to be sure, but the evidence available in company records does not substantiate any claim that they were frequent enough or

---

[23] "Price of British and Foreign Metals," *MJ* 18 (15 January, 29 April, 24 June 1848), 31, 207, and 303, respectively; Gilmore, "British Mining Ventures," pp. 152–155.

protracted enough to contribute significantly to the company's downfall.

The delivery of supplies from overseas was always subject to delay and sometimes, as in the event of war between Mexico and a foreign power, entirely cut off. Requisitions were usually sent from Real del Monte with the regular monthly dispatches that were carried on British packet ships sailing between the Mexican Gulf coast and English ports, usually Falmouth. The interval between the chief commissioner's writing an order and receiving the goods averaged from six to eight months, depending on the following: (1) the delay in passage both ways across the Atlantic due to the speed of the vessel employed—freight ships being slower than packets—sailing schedules, and weather conditions; (2) the time required to process the order in London; (3) the purchase of the goods, often in Cornwall; (4) the delivery of the merchandise to the British port of embarkation and its loading; and (5) the discharging of the merchandise in Mexico and its transport to the Real.

Twice during its twenty-five–year operation in Mexico the British company had its supply lines disrupted owing to wars engaged in by its host country. The first conflict that affected the firm was the "Pastry War" between Mexico and France, which occurred during 1838 and 1839. The second was the more significant war between Mexico and the United States, which lasted from 1846 to 1848.

The blockade imposed on Veracruz by the French fleet in 1838–1839 during the "Pastry War" worried Real del Monte officials but did not break the company's supply link with its home base. Indeed, the English officers in Mexico admitted that, despite the fact that two ships carrying equipment for the concern had been turned away from Veracruz, the mining camp had enough of everything except iron. To offset the shortage in that category, Commissioner John Rule started building a small foundry for the purpose of rehabilitating the large stock of old iron accumulated over the years. Evidence in the company papers is inconclusive, but apparently Real del Monte continued to process and use its second-hand iron during the last decade of its existence in Mexico. In general, then, whereas its officers in Mexico called the French blockade a "sad thing," the English mining company had no great difficulty in combatting a temporary shortage of general stores.

In an odd way, the Real del Monte Company actually made a small gain from the pseudo-war. British packet ships, which carried passengers, mail, and frequently mercury, were allowed to pass through the French fleet. By taking advantage of a May 1838 law designed to encourage slipping mercury and other vital supplies through the blockade, the company claimed and collected in tax credits a bonus of $5 for every quintal of quicksilver it was able to import on the privileged British packets.[24]

In declaring war against Mexico in May 1846, the United States imposed a blockade on the Gulf ports of Veracruz and Tampico.[25] For a time the supply line from England was therefore cut. Two ships carrying goods intended for the Real were kept from landing at Veracruz, and a third was detained in England on receipt of the news of events in the Gulf of Mexico. Commissioner Rule complained that the mining camp would be seriously inconvenienced by the loss of three consecutive shipments of general supplies, but he also admitted that, as the British packet ships were still allowed to land quicksilver, no shutdown of the principal works was anticipated. Paradoxically, the Americans' capturing of Veracruz in 1847 and permitting European ships to land prevented that inconvenience from becoming a stranglehold.

The capture of Veracruz by United States forces in March 1847 may have put an end to one kind of threat to the England–Real del Monte supply line, but it did not guarantee that there would be no other threats or no further aggravations. The company suffered three more supply problems that were quite aggravating. For a time just after the American occupation of Veracruz, the English

24 1838 CG 35; 1838, 1839 CG 39; Ley de mayo 12 de 1838, in Dublán and Lozano, *Legislación mexicana*, III, 508–509.

25 George L. Rives, *The United States and Mexico, 1821–1848: A History of the Relations between the Two Countries from the Independence of Mexico to the Close of the War with the United States*, II, 160, 291–292.

firm's agent in that port, Muñoz and Company, could not find a carrier willing to risk a trip between Veracruz and the Real along a road that had become "infested with robbers." Then, the company had to seek safe-conduct passes from the Mexican government; these allegedly would insure its supply wagons from being molested by "authorized Guerrilla bands." The bureaucratic annoyance was bad enough, but the passes did not always guarantee "safe conduct." In November 1847 a company wagon en route from the coast to Real del Monte, and furnished with an official document, was robbed about seventy-five miles from its destination. All of the clothes belonging to the transport party and $1,000 carried by its leader were stolen.

Still another obstacle stood in the way of transport of supplies. In January 1848 a company wagon train carrying stores from England reached the Real, but instead of making the trip from Veracruz in the usual thirty-one or thirty-two days, it took forty-five. The extraordinary delay occurred because the Mexican forces had destroyed a bridge and broken up the road in many places, "to prevent the passing of the Americans into the interior." Under those conditions, the chief commissioner decided not to send the company wagons back to the coast, but rather to contract for the transport of supplies by private carriers. That step was of dubious advantage to the concern, however, for freight charges appear to have risen enormously during the war. The cost of shipping quicksilver from Veracruz to Real del Monte was, in early 1848, for example, $60 a *carga*, or $20 a quintal, whereas in normal times the freight and handling charges were only $8 a quintal.[26]

[26] 1846–1848 CG 48.

9. Real del Monte
and Mexico

THE PRESENCE OF THE BRITISH REAL DEL MONTE COMPANY IN
Mexico was felt most strongly in the immediate vicinity of its
operations, the Real del Monte–Pachuca mining district. Its influence, however, spread to a much wider circle through its purchase
of salt from Yucatán and Colima and blasting powder from near
San Luis Potosí. The recruitment campaign of 1827 reached workers not only in the immediate vicinity and in nearby Atotonilco el
Chico, but farther away in the capital and Zimapán and even at a
camp as distant as Guanajuato. In marketing its silver the English
concern exerted a strong influence on the Casa de Moneda (mint)
of Mexico City and even affected the system of conveying precious
metals from the capital to Veracruz for export. Impact and influence were not, of course, one-sided. The British company felt the
effect of individuals and of institutions in its immediate neighborhood and beyond, particularly those in Mexico City, whose relative
closeness to Real del Monte was both a blessing and a curse.

In the various governments of Mexico—national, state, and local —the company found neither an implacable enemy nor a constant friend. On the whole, the English concern got along best with the state, or department, of Mexico; reasonably well with the municipality of Real del Monte and with officials at Pachuca and Tulancingo; and worst with the several national administrations. Its contacts with the governments in Mexico City (and it should be noted that there were dozens of them during the period of political instability that followed Mexican independence) were less immediate and therefore less important than those at the state or local levels. When, for example, the firm was involved in its two most difficult labor disputes, in 1827 and in 1840–1841, it turned to the chief executive of the state of Mexico for aid. Company dealings with the municipal authorities at the Real or with the district officials in Pachuca and Tulancingo were frequent, almost daily.

Communications between company officers and government officials at the mining camp, or in Pachuca, Tulancingo, and the state capital abound in the company papers. Those directed to and received from the central government are rare. Most of the cases in which the company communicated directly with officials in Mexico City occurred in the early years, as, for example, during the landing and transport of the first shipment of machinery and equipment. Usually the British firm approached the capital through intermediaries—in most cases the diplomatic and consular representatives of Great Britain in Mexico. Company commercial agents and the third Count of Regla were sometimes pressed into service. But the company's correspondence contains many more appeals directed to British consuls or chargés than to Holdsworth, Fletcher and Company or to Pedro Romero de Terreros.

Three topics should serve to illustrate the relations between the English mining concern and various levels of government in Mexico: (1) the attitude of Mexican officials toward the mining industry in general and the Real del Monte Company in particular, (2) taxation, and (3) the company's problems in marketing its silver. The first subject has mainly but not exclusively to do with the English firm and the government of the state, or department, of

Mexico. The second concerns the company and officials at nearly all levels, from municipality to nation. The third deals almost entirely with negotiations between the company, its advocates, and the central government.

The Company's Reception in Mexico

The attitude of the earliest national administrations of Mexico, characterized by an anxiety to see the rehabilitation of the ruined mining industry and by a willingness to allow foreigners with money to help with that task and to profit thereby, provides a general background to the reception given the British Real del Monte Company. Perhaps more important, though, is the way in which the state of Mexico looked upon mining within its borders and specifically upon the operation at the Real, not just at the time the British concern established itself in that state but over the whole period of its existence.[1]

[1] Real del Monte was within the jurisdiction of the state, or department, of Mexico. During the periods in which the federalist Constitution of 1824 was in effect (1824–1836 and 1846–1849), Mexico was known as a state; during the period in which the centralist constitutions of 1836 and 1843 were in effect (1836–1846), it was called a department. The state government exercised considerable autonomy, while the departmental government was little more than a local administrative agency of the strong central government. Enrique Olavarría y Ferrari, *México independiente, 1821–1855,* vol. 4 of *México a través de los siglos,* pp. 595–600).

A very large state in 1824, covering approximately 39,500 square miles, Mexico was bordered on the north by Querétaro and Veracruz, on the east by Puebla, on the south by the Pacific Ocean, and on the west by Michoacán. It was divided into eight districts—Acapulco, Cuernavaca, the Federal District, Huejutla, Mexico, Toluca, Tula, and Tulancingo—which in turn were subdivided into thirty-six counties. Though lacking in autonomous powers, the department of Mexico was even larger than the state had been, for to its area was added the territory of Tlaxcala. It was composed of thirteen districts—Acapulco, Chilapa, Cuautitlán, Cuernavaca, Mexico, Mextitlán, Taxco, Temascaltepec, Texcoco, Tlaxcala, Toluca, Tula, and Tulancingo. The district of Tulancingo was divided into three counties, one of the same name, Pachuca, and Apám. The seat of the state, or departmental, government was located intermittently in Mexico City, Texcoco, Tlalpám, and Toluca. The principal officials with whom the English company dealt over the years were the governor, the prefect of Tulancingo, the subprefect of Pachuca, and the mayor of Real del Monte (*Memoria en que el gobierno del Estado libre de México, da*

Soon after independence the state of Mexico looked with enthusiasm upon the mining industry, and in particular its rehabilitation by foreign capital. In his annual report for 1825, Governor Melchor Muzquiz singled out for special attention the Tulancingo district, in which Real del Monte was located. The thirty-eight mines being worked there (of the seventy-two known to exist) were, he said, the most productive and, owing to the large sums invested in them by companies and individuals, would doubtless provide a stimulus not only to the surrounding towns but also to the agriculture, industry, and commerce of the entire state. Muzquiz thought that the government ought to encourage the revival of the mining industry; the best way to do so, in his opinion, was to establish funds that would allow the mine owners to exchange their silver for money without delay (*fondos de rescate*). His views were reflected in a decree issued by the state Congress on 1 July 1825, authorizing the establishment of silver exchanges in Pachuca, Taxco, Temascaltepec, and Zimapán. The governor was to propose the amounts of money to be placed in the various funds, and all silver acquired by them was to be coined in the state's own mint, whose construction was authorized. The importance of the company in that chain of developments is shown by the fact that in February 1825, several months before the decree was promulgated, the state administration set up a *fondo de rescate* of $20,000 in Pachuca and one of $15,000 in Zimapán.[2]

Demonstrating a continued interest in mining within its borders, the state of Mexico enacted a law in 1826 which set forth provisional arrangements for regulating the industry. Mining matters were placed in the hands of the governor himself. The territorial

---

cuenta de los ramos de su administración al congreso del mismo estado [hereafter the annual reports of the governor of the state of Mexico, which usually cover the year prior to the presentation date, will be referred to as *Estado de México 1826*, etc.], p. 9; Decree of 23 December 1837, *Colección de decretos de los Congresos Constitucionales del Estado libre y soberano de México*, II, 396–397).

[2] *Estado de México 1826*, pp. 11, 46; Decreto de 1° de julio de 1825, *Decretos del Congreso Constituyente del Estado de México revisados por el mismo congreso é impresos de su órden*, I, 78.

mining deputations already operating in the various camps were to pursue their activities, but under the direct supervision of the state government. The regular courts in the mining districts were given jurisdiction over the legal aspects of the industry. While that step was being taken, the administration reminded the legislature that the most important mining properties were located in the Tulancingo district and that the heavy investments being made there and elsewhere by foreigners made it imperative for the Congress to protect the entrepreneurs, regardless of their origin.[3]

When the Real del Monte Company first clashed with the Mexican working force, the government of the state was still favorably inclined toward foreign-operated mining enterprises. In reporting to Congress on the fiscal year beginning October 1826, Governor Lorenzo de Zavala expressed the opinion that the foreign-managed gold and silver mines in the Tulancingo district, then yielding their first ore, would in time be the principal source of wealth of the entire state. He spoke directly of the Real del Monte Company in his account of the shortage of workers and the labor strife that had occurred in the Real. He chided the company for its "exaggerated" complaints regarding the labor shortage, the workers' practice of taking shares in the production of the mines, and the "insolence of labor" as a threat to public order at the Real. Yet Zavala concluded his remarks by saying that "the government . . . is satisfied with the moral, political, and religious conduct of the foreigners who are occupying themselves in various branches of our mining industry. Their industrious hands have given life to places that formerly were nothing but wilderness."[4]

The state government further gave concrete expression to its desire to promote the mining industry by constructing a mint in Tlal-

[3] Decreto de 28 de julio de 1826, *Decretos del Congreso Constituyente del Estado de México*, I, 103; *Estado de México 1827*, pp. 5–6. For a discussion of the Spanish colonial legislation and custom that underlay the legal and administrative framework within which the mining industry of newly independent Mexico operated, see Walter Howe, *The Mining Guild of New Spain and Its Tribunal General, 1770–1821.*

[4] *Estado de México 1828*, pp. 8, 11–12.

pám. The governor's report to the legislature in the spring of 1828 was optimistic regarding the future of that establishment. Yet, while the mine owners were showing confidence in the mint by sending their silver there, they would continue to do so only so long as they received prompt payment for their product. Zavala insisted that a reserve of at least $100,000 be kept at the Tlalpám mint to pay for the bars of silver introduced, particularly those from Pachuca. He showed an awareness of the problems of mine owners in general, and in particular seemed to understand those often faced by the company in its dealings with the Mexico City mint, when he said that the slightest delay in payment for silver could cause serious damage, since immediate cash was needed for wages and other operating expenses.

Within a few years, however, the Tlalpám mint was closed and the state government's enthusiasm for mining somewhat tempered. Governor Muzquiz told the Congress in 1831 that poor judgment had been shown in the establishment of a mint so close to the one in the capital and with such a small fund for paying for the silver introduced. The mint had been shut down in 1830, he noted, but only after sustaining a loss of $149,775. As to mining in the nation as a whole, investments made by foreigners between 1824 and 1826 had given considerable impetus to the industry. Yet the success of the non-Mexican enterprises was not commensurate with the enormous sums invested, owing to a lack of practical knowledge on the part of the foreign directors.

Though less concerned with the mining industry, the state sought to maintain the *fondos de rescate* in Pachuca, Taxco, and Zimapán for a number of years after the closing of the Tlalpám mint. The Pachuca office of the treasury received particular attention, since it served the most productive mining district. A system was devised under which the Pachuca silver exchange would be financed by taxes collected both in that town and in Tulancingo; the silver it received would be sent to the Mexico City mint and the cash delivered by the Casa de Moneda would be turned over to the general exchequer of the state. That plan, like the one for the maintenance of the *fondos de rescate* in other places, seems to have failed because of the state government's inability to provide the necessary financial support.[5]

Up to the time its autonomous powers were abolished, the state of Mexico retained some interest in the mining industry; yet its concrete accomplishments in encouraging enterprises like the British company were few. The isolated pieces of legislation that it passed—which were probably never carried into practice—elicited no comment from officials of the British company. A general education law of 1834, for example, provided for instruction in mineralogy, including two years' practical training in the various mining camps. The Congress that year authorized the administration to enter into agreements with financiers, who should, other things being equal, be Mexican citizens, for the establishment of private *fondos de rescate* in the mining centers. In 1835 the administration was instructed to set aside from the state's tax receipts a fund with which to purchase quicksilver in several small villages in the southern part of the state and in the town of Cuernavaca, and also to grant a $3,000 prize for each discovery of a mercury vein that, in the judgment of experts, lent itself to profitable exploitation.[6] On the state's becoming a department, the enactment of laws affecting the mining industry ceased until 1846.

During the brief 1846–1849 federalist period, in spite of the fact that a war was in progress most of the time, the state's interest in the mining industry was reawakened. An attempt was made to reestablish the system of special courts for mining matters, which had not been in effect since the end of the Spanish colonial regime. The plan was not carried out, however, and the territorial deputations, which still existed in Pachuca, Sultepec, Taxco, and Zimapán, continued to assist the regular judiciary in handling mining cases. Fur-

[5] *Estado de México 1828*, pp. 46, 53; *1831*, pp. 13–14, 58; *1832*, p. 20; *1833*, p. 49; *1834*, p. 15. As a measure of the state's declining interest in mining, it should be noted that these volumes do not contain a section devoted exclusively to that industry, whereas the annual reports of the 1820's do.

[6] Ley organica de la instrucción pública del Estado de México, 13 January, 1834, Decree of 17 December 1834, Decree of 18 May 1835, *Colección de decretos de los Congresos Constitucionales del Estado libre y soberano de México*, II, 285–299, 361–362, 367.

ther evidence of the renewed attention paid the industry was the passing of legislation in December 1847 that authorized the establishment of a mint in the state capital. The new institution was to be constructed and operated by private parties, acting under a contract with the state government. This effort also failed. Finally, the state itself planned to take a hand in reviving the defunct mining district of Temascaltepec by completing, at its own expense and with prison labor, an adit through which to explore some of the formerly productive veins.[7]

A report covering the years 1846–1848, which the administration submitted to the state legislature in May 1849, spoke at length of the mining industry. Conspicuously absent is any discussion of mining activities in Real del Monte, although an appended list of fifty mines in that camp shows thirty-seven as being operated by the British company, five as being worked by their original owners, and the rest idle. The concern shown in 1827 and 1828 toward the British Real del Monte Company was now transferred to the mining district of El Oro, some forty miles northwest of Toluca, near the border between the present states of Mexico and Michoacán, where a new company had recently begun the rehabilitation of old properties.[8]

Taxation

The Real del Monte Company had little reason to complain about the direct charges assessed on its produce: a production tax, *minería* (a tax to support the Mexican Mining Guild), assay fees, and payments for the services of minting and separating gold from the silver bars. The newly independent government of Mexico had considerably lowered all these taxes, direct and indirect, from the levels set in the colonial period. The British company's quarrel was

[7] Decrees of 1 October 1846, 7 December 1847, *Colección de decretos del Congreso Estraordinario del Estado libre y soberano de México*, III, 11, 226–227; *Memoria de las secretarias de relaciones y guerra, justicia, negocios eclesiasticos, é instrucción pública, del gobierno del Estado de México, leida a la honorable legislatura en las sesiones de los dias 1 y 2 de mayo de 1849* (cited hereafter as *Relaciones del Estado de México 1849*), pp. 19, 21, 48.

[8] *Relaciones del Estado de México 1849*, Table 3, pp. 20, 47.

instead with fluctuations in the taxes on exports of either bullion or coin, attempts to impose special charges or forced loans, import duties and restrictions on the acquisition of badly needed equipment unavailable in Mexico, and the *alcabala* on materials purchased within the country.

The amount that the company paid in taxes varied somewhat from year to year, depending on the output of silver and the mode of disposing of that product. A reasonably accurate estimate of those taxes can be arrived at by looking at the year 1836, when the concern was struggling to make use of its legal right to ship all of its silver out of the country in the form of bullion and was therefore citing a good deal of data on its financial and tax-paying situation. In July company officials stated that they were paying just under 12 per cent of the value of the produce in direct taxes. This rate was confirmed two months later, when Commissioner John Rule noted that Real del Monte was paying some $66,000 a year in direct taxes on its silver (amounting to approximately 12 per cent ad valorem). The assessment of $7,000 in import duties on stores from England and of $1,000 in "aduana duties at the mines and haciendas" (by which *alcabala* levies on locally purchased supplies were probably meant) added a tax payment of slightly more than 1 per cent.[9]

The company paid little, if any, of its direct mining tax—3 per cent of the value of its actual production—to the national government. While decrees of November 1821 and October 1824 provided for the collection of that tax by the central government, as early as 1825 the state of Mexico was beginning to press for the right to receive the payment. It was not until July 1828 that federal legislation turned over the assessment of the tax to the various states; yet the state of Mexico appears to have undertaken the task on its own during the three-year interim. That it continued jealously to guard

[9] 1836 CG 35, 36. An English traveler writing in 1834 estimated that the company was paying 13 per cent in duties to the Mexican government; neither import charges nor the *alcabala* were mentioned (Henry Tudor, *Narrative of a Tour in North America; comprising Mexico, the Mines of Real del Monte, the United States, and the British Colonies: With an Excursion to the Island of Cuba*, II, 307–308).

its claim to the receipts is indicated by an August 1831 decree of the state legislature authorizing the administration to make the necessary arrangements with the federal government for the collection of those monies allotted it under the July 1828 federal law.[10]

During its early and more affluent years, the British concern was disposed to making extraordinary payments to the Mexican government. In the fall of 1828, for example, the chief commissioner arranged with two English commercial houses in Mexico City for "a subscription of $2,000 from the Real del Monte Company towards the present exigencies of government." Later on, when it had become keenly aware of its lack of fortune, the company was reluctant to make such payments. In mid-1836 company officials appealed successfully to the British representative in the capital for exemption from "contributing to the forced loan now in progress of being levied throughout the Republic."

The concern was not always able, however, to escape the special assessments aimed at it. In 1844 the treasurer-cashier explained to the London management that two entries under the head of "general expenses" made three years earlier were payments to the government. The first entry, Brenchley said, was for a "poll tax, since ceased." The second was for an income tax on the salaries of the company officers. By placing "a very limited interpretation on the term 'officers,' " the chief commissioner paid the tax on the "half salaries of 19 Company servants." In July 1847, as a result of a general forced loan imposed by the federal government on all property in Mexico, the company was assessed $1,600 for the Regla hacienda. Commissioner William Rule settled that matter by paying $100 to the prefect of Tulancingo, on condition that "no further demands were made against the mines or haciendas."[11] If the English

[10] *Estado de México 1826*, pp. 45–46; *1827*, Table 11; *1829*, Table 7; Decree of 26 August 1831, *Colección de decretos de los Congresos Constitucionales del Estado libre y soberano de México*, II, 173.

[11] 1828 CG 12; 1836 CG 35; 1844 CG 47; 1847 CG 48. Not all of the mining companies in Mexico were as fortunate as the Real del Monte concern in evading the forced loan of July 1847. The United-Mexican Mining Association contributed $2,000 toward a $56,000 assessment made on the town of Guanajuato. With the governor's assurance that the loan would be repaid in a short

firm was not able to avoid entirely those special assessments, it certainly found means to make only token payments.

The tax that was probably most annoying to the firm was the *alcabala*. For a time it appeared as though the company would be spared this sales tax, for in August 1827 the legislature of the state of Mexico exempted many articles used in mining. Freedom from the *alcabala* proved, however, to be more apparent than real. In less than a year Commissioner Tindal was obliged to appeal to Governor Zavala of the state of Mexico against the Huasca tax collector's efforts to force the payment of the *alcabala* on goods sent to the Regla mill. Moreover, in 1832 the company offered the state $1,000 a year for the period between September 1827 and the end of 1830, during which time no duties had been paid on "goods introduced into these mines."

During the 1840's, the firm suffered the adverse effects of the Mexican government's levying an *alcabala* on all supplies used in mining and prohibiting the importation of practically all hardware, much of which could neither be purchased nor made at the mining camp. The company was especially hard pressed for such articles as wire rope (just being introduced at Real del Monte), anvils, shovels, and chisels.

The various methods employed to deal with the problem produced uneven results. First, exemptions from the laws imposing the new taxes and prohibitions were sought. When this effort failed, the company lodged a formal request with the government for relief from the tax and, at the same time, asked for a moratorium on the silver-production tax. Neither of the appeals had met with success by the time war broke out between Mexico and the United States, an event that caused the British firm's petitions to be dismissed.

---

time by credits against the taxes levied on silver, the Guanajuato "mining interests" alone advanced the entire sum of $56,000 demanded by the federal government ("Mining Correspondence, Foreign Mines: United-Mexican Mines," *MJ*, 17 [11 September 1847], 428). Nor was the Real del Monte Company the only property-holding establishment in the state of Mexico that was reluctant to contribute to the forced loan. The state was authorized to collect $200,000; by October 1847, when the drive was suspended, only $91,347 had been received or promised (*Hacienda del Estado de México 1850*, p. 7).

With considerable adroitness, the British evaded the payment of the *alcabala* and circumvented the prohibition of hardware imports whenever they could. In January 1844, for example, the chief commissioner notified London that by describing as "machinery" some much-needed wire rope the company's Veracruz agent had been able to pass a shipment through customs. Although a July 1843 law applied the tax even to timber, firewood, and charcoal taken from company land, the English withheld payment of any of that tax as long as possible. The final mention of the extended *alcabala* in the company papers, made at the end of March 1845, shows that local customs officials at Real del Monte and Huasca were awaiting a decision on a petition sent to the minister of finance in Mexico City and that no payments had yet been made.[12]

Minting and Export of Silver

However receptive the national and state governments were to Real del Monte's participation in the resurrection of the Mexican mining industry and however successful the English company was in evading ruinous taxation, the fact remains that the firm's representatives complained endlessly about their relations with public officials at all levels. Their lamentations were probably loudest when they sought and failed to get the kind of cooperation they thought they deserved in their struggle to find the most convenient and economically beneficial method of marketing silver. The company's marketing practices were complex, and the purpose of their treatment here is not to explain in great detail how a foreign mining company disposed of a rather special product but rather to show how its marketing practices led to strained relations between the company and government officials.

Three alternative methods of handling silver, each with its advantages and drawbacks, were tried. The British could introduce bullion into a mint and take payment for each deposit in Mexican coins, some of which would be exported to Great Britain and some

[12] Decree of 23 August 1827, *Colección de decretos de los Congresos Constitucionales del Estado libre y soberano de México*, II, 24; 1827, 1828 CG 12; 1832 CG 15; 1844, 1845 CG 36; 1843 CG 39; 1843, 1844 CG 48.

returned to the mining camp to meet the day-to-day expenses of operations there. In theory, converting silver into money for local use was beneficial to the firm. But the English had to deal almost exclusively with an ancient mint that was so woefully inefficient that long delays between depositing metal and receiving money were common. From the point of view of the concern in Mexico, moreover, the practice of coining silver destined for shipment to the home country was economically ridiculous. The second alternative was to export uncoined bullion directly to Great Britain. Economically speaking, that was the most favorable marketing practice under most circumstances, but it took the company into political struggles over the welfare of the Mexico City mint and over military escorts for *conductas* (mule trains carrying silver or money) to the Gulf coast. The third possibility was to sell bulk metal in Mexico City. This practice was looked upon for the most part as a last resort, turned to usually when minting was particularly slow or when short-term fluctuations in the rate of exchange between British pounds and Mexican pesos made drawing bills against the value of exported silver disadvantageous.

Minting and the export of uncoined bullion brought the company into contact, and sometimes conflict, with the national government of Mexico. The British mining company dealt directly with two mints, the national institution in Mexico City and the briefly operated provincial mint located in the capital of the state of Mexico, at the time in question Tlalpám. Company officials were not really satisfied with either. The two mints suffered from a chronic shortage of capital, necessary if they were to exchange cash for bulk silver on delivery. In addition, the Casa de Moneda in Mexico City was so antiquated that it could not make coins fast enough from the silver it received to return prompt payments to the mine owners or operators who did introduce the metal.

The Tlalpám mint was a product of a general movement that began with the outbreak of the wars of independence. After 1810 the disruption of communications and transport between the outlying districts and the colony's only mint, located in the capital, forced the viceregal government to open mints in some of the distant mining camps. Between 1810 and 1815 six such provincial establishments were opened, and four of them, at Durango, Guadalajara, Guanajuato, and Zacatecas, were operating when independence was won. Under the newly created Mexican nation, the proliferation of mints continued.[13]

Legislation authorizing the operation of a mint by the state of Mexico was decreed by the first constituent congress of that state on 1 July 1825. The original plan called for the mint to be built and run by a private individual or company, acting under a contract drawn up by the governor. Nearly two years passed, during which time only one candidate came forward. Although his proposal was acceptable to the state government, he was unable to carry through with his intention to construct the coining establishment. The governor therefore asked that the legislation be amended to allow the state itself to build a mint. Consequently, on 26 May 1827 the congress of the state of Mexico issued a new decree authorizing the construction and operation of a *casa de moneda* with state funds. Work was begun in July of that year to convert a ranch owned by Governor Lorenzo de Zavala into a minting plant. Before the end of the year, coins from the new money mill were being circulated in the state. The Tlalpám mint, officially opened in February 1828, remained in operation until July 1830, when it was closed upon the transfer of the state government to Toluca. During its short lifetime, it coined slightly less than $1 million in silver and approximately $200,000 in gold.

For a short time the Tlalpám mint seemed to hold out great promise to the English. At about the same time that the Real del Monte concern was sending its first shipment of silver to the national mint in the capital, in the fall of 1827, Commissioner Tindal informed London that he was seriously considering diverting the entire production to the plant being built by the state of Mexico. He noted that Tlalpám seemed to be supported by a larger capital than the older national Casa de Moneda, that the state of Mexico gave every indication that it would pay promptly for silver re-

---

[13] Santiago Ramírez, *Noticia histórica de la riqueza minera de México y de su actual estado de explotación*, pp. 47–52.

ceived, and that Governor Zavala looked upon their firm as so promising that he had already established at Pachuca a treasury to receive metal from the Real. But the Tlalpám institution failed to live up to Tindal's expectations, and the last shipment sent to the state mint was a few bars of silver recorded for March 1829.[14]

Most of the coinage of the firm's metal took place in the Mexico City mint, an institution, as previously noted, not particularly famous for efficiency or for promptness of payment. In 1823 a visitor observed that it was using wooden, mule-powered machinery to draw the metal into long, thin strips and hand-operated screw presses to cut it into round pieces. Writing twenty years later, a French metallurgist closely connected with Mexican mining said that the national mint, "reduced to a tenth of the importance it had at the beginning of the century, owing to the dispersal of coinage," retained the same number of employees, the same equipment, and the same weights and measures it had under the Spanish government. The Mexican mining engineer Santiago Ramírez claimed that even though the government twice appropriated funds for the purpose, the obsolete equipment was not replaced until 1850, after the mint had been leased to private individuals.[15]

Apparently with some reluctance, the company entered into negotiations with the Casa de Moneda during Charles Tindal's administration. Tindal's reluctance was caused initially by a four-week delay in the receipt of payment for pure silver. If the bars contained gold, there was a six-week delay. During its early years in Mexico, the British company had strained relations on the payment issue with officials of the mint itself and with those in the national government who supported the coining establishment.

---

[14] Decreto de 1° de julio de 1825, *Decretos del Congreso Constituyente del Estado de México*, I, 78–79; *Estado de México 1828*, pp. 52–53; Decree 45, 26 May 1827, *Colección de decretos del Congreso Constituyente del Estado libre y soberano de México*, I, 19; Ramírez, *Riqueza minera*, p. 52; 1827 CG 12; 1829 CG 15.

[15] W. Bullock, *Six Months' Residence and Travels in Mexico*, I, 195; St. Clair Duport, *De la production des métaux précieux au Mexique, considérée dans ses rapports avec la géologie, la métallurgie, et l'économie politique*, p. 175; Ramírez, *Riqueza minera*, pp. 44–45.

Leaders at the Real complained of their troubles while notifying London that the pressing need for cash at the mining camp forced them to sell silver at a discount rather than await payment from the Casa de Moneda. The national mint's tardiness in exchanging cash for bulk silver becomes understandable if a study is made of the institution's own accounts of the late 1820's and early 1830's. The mint showed a loss of $22,336 for the fiscal year 16 October 1831–15 October 1832.[16]

The mint's payment record had improved so much in the late 1830's that Commissioner John Rule told London he favored presenting ingots to the mint rather than dispose of the company's silver in another manner. Despite Rule's favorable report, friction between the company and the Casa de Moneda continued. Another issue arose during the thirties, the much more difficult question of shipping uncoined bullion out of Mexico. Rule expressed the problem well in 1837, when he argued that the minting of some of the bullion from the Real "would be satisfactory to influential parties in the country who view with alarm the export of so much silver."[17]

The company preferred to ship its product, uncoined, direct to Great Britain. The unfettered export of bullion, however, ran counter to Mexican tradition and was often prohibited by the laws of the nation. In the colonial era, nearly all of the precious metals intended for export had, by legal requirement, been coined. Immediately after the end of Spanish rule, the provisional governing body of Mexico issued a decree allowing the export of precious metals but imposing a tax of 5 per cent on silver bullion. That freedom was short-lived, lasting from December 1821 to January 1822.

The Mexican government thereupon established a policy of restriction on, or outright prohibition of, bullion export, which was to continue until the late 1870's. During the same period, the ex-

---

[16] 1827 CG 13; 1830 CG 23; 1834 CG 33; *Memoria del secretario del despacho de hacienda, leída en las cámaras del Congreso general el día 20 de mayo de 1833* (hereafter the annual reports of this ministry, which usually cover the year prior to the presentation date, will be cited as *Hacienda 1833*, etc.), p. 9.

[17] 1838, 1839 CG 39.

port of coins was allowed, even encouraged, except for about one month (between 16 February and 22 March 1822), when no money could leave Mexico without permission of the Regency and unless merchandise of the same value were brought into the country. This brief prohibition, which failed in its objective, was designed to prevent the sudden flight of capital in the hands of departing Spaniards.

A decree dated 19 July 1828, revoked the 1822 law barring the shipment of uncoined precious metals. Silver or gold bullion could be exported upon the payment of a 7–per-cent duty. The government retained the free-export policy for less than four years; in March 1832 it again disallowed bullion exports but stipulated that special permission to export uncoined gold and silver might be extended to individual parties or companies. Thereafter, the laws and practice with regard to the export of bullion underwent a number of variations, among them the revocation, and then the reinstatement, of the right of the executive branch of the government to issue export permits; the granting of licenses for the shipment of a certain number of bars of silver from the country, regardless of the port of exit; and free export from districts having no mint. A series of laws and decrees promulgated in the 1870's finally put an end to all restrictions on the export of precious metals in whatever form.[18]

When Real del Monte first availed itself of the privilege of exporting bullion under the July 1828 law, it began a long battle with various government officials, the national mint, and certain powerful private individuals. To the company the issue was usually purely economic. For the most part, the company realized more for its silver by exporting it uncoined than by minting it. In 1830, for example, the firm gained $7,560 on a shipment of fifty-four bars over the sum it would have received had the same amount of silver been coined in Mexico. On another occasion, in 1832, the benefit derived from exporting bullion that contained gold was clearly shown. John Rule estimated that the gold content of forty-

18 Joaquín Casasús, *La cuestión de la plata en México*, pp. 351, 352–355; Miguel Lerdo de Tejada, *Comercio esterior de México desde la conquista hasta hoy*, p. 39.

one bars recently shipped to the company would have earned $245 in Mexico, whereas in England that amount of gold had brought some $2,345, almost 5 per cent of the total value of the bullion. The high cost of chemical and other materials in Mexico; the amount of gold left in the silver ingots, depending on the ore-reduction process used; and advanced European parting techniques are given as reasons for such extreme differences in price.[19]

To the company's opponents there were several issues. The Casa de Moneda looked upon the question of bullion coinage or bullion export as a matter of survival. Support for that view is gained from the 1837 report of the minister of hacienda, who stated that the mint was sunk into decadence and had coined less than $1 million, because all the nearby mining camps except Real del Monte were not producing and because the government had been granting privileges for the export of bullion, which he termed the "final blow" to the Casa de Moneda.[20] Clearly, then, there was a connection between the British company and Mexico's oldest and proudest coinage establishment. But how close was that connection? In the middle of the 1830's, a time of strife between the company on the one hand and the Casa and its allies on the other, it was close indeed. The direct relationship between the means by which the English mining firm marketed its product and the health of the Mexico City mint may be seen in a comparison of the company's income, derived as it was almost entirely from its gold and silver output, and the quantities of those metals that were coined in the capital (see Table 7).[21]

Government officials tended to see the question in a political light. As John Rule put it, whenever the company shipped uncoined silver and gold out of the country it had to "proceed against a strong popular clamour," which insisted that bullion export was responsible for a shortage of silver coins and an abundance of debased copper money in Mexico.

[19] 1830 CG 13; 1829 CG 15; 1832 CG 15; Duport, *De la production des métaux*, pp. 169–174.
[20] *Hacienda 1838*, pp. 26–28.
[21] *Hacienda 1844*, pp. 103–105; Table 1 of this study.

TABLE 7

*Relationship between Real del Monte Income
and Casa de Moneda Coinage, 1834–1838*

Year	Coinage	Income
1834	$ 763,196	$377,116
1835	694,670	478,039
1836	653,090	530,237
1837	728,937	717,405
1838	1,068,815	838,033

SOURCE: *Hacienda 1844*, pp. 103–105. Compare with Table 1.

Some merchants who aligned themselves against the British mining company also viewed the matter in strictly economic terms. A prominent Mexico City commercial firm, Manning and Mackintosh (which was also a British firm), and a broker named Lasquitty both tried to prevent the mining concern from obtaining permission to export bullion—and both for the same reason. Each had, from time to time, export licenses and wanted Real del Monte to supply them the silver from which an export profit could be made.[22]

After scrambling for an occasional grant of a limited export license following the 1832 general prohibition on shipping uncoined silver out of the country, the company began a campaign to end an intolerable situation. It would obtain a long-term export privilege from the Mexican government; moreover, it would delve into politics to do so. Late in 1835, company officials drew up and formally presented a petition to the government, a document that described efforts to build a great and profitable mining establishment in general and the harm done the British firm by adverse marketing conditions in particular. John Rule and his aides then marshaled all the political support they could to argue the company's case before the Mexican government. The British minister, Holdsworth and Fletcher, the Count of Regla, and a friendly politician, Félix Lope y Vergara (described by Rule as "the leader of the independent party in Congress"), were all pressed into service.

[22] 1836 CG 39.

Before the onset of summer in 1836, the campaign was won. The minister of finance submitted to a joint session of the two houses a petition on behalf of the British firm, drafted by the Count of Regla, and a note from the British minister supporting the same cause. The bill was first read on 5 May, discussed four days later, and read for a second time and put to a vote on 22 May. It was carried (fifty-four to seventeen) in another joint session, but with the proviso that, while the executive department might grant Real del Monte permission to export bullion for a period of ten years, that concession was to end the moment a *fondo de rescate* was established in the treasury office at Pachuca.[23]

The British Real del Monte Company, then, succeeded in obtaining its special privilege from the Mexican government. According to the terms of the law dated 6 June 1836, the firm received a ten-year right to export all of its silver in the form of bullion. It would, however, have to pay in advance a sum equal to the duties it would be charged were it to ship metal out of the country in the form of coins.[24] After victory was seemingly assured, Commissioner John Rule thanked Lope y Vergara and the Count of Regla for their efforts. To the latter he expressed special gratitude, attributing to him and his friends the success of the appeal.

Obtaining a special privilege from the Mexican government and using it proved to be two quite different things. Real del Monte estimated a total duty of approximately 12 per cent of the value of its metal, 5 per cent paid in Pachuca and the remainder paid either in the capital or in some other location designated by the national administration. Having been assured by the minister of hacienda that the new fees would be no higher than the firm had anticipated, the English company made an advance payment of $8,000. When he came to interpreting that part of the 1836 law that defined duties,

[23] 1835, 1836 CG 35; 1836 CG 36, 39; Juan A. Mateos, ed., *Historia parlamentaria de los congresos mexicanos*, XI, 310, 340, 344, 381–382.

[24] Ley sobre exportación de platas pertenecientes á la Compañía del Mineral del Monte, junio 6 de 1836 in Basilio José Arrillaga, comp., *Recopilación de leyes, decretos, bandos, reglamentos, circulares y providencias de los supremos poderes y otros autoridades de la República Mexicana*, p. 444.

however, the minister set the fee at 12 per cent plus the amount of the Pachuca taxes, that is, a total of 17 per cent. John Rule thought he saw the hand of the Casa de Moneda and its friends in what seemed to him at best a mistake and at worst a plot to cheat Real del Monte out of its fairly gained advantages. He appealed to the British minister and informed London of the unfortunate turn of events.

The firm re-formed its lobby and fought vigorously, but vainly, for a reduction of the 17–per-cent fee. Handicapped by the death of Lope y Vergara, the English company and its allies simply could not overcome the forces combined against them—the Casa de Moneda, some government officials, and some private individuals in the capital. Before the end of 1836, company officials admitted defeat. In doing so, John Rule commented bitterly to the Count of Regla that, as merchants in Mexico City were obtaining export licenses with "a moderate payment of duties," the whole episode showed "the low esteem in which the Government holds mining."[25]

Mollified in their disappointment by the government's willingness to issue Real del Monte an export license for four hundred bars of silver at a fixed duty of 8 per cent over and above the Pachuca taxes, company officials began a new campaign. Efforts to win one such license after another carried the English firm into the murky waters of behind-the-scenes Mexican politics. In June 1842, for example, the minister of hacienda granted the British concern the right to ship five hundred bars from the port of Veracruz, on paying a 7.5–per-cent duty in advance. Both the foreign company and the administration of Antonio López de Santa Anna were promptly attacked by the prominent newspaper *El siglo XIX*. Not only did the government suffer a financial blow—the loss of between $15,000 and $100,000, depending on whether the bars were pure silver or had substantial gold content—the journal charged; but also withholding that amount of metal from the Casa de Moneda, which was virtually sustained by silver brought it from Pachuca, might force the institution to close down. Moreover, the export privilege would deprive the country of badly needed circu-

[25] 1836 CG 35, 36, 38, 39.

lating medium. The transaction was defended by the official gazette. The editors of *Diario del gobierno* contended that the government was near bankruptcy and that the advance payment received from the Real del Monte Company would prevent its having to force the veteran soldiers who were defending the northern border against an invasion from Texas, "that vanguard of the colossus threatening the national independence," to live as vandals off the frontier towns.[26] Despite that dramatic defense given its silver-export arrangement by the government newspaper, the English company found the pursuit of export licenses to be for a time more difficult.

During the following year (1843) the company sought unsuccessfully to bypass ministerial-level government officials' resistance to the company's request for a new export permit by approaching the president of the Republic. In doing so, Real del Monte became involved in a distasteful, not to say sordid, pursuit of favors from the wily Santa Anna. The mining concern wanted an export permit without advance payment for it; the general-president wanted money now. Trouble developed from political opposition to any bullion export and from tension between the Mexican government and British diplomatic representatives over an alleged insult delivered the latter at a social event. Undaunted by rebuffs in Mexico City and by the fact that Santa Anna made one of his many retreats from the center of the political scene, company officials sought the aid of Rodolfo Muñoz, the head of the firm serving as their agent in Veracruz and a man known to be welcome at Santa Anna's nearby Manga de Clavo hacienda, to which the general frequently retired. When Muñoz failed to persuade his high political friend to grant the British company favorable export terms and drop his demand for an advance payment, Commissioner William Rule appealed to a member of the Murphy family, which, it will be

[26] 1836, 1842 CG 36; 1836 CG 39; "Editorial," *El siglo XIX*, 23 June 1842, p. 4; *Diario del gobierno de la República Mexicana*, 25 June 1842, pp. 223–224. While the prosperity of the Mexico City mint was closely linked to the silver production of the British Real del Monte Company, by 1842 that relationship had become less direct. In that year, the mint coined just over $2 million in gold and silver; production at the Real was a little less than $860,000 (*Hacienda 1844*, p. 105; Table 1 of this study).

recalled, had leased the Morán mine to the British firm. Murphy, reputed to be another confidant of Santa Anna, did no better than Muñoz.[27] Only then did Real del Monte drop the sticky matter and wait for a more favorable moment.

In fact, that moment never came. Although the mining concern and its agents made several more attempts to gain shipping permits on favorable terms, through March 1846, they were consistently unsuccessful. During the final few years of its existence in Mexico, the British company turned back to the two other alternate methods of marketing its silver: selling it to those parties in the capital who were able to obtain export licenses and introducing it into the Mexico City mint.[28]

A final example of the tension resulting from the company's preference for exporting uncoined bullion on its own account lies in the manner in which the company dealt with the double problem of transporting silver from the mining camp to Veracruz and of providing armed guards for that purpose. Generally, Real del Monte preferred to send its product direct to the coast in its own private *conducta*, the Mexican government providing troops for an escort. The national administration, on the other hand, preferred that the mining concern deliver all its silver to the capital, providing its own transport and armed guards; bullion destined for export would then be sent by public *conducta* to Veracruz. Arguing that the government-favored Real del Monte–Mexico City–Veracruz route was too expensive, too time consuming, and too insecure, Real del Monte first tried to establish its own regular silver transport system between the mining camp and the coast. When this proved to be impracticable, in no small measure because of the difficulty of maintaining discipline among the Mexican and English employees serving as armed guards, the firm sought a compromise with the government. It would transport silver (under the government's or its own protection) from the Real to a convenient point along the regular *conducta* route between Mexico City and Veracruz, where

27 1843 CG 48.
28 1844, 1845 CG 36; 1844–1846 CG 48.

company mules or wagons would join one of the public bullion trains traveling from the capital toward the coast.

Between about 1837 and 1844, Real del Monte and the government seem to have developed and carried out the compromise *conducta* system proposed by the British—but not without conflict. Whenever it could persuade the administration in Mexico City to order escort troops to Real del Monte or to Apám (never an easy task), the company hauled its silver over the carriage road it regularly used for transporting supplies between the mining camp and Veracruz, joining the public bullion train at Perote. Whenever the company could not obtain government troops at or near the Real, it carried and guarded its silver through Apám to San Martín Texmelucan, there to meet the Mexico City–Veracruz *conducta*. In either case, although the Mexican government furnished most of the armed guards, the company paid for all or part of that service. A fifty-five–bar shipment made in December 1836 by the Perote route, for example, cost the concern .12 per cent of the estimated value of the silver, or $85.[29]

The disputes over routes and armed guards which, from the mid-1830's to the mid-1840's, took place between the British mining firm and the national administration in Mexico City seem to have been more annoying than damaging to both parties. Nonetheless, they did add something to the over-all company-government friction and did influence the whole system of convoying precious metals from the capital to the Gulf coast for export.

[29] 1837–1844 CG 35–39. For the various routes over which Real del Monte silver traveled from the mining camp to Veracruz, see Map 5.

10. Dissolution

THE ENDING BEGAN WITH A DISPUTE BETWEEN THE HEAD OF THE
Mexican establishment and the London office. The mining company's fourth chief commissioner left the Real del Monte Company
when it was severely weakened by more than twenty years of generally profitless operations and confronted by an immediate financial crisis. The firm showed some earnings in 1846, but in 1847 suffered the heaviest loss in nearly a decade. As the situation failed to
improve during the year, but instead grew worse month by month,
the Court of Directors apparently lost confidence in Rule's management of affairs in Mexico. The immediate issue between London
and Real del Monte was minor; the court disapproved of Rule's
having given a bonus to underground mine captains at a time of
such immediate shortage of disposable funds. But much more
weighty matters were pressing in upon the chief commissioner and
upon the company in general. Real del Monte was unable to carry
into effect the two measures that Rule and his superiors in London

considered necessary if the concern were to be placed on a sound financial footing and thus saved: the installation of an eighty-five-inch steam engine at the Acosta mine shaft and the completion of a large barrel amalgamation plant at the Sánchez and San Antonio haciendas, to allow the profitable reduction of the low-grade ore available in large quantities.[1]

Because of the disaffection in the London office with William Rule, it was not he but John Buchan who, after a brief interim administration, headed the overseas operations during the final days. Rule submitted his resignation sometime in the fall of 1847, under what were probably not the most amicable of terms. Even before receiving word that his resignation had been accepted, Rule left the Real in January 1848, saying that he was anxious and ill. As though symbolic of his company's fate, within a year Rule died in Pachuca.[2] John Buchan, who had been associated with the company as early as the celebrated first transport party of 1825, arrived at the mining camp in May 1848 to take over the foundering concern. His first dispatch, dated 11 May, was discouraging. The new commissioner acknowledged the absolute necessity of cutting expenses but found that all mining and milling activities were so interrelated and all so closely linked with the general, and costly, drainage problem that he found expenditure reduction "a most difficult point to decide or meddle with."[3]

Final Efforts to Save the Company

Against this background of a fatally ill chief commissioner and an apparently dying mining establishment, stockholders and creditors in England struggled with the question of whether to let the company slip away or try to revive it. It is not difficult to imagine

[1] 1847 CG 48.

[2] 1847, 1848 CG 48; *El siglo XIX*, 4 August 1849, [p. 4].

[3] "Mining Correspondence, Foreign Mines: Real del Monte Mines," *MJ*, 18 (24 June 1848), 301. The *Mining Journal* does not state that the correspondence from the company's commissioner in Mexico was specifically from Buchan, but its contents and a letter written the following day by the interim administrators, Russell Brenchley and William Woodfield, leave little doubt as to its author (1848 CG 48).

the state of anxiety in which the Annual General Court of Proprietors assembled on 24 June 1848. At the outset, Chairman Robert Price announced that John Taylor, who had resigned as manager, wished to be considered a candidate for one of the three posts on the Court of Directors that had fallen vacant. Though he had little hope for the firm, crippled as it was by adverse conditions and with no prospects of raising more capital, Price said that under those "cheerless circumstances" he was happy to recommend Taylor, "who was willing to struggle to the last."

Following the election of Taylor and two other members of the court, Secretary Phillips read the report of the directors, which laid before the proprietors a generally pessimistic view of the company's future. A combination of conditions had so affected the financial status of the concern as to "render necessary prompt measures of retrenchment, probably involving the suspension of all works that are unproductive of profits." In the reduction of abundant but low-grade ore "great reliance" had been placed on the barrel amalgamation and other processes, special machinery having been provided and the haciendas fitted out. The war between Mexico and the United States, however, had prevented unloading at Veracruz, and the machinery was thus detained in Havana and in England for many months. Other effects of the war mentioned in the report included a rise in prices, difficulty in obtaining quicksilver, and "great insecurity of property—all tending to make an increase of expenditures unavoidable, and to lessen the returns of silver, for want of materials essential in the reduction of ores."

Yet by far the "greatest detriment" stemmed from the extraordinary volume of underground water. In May 1846 when it was thought that the engines were already overworked, 2,643 gallons of water were being raised per minute; by December 1847, the rate had increased to 3,149. The company had therefore ordered the eighty-five–inch engine, which would have been dispatched to Mexico had it not been for the "disturbed state of that country" and for the deteriorated financial situation of the company.

Pointing out with regret a $38,763 loss for the first quarter of 1848, the directors saw little prospect of immediate improvement.

Not only were the funds then available insufficient to correct the situation, but it was doubtful that an attempt to raise new capital would meet with success. The court had therefore issued "positive instructions" to suspend the deep drainage and to cut back operations, unless the mines themselves could defray the cost of their continued working. If ore were extracted from accessible points and expenditures rigidly controlled, it might still be possible to realize profits. Otherwise, it would be best to dispose of the concern.

The directors were unwilling to give up. They ended their report with a strong statement of "conviction, that, notwithstanding the unsuccessful results of all their efforts to place this company's affairs on a sound and satisfactory footing, there still remain the elements of a great and profitable concern." This optimism was not communicated to the stockholders, who empowered the Court of Directors "to sell all, or any part of the property, or to take any other steps which, in their judgment, may appear to be for the interest of the company."[4]

Throughout the month in which this meeting was taking place in London Buchan was trying to cut costs at Real del Monte in a desperate attempt to keep the concern going. It was not an easy task. The expenses of drainage, *alimentos*, and general operations, which amounted to $3,631 a week, could not be further reduced so long as the deep drainage (at a cost of $2,431 itself) was continued. These constant expenditures would have to be matched against the profit from the mines. In seeking a way to make the mines produce enough to meet the fixed outlay, the commissioner decided that the northern tier of the Regla mines, including all of the shafts from Acosta to Sacramento, was the best property held under lease. Besides Morán, those mines were the only ones likely to help the company in the present emergency. In them the first officer suspended all tutwork explorations and reduced the area of ore extraction to the most promising points on the Santa Brígida and Acosta veins. Despite a small amount of good ore, the Vizcaína was still much fractured and generally poor. The loss suffered by the concern for

4 "Real del Monte Mining Company," *MJ*, 18 (1 July 1848), 313.

May was $17,489, and although that for June ($4,491) was considerably smaller, it was nonetheless a deficit.[5]

On 19 August, after receiving Buchan's first two monthly reports from Mexico, the directors convened a special meeting. Once assembled on 28 August the stockholders heard another distressing report from the court. Since the June meeting, the statement began, Buchan had informed the London management of "the steps he had taken for the preservation of the concern, but . . . all his exertions had been ineffectual to bring the expenditures within the returns." The chief commissioner believed, however, that new capital applied to the opening of the mines, the extraction of a larger quantity of ore, and the extension of hacienda power could make the concern profitable; with the resources available in Mexico alone, such improvements were impossible. After summarizing more of the information furnished by Buchan, the directors noted that the debt overseas amounted to upwards of $80,000 and that a large sum was owed the loan note and debenture holders. They therefore believed that the "most prudent course" was to sell the concern to parties either in Mexico or in England. At the same time, they asked whether any parties were "disposed to offer arrangements" for carrying on the present concern before a decisive vote was put before the stockholders for its dissolution.

The remainder of the August stockholders' meeting resolved itself into an argument between certain proprietors, who wished to make an attempt to raise more capital and carry on, and some of the loan note holders, who urged an immediate sale of the company's assets and the settlement of all legal claims against the company, including of course their own notes. Interestingly, the company officers seem to have favored the position of the loan note holders. The discussion began when Chairman Price observed that the concern was in a calamitous situation: the mines in Mexico held out a promise of success, but there appeared to be no way of

[5] "Mining Correspondence, Foreign Mines: Real del Monte Mines," *MJ*, 18 (29 July, 26 August 1848), 356, 399–400.

realizing it under the present ownership. He went on to say that money had been so frequently raised and so much privileged capital was outstanding that the directors were reluctant to propose new calls for funds. In view of these circumstances, the court thought it prudent to dispose of the concern, if possible, and to liquidate the claims with the loan note holders.[6]

Hardly had the September 25 meeting of stockholders been called to order when Chairman Price reiterated the directors' opinion that it was absolutely necessary to terminate the company's affairs. He therefore resolved "that this company, under the title of the Real del Monte Mining Company, be dissolved." In an attempt to delay a vote on the motion the latest letter from John Buchan was read. Dated 11 August 1848, that dispatch was no more encouraging than his earlier ones had been. No improvement had taken place during the preceding month in any of the mines. The weekly loss remained at $1,740, a sum that could not be reduced so long as the deep drainage was necessary to continue explorations for new ore ground. How long he ought to carry on this discovery work was, the commissioner assured the London management, "a most anxious question; as the last hope of the company, I am, indeed loath to give it up, and yet the continued delay in obtaining a result is very embarrassing."[7]

Buchan's disheartening letter crushed the opposition to the chairman's resolution, which was carried unanimously. Before the meeting was adjourned, to reconvene on 23 October for the purpose of voting in favor or against confirmation, the chairman offered advice to those who might be inclined to form a new company for the working of the Real del Monte mines. He suggested they complete the Aviadero adit, which would eventually drain all of the works in the district. It would take approximately three and one-half years and $300,000 to complete the task, but once it was accomplished,

6 Notice, "Real del Monte Mining Company," *MJ*, 18 (19 August, 2 September 1848), 385, 413.

7 "Mining Correspondence, Foreign Mines: Real del Monte Mines," *MJ*, 18 (30 September 1848), 457.

Price said, the new owners would have a most profitable concern—
and also the benefit of the "present company's large outlay, and all
their woeful experience, which would teach them what to avoid, as
well as how to proceed."[8]

The stockholder's meeting of 23 October took no action other
than to adjourn for a week, in order to await the latest word from
Mexico before taking the definitive step of disbanding. Buchan's
dispatch of 9 September held out no more hope than had his earlier
letters. With Buchan's discouraging report before them, two meetings were held on 30 October. At the first, attended by the holders
of company loan notes and debentures, Price explained the position
of the company with regard to its property. Any surplus that might
arise from the liquidation would go to the firm's creditors, the pos-
sessors of red debentures receiving first preference and the holders
of black debentures second. A letter published in the most recent
issue of the *Mining Journal* was then read. In it a John H. Fagan
said that, if the company were dissolved, he and some of the large
shareholders were prepared to make an effort to carry on the concern by means of a new company. It was considered advisable to
await Fagan's plan. The creditors' meeting ended with no vote except one of thanks to the chairman. Immediately thereafter a meeting of the original proprietors was held. Its business was simple
and quickly accomplished: the resolution calling for the dissolution
of the company was unanimously confirmed.[9]

Attempts in England to Form a New Company

A display of interest in resuscitating the British Real del Monte
came close behind the proprietors' irrevocable decision to disband.
On the day after the final stockholders' meeting, Fagan published a
prospectus for the formation of a new company, with a capital of

[8] "Real del Monte Mining Company," *MJ*, 18 (30 September 1848), 457.
[9] "Real del Monte Mining Association," *MJ*, 18 (28 October 1848), 504;
"Mining Correspondence, Foreign Mines: Real del Monte Mines," *MJ*, 18 (28
October 1848), 505; "Proceedings of Public Company," *MJ*, 18 (4 November
1848), 517; "Letter to the Editor: Real del Monte Mining Company," *MJ*, 18
(4 November 1848), 520.

£100,000 ($500,000), divided into nonassessable shares worth £1 apiece. Among the attractions that the document held out to investors was the intelligence that the new firm would be "relieved from the incubus of a debt of £450,000 [$2,250,000], with an accumulating interest at 4 per cent"; that the "inefficiency of the drainage power," which had been the "principal cause of the failure" of the old concern, would be remedied by the completion of the Aviadero adit, rather than by the dispatch of the new steam engine from England; that the driving of the great adit to the Vizcaína vein would permit the exploration of secondary veins as well as the prompt drainage of the major veins of the northern part of the district, thus producing enough ore to cover the costs of the entire undertaking; that a review of company expenditures and income between 1841 and 1847 showed that "very little would have turned the scale in favour of the Company"; and that the fall in the price of quicksilver would be of immeasurable aid, probably reducing the cost of ore treatment sufficiently to allow the new concern to meet its obligations or make a small profit even before the Aviadero was completed. Fagan proposed purchasing the plant in Mexico and the interests of the old shareholders, reorganizing the management at Real del Monte, and hiring John Phillips, whose knowledge of the establishment would "enable the New Company to act with vigor, certainty, and economy."[10]

Fagan's plan for a new, debt-free Real del Monte Company seems to have gotten a mixed reception. The 4 November issue of the *Mining Journal* carried his proposal and that of 11 November an announcement that the holders of shares, debentures, or both in the old concern had only until 18 November to claim preference in the purchase of shares in the new undertaking.[11] Yet, in early December the *Journal* published an unsigned letter that may have reflected the view of a number of potential investors and explained their hesitation to take up shares in a revamped company:

[10] *Real del Monte Company (Ex.-Debt.)*, pp. 1–3.
[11] Two advertisements re "Real del Monte Mining Company—(Ex.-Debt.)," *MJ*, 18 (4 November 1848), 524–525.

Should a new company be formed out of the wreck of the old, it is to
be hoped that men who thoroughly understand their business will
have the management of the affairs in Mexico, and not a chairman in
London, who never saw a mine [Fagan]; or a secretary who has only
studied, but not applied, chemistry [Phillips].[12]

A week later the trustees (former directors) of the old company
announced their willingness to receive proposals "for the purchase
of the whole of the company's rights, interests, property, and effects
in Mexico."[13] The publication of that notice suggests that the attempt by Fagan and his associates to revive the British firm had
come to an end.

Early in 1849 a second effort was made to form a new company,
this one led by John Phillips. The October and November 1848 dispatches from Real del Monte had held out the hope that the concern
might not only be steadied but even made profitable. The two most
important pieces of information that Buchan had furnished the
mining circles in London were that, by suspending the deep drainage, he had been able to balance expenditures and income, and that
an important ore discovery had been made above the water level in
the Santa Inéz mine. The commissioner had stated emphatically
that, were he to receive financial assistance from England with
which to pay off the concern's liabilities in Mexico and to increase
the barrel amalgamation establishment in the company's mills, he
would soon make a profit.[14]

It was after the publication of the two reports from Mexico that a
meeting of "persons interested in purchasing and carrying on the
mining works at Real del Monte" was convened for 27 February
at the George and Vulture Tavern, Lombard Street, London. The
thirty persons in attendance had in mind taking the first steps toward forming a new company. They accomplished next to nothing.

[12] Letter to Editor re Real del Monte Mining Company, *MJ*, 18 (2 December
1848), 566.
[13] Advertisement, *MJ*, 18 (9 December 1848), 573.
[14] "Mining Correspondence, Foreign Mines: Real del Monte Mines," *MJ*, 18
(25 November, 30 December 1848), 553 and 613.

The meeting began with a dispute over who might serve as chairman, there being objections to any former director of the old company and to Phillips on the grounds that they were too closely associated with the firm from which a new company would purchase property and interests. When no agreement was reached, "the proceedings resolved themselves merely into a lengthened and somewhat desultory conversation, as nothing official could be done." In the end, several of the participants (including James Colquhoun) were appointed to an unofficial committee to prepare the ground for a second session, at which something tangible might be done.

Despite the editorial support of the *Mining Journal* and an even more encouraging report from Buchan, the second meeting was never called. The last word on the subject was a letter in the *Mining Journal* from "An Old Stockholder," urging investors to come forward with sufficient pledges to allow Phillips to convene another, and, it was hoped, more fruitful, meeting.[15] No such gathering took place, and the last opportunity to resuscitate the company from London slipped away.

Transfer of Property

While the final attempt to revive the British concern was being carried to its unsuccessful conclusion in London, John Buchan was seeking to dispose of the company's property in Mexico. Sometime in early 1849 (probably with his 12 January dispatch), he forwarded an offer of purchase made by Alejandro Bellangé. At the end of March, the directors instructed Buchan to accept it and promised to send him at the earliest opportunity power of attorney for the transaction. In early May, the chief commissioner acknowledged the receipt of the document, adding:

I have only to express my deep regret that the old company is reduced

---

[15] Two advertisements, "New Real del Monte Mining Company," *MJ*, 19 (17 February, 3 March 1849), 73, 101; Editorial, *MJ*, 19 (3 March 1849), 104; "Mining Correspondence, Foreign Mines: Real del Monte Mines," *MJ*, 19 (10 March 1849), 115; Letter to the Editor re "New Real del Monte Mining Company," *MJ*, 19 (17 March 1849), 129.

to the necessity of making so great a sacrifice in the disposal of their property; the more so, as I feel fully persuaded that their long and exemplary perseverance would have reaped its due reward, with one more effort. The die is, however, now cast, and it only remains for me to pass over the concern to the new parties, which I shall do as soon as possible, and hope to encounter no difficulty in carrying out all the arrangements.[16]

If Commissioner John Buchan was making his last, desperate attempt to save the Real del Monte concern for its original owners, he was also preparing to participate in the new company that would take it over. In Mexico City on 1 June 1849, he joined with a group of Mexican businessmen—Nicanor Béistequi, Manual Escandón, P. de la Roche, and Alejandro Bellangé—and with a British subject, Edwin C. Mackintosh, to found a "Comp. de Minas de Real del Monte." Those men represented the companies that handled the Mexican government's tobacco monopoly and operated the national mint and parting establishment. The new company, it was agreed, would have an original capital of $700,000, made up of 350 shares worth $2,000 each. Half of the total capital, or $350,000, was to be set aside to purchase the supplies, machines, haciendas, and equipment of the old company and also to cover its outstanding debts, in accordance with an inventory and statements submitted by officers of the British concern. The other $350,000 would be applied to the working of the mines. All of the shares were assessable, should more capital be needed, but a limit of $2,000 per share was fixed on such assessments.

At the organizing session the founders of the Mexican Real del Monte Company distributed among themselves 200 of the original 350 shares, declaring them nontransferable. The remaining 150 were set aside, to be taken up by persons wishing to join the company at a later date, with the proviso that, should these shares not be sold within a reasonable period of time, they would go to those in possession of the other 200, in the same proportion as their original holdings. That preliminary division was as follows:

[16] "Mining Correspondence, Foreign Mines: Real del Monte Mines," *MJ*, 19 (23 June 1849), 296–297.

To Manuel Escandón, for the Tobacco Company   100 shares
To Alejandro Bellangé, for the Minting and
    Parting Company   95 shares
To John Buchan, for himself   5 shares
                                                                  ————————
                                                                  200 shares

Having settled all other matters of business, the original proprietors of the Mexican Real del Monte Company elected Béistegui, Escandón, and Bellangé to the first Board of Directors.[17]

In possession of a power of attorney dated 28 April 1849, Buchan, on 4 July, met with Bellangé and Miguel Bringas, acting on behalf of the Minting and Parting Company and the Tobacco Company, respectively, and agreed to terms for the transfer of property, rights, and obligations from the defunct British Real del Monte to the newly formed Mexican concern. All the shares and rights of the former firm, acquired through various contracts concluded with the Count of Regla and other parties, as well as all property owned by the company in Mexico, would be turned over. Bringas and Bellangé accepted the obligation to fulfill all of the contracts entered into by the British company and to assume all debts and responsibilities outstanding on that date. The new ownership thus bound itself to cover the old firm's debts, which were estimated at $100,000, and also to pay the sum of $30,000 to the former directors of the British firm on 8 November.[18] By those actions Buchan terminated the operations of the British company in Mexico.

The British Real del Monte, in ceding its overseas holdings, sacrificed valuable property for a pittance. It had evaluated that property as follows:

Permanently installed machinery and equipment
    at various mines and mills $309,560
Stores at warehouses, mines, and mills   148,137
Nonmining real estate   22,800
                                                            ——————————
                                                            $480,497

[17] Acta de los socios del Real del Monte, 1° de junio de 1849, RdM, Accounting Dept. File IV-C-1, pp. 1–4.

[18] Acta cesión de traspaso de derechos, 4 de julio de 1849, RdM, Accounting Dept. unnumbered file, fols. 1-3v, 8v.

A neutral appraiser, considering the company's evaluation of its stores too high, reduced the figure by 10 per cent, to $133,324. Although he did not believe the value placed on the permanent machinery and equipment to have been exaggerated, he thought that it could not be realized immediately because of the suspension of drainage in the deep levels of the mines, and he therefore decreased the amount to $216,676. Thus he arrived at the sum of $350,000 as the true and real value of the English concern's property.

At the time of its sale, the company had known liabilities of $102,359. But it was owed an enormous sum by various mine owners, who had granted the concern the right to be reimbursed for part of its initial investment and for certain other expenses before profits were divided. The largest single "debt" was $3,747,285, owed by the Regla family; the Murphy family, to whom the Morán mine belonged, owed $670,000. The total credit with the mine owners, which, of course, could not be collected unless the concern were to become profitable, was $4,640,285. In addition, the House of Regla owed the British concern $30,000, a private debt contracted by the late third count.[19] When the British firm turned over its holdings, these, then, were its assets and semicredits in Mexico:

Neutral appraisal of property	$ 350,000
Owed by mine owners	4,640,285
Private debt of Regla family	30,000
	$5,020,285

Combining the firm's solid assets in Mexico with its semicredits and deducting its known liabilities, one concludes that the British company was worth $4,917,926 at the time it passed its property, rights, and obligations to the newly created Mexican firm. The final result of a quarter-century's operations by the Company of Adventurers in the Mines of Real del Monte was the receipt of $30,000 for a concern in Mexico whose assets and semicredits totaled nearly $5 million.

[19] Acta de socios, 1849, RdM, Accounting Debt. File IV-C-1, pp. 5–15, 19–32; Acta cesión, 1849, RdM, Accounting Dept. unnumbered file, fol. 9.

The Ironic Failure

In evaluating the final results of the British Real del Monte Company's existence in Mexico, two subjects must be given direct attention. The first is a summation of the tangible and intangible elements that explain why the concern was unable to conduct a profitable operation. The second is a consideration of whether, even on economic grounds, the English firm must be described as a total failure.

Why, with ample initial capital, with a body of stockholders willing to submit to additional calls for funds, and with the important technological advantage of the steam engine, did the Company of Adventurers in the Mines of Real del Monte not succeed? The anatomy of the failure comprises several parts. Taken together, weaknesses in the managerial structure of Real del Monte must be marked down as contributing to its eventual collapse. Those weaknesses were in part due to something unavoidable—the sheer distance between the home office and the site of actual mining operations. There simply had to be irritating and sometimes harmful delays in communications, in dispatching essential equipment, and in making basic policy. Perhaps the most serious fault in the firm's management was the refusal on the part of the London administrators to grant much discretionary authority to the head of the establishment in Mexico. Although the man who held the post of manager in England had first-hand knowledge of mining matters in general, he had only second-hand knowledge of silver mining in Mexico. Yet John Taylor insisted on being consulted on large and small things that occurred at Real del Monte. Otherwise, the remainder of the London staff was business-minded and did not seem really to trust the professional miners, like John and William Rule, who came to lead the staff in Mexico.

The organization of its mining operations presents a definite and tangible element of the company's downfall. Briefly, the firm made a serious error when it set out in the beginning to reach the deep workings of the ancient Vizcaína vein. The exorbitant cost of that venture, together with the fact that the ore finally encountered was

less rich and extensive than the concern had been led by the Reglas
to believe, made it impossible to explore thoroughly virgin territory, like Rosario, Santa Inés, and San Ramón, or to construct the
large-scale barrel amalgamation plant for the reduction of the low-
grade ore that it did find—either course perhaps spelling the difference between success and failure. In the end, Real del Monte could
not even afford to maintain the steam-drainage system that its type
of mining demanded. All the same, the profits that the Mexican
company made from virtually the same properties worked by the
English before them suggest that the line between good and bad fortune in the Real del Monte–Pachuca district was thin indeed.

Except that it did not go far enough in its efforts to find a substitute for the traditional patio amalgamation process, the company
could not blame its failure on its milling operations. Perhaps the
correct phrase is "could not go far enough," for here too the English
were handicapped by the heavy initial outlay of funds. John Rule
saw clearly the necessity of basing the concern's solvency on a system of economically reducing the low-grade and sometimes "rebellious" ore available. His brother William started to build the barrel
amalgamation plant that would do just that. But there simply was
not available enough money by the late 1830's and eary 1840's to
complete the job. The British found that the barrels were an effective and profitable means of reducing ore disastrously uneconomi-
cal in the patio. Thus they were led to acquire and begin exploiting
the Rosario mine in Pachuca. But because they were unable to
build a really large barrel amalgamation establishment they were
compelled to curb ore extraction and explorations in their new
property. The British concern went out of business and left it to its
successor to discover, in Rosario, one of the greatest bonanzas in the
history of Mexican mining.

It is difficult to measure precisely the effect that labor relations
had on the English concern's decline and eventual downfall. Although officials at the mining camp, along with inspectors from the
outside, charged that wages paid to both Europeans and Mexicans
were too high, they also admitted that company workers received
no more than those in similar occupations in other parts of Mexico.

Disciplinary problems with Cornishmen and outright conflict with Mexican *barreteros* were irritating, time consuming, and somewhat damaging. But they hardly broke the company. Perhaps it must be concluded that labor problems contributed to the firm's failure in ways that are both tangible and intangible.

The effects of supply problems seem more directly measurable. There is, however, a difference between the way the Court of Directors and other officers in London explained those problems to the stockholders as the company was going out of business and the way that they appear from the vantage point of the present study. Two issues were singled out for special comment in 1848: the break in the overseas supply line caused by the war between Mexico and the United States, and the extremely high price of mercury due to the Rothschild monopoly. The first seems to be something of a red herring. London claimed that war-caused political turmoil in Mexico led to the decision in 1847 not to ship the much-discussed eighty-five–inch steam engine to Mexico. That argument appears now to have masked the real reason for retaining the machine in England—the lack of funds for carrying it from the Gulf coast to Real del Monte and for installing it at the mine site. The costliness of quicksilver cannot be denied. The company was definitely hurt by having to pay a monopoly price for that crucial product. All in all, it might well be said that supply problems helped to sink the English concern. But would they have had the same effect on a company that had not, before they became important, already overloaded itself with heavy expenditures in the first few years after its launching?

Complaints on the part of Real del Monte officers about poor or no cooperation from the Mexican government at various levels, about taxes imposed on the company's product and property, and about the difficulties faced in marketing silver were frequent and loud. Incidents of strife between company men and their neighbors at Real del Monte often occurred. But neither should be allowed to hide a very important point—that political turbulence was less a factor in the company's failure than one might expect. At no time did a pronunciamento or other political commotion force the concern to close down its operations. The chronic domestic instability of Mexico affected the foreign firm only in its collateral activities—altering, for example, the schedules for the shipment of freight, bullion, or cash; delaying the receipt of payments from the national mint; or causing petitions addressed to the government to be set aside.

To return to the question that began this discussion: why did the British Real del Monte Company fail? Three reasons can be put forward. The first is the most tangible: the concern spent all of its initial capital and much of that subsequently raised before it made any substantial income. Indeed, the loss of $4,316,109 by the end of 1832 was nearly 85 per cent of the total deficit of $5,079,283 suffered by Real del Monte in its operations in Mexico.[20] That quickly gained financial burden was like a counterweight acting against any measure that might subsequently be devised to cope with the real problems of mining and milling—for example, the expense and inefficiency of the patio amalgamation process—that faced the company in Mexico. The second reason is still tangible, but a little soft: the combination of the big and little problems in all phases of the concern's operations, none of which was in itself weighty enough to bring down the company. The third reason is impalpable: the first two reasons taken together would not have presented an insurmountable obstacle to success—if Real del Monte had been lucky in the lottery that mining is.

Judged by strict financial standards, the British company has to be considered a total failure. After all, it lost approximately $5 million in its twenty-five years of mining in Mexico, and it defaulted on most of a debt of some $2.2 million built up in England. The fact that the concern in Mexico was, in a certain sense, owed about $4.6 million by Mexican mine owners cannot be pressed too far. As noted above, that figure represents only a sum that Real del Monte might have kept to itself before dividing profits with those mine owners—had there been any profits. But is there not another way of looking at the British firm's performance in Mexico?

[20] See Table 1 of this study.

That a perspective other than the strictly financial one calls into question the characterization of "failure" is suggested by a remark made by the Bolaños Company executive who examined and reported on the company in 1839. Commenting on the rather numerous body of European artisans found in the mining camp, he said that such a large force was made necessary by the fact that "the Real del Monte mining concern is the most extensive perhaps in the whole Mexican Republic as regards the number of mines and engine power which is necessary for working them."[21] While it is beyond the scope of this study to test the accuracy of Schuchardt's estimate, it is possible to compare what the British found at Real del Monte in 1824 with what they left there in 1849.

The establishment acquired by the British at Real del Monte was described in 1824 with such terms as "ruin" and "abandonment." Neither word would be remotely appropriate to characterize the one turned over to the Mexican company a quarter of a century later. Two inventories are available which, while they have been prepared in different ways, allow a fair comparison between the operation taken over by the English in 1824 and that passed on to a new Mexican firm in 1849.

The two most important points at which to look for similarities and differences are also the most obvious—in the mines and mills. Below is the 1824 description of two properties worked extensively by both the Regla family and by the first foreign contractors:

Dolores Mine (Vizcaína vein): Shaft in use to depth of 147 yards its mouth entirely fitted up with masonry arches; walls, all that remains of the galleries, stables, and granaries, in ruin.

Acosta Mine (Acosta and Santa Brígida veins): Shaft filled with rubbish; nothing remaining but ruined walls of galleries and shops.[22]

---

[21] 1839 CG 39.

[22] Ynventario y entrega formal que hizo el Sr. Conde de Jala y de Regla, á Don Jaime Vetch como director principal de las minas y haciendas de beneficio de metales en los Reales del Monte y Zimapán . . . in Libro en que se hallan, el preliminar con que la Sociedad de Aventureros formada en Londres convino celebrar una compañía . . . con el S. D. Pedro Terreros Conde de Jala y de Regla . . . ; la escritura pública con que se afianzó el contrato, y los ynventarios judiciales (cited hereafter as Ynventario), RT, pp. 95–124.

The same two properties were pictured in the 1849 inventory as follows:

Dolores Mine: One seventy-five–inch-cylinder steam engine, engaged in general drainage; its three boilers; buildings for dwellings and to house machine, boilers, and furnace; three sets pumping apparatus.

Acosta Mine: One fifty-four–inch-cylinder steam engine; its three iron boilers; one thirty-inch-cylinder steam engine; its two boilers; two sets pumping apparatus.[23]

The 1824 descriptions of the Regla and Sánchez mills are immensely detailed, but they deal mainly with abandoned edifices, some falling into disrepair. Very striking is the relative lack of serviceable machinery. Here are a few passages from that long document:

Regla Hacienda: Patio for quicksilver reduction, with forty-five masonry arches to support roofs, now in ruin. Wooden floor partly serviceable, partly in ruin. Pillars supporting arches partially worn away at base, owing to salt. *Grinding establishment.*—One wheel in working order. Five stamp heads. Iron hoops. One steelyard. One crowbar. Six hand drills. Quoins. One chisel. One pickax. One tapper. One adz. Drags. Seventeen pivots for turning upright centerpieces of arrastres, Ten in use. One ore-chute and two sieves, with cloth, for pulverizing.

Sánchez Hacienda: Dwelling, with two habitable rooms. Storeroom, with bell retort for silver amalgam; reverberatory; heater; sieve with cloth, all serviceable. . . . One copper-pyrite oven, roof in good condition. Corral, with stable and roof in good condition. One serviceable room for storing salt. Six bearings for machine shaft, with six new sets of teeth.[24]

In the 1849 inventory, on the other hand, the theme is working machinery in operating plants:

[23] Nota de las contratas de minas, haciendas, etc., maquinaria y otros bienes pertenecientes á la Compañía Inglesa del Mineral del Monte, 7 de febrero de 1849; Inventario y avalúo de las existencias y bienes de la negociación del Real del Monte, mayo 26 de 1849 (cited hereafter as Nota y Inventario), in Acta de socios, 1849, RdM, Accounting File IV-C-1, pp. 5–15, 17–32.

[24] Ynventario, RT, pp. 95–124.

Regla Hacienda: In working order, with patio, washing area, mortars, and forty water-powered *arrastres* capable of reducing 120 tons per week. Foundry with ten furnaces, iron-cylinder blast powered by water; capable of smelting from 27 to 30 tons per week. Machinery to power sixteen barrels; four-cylinder engine to provide blast for furnaces; one thirty-inch-cylinder steam engine, not in use and somewhat out of repair; one rotary steam engine, not in use and somewhat out of repair; one boiler, not in use; spare parts for pumping apparatus, not in use.

Sánchez Hacienda: In working order, with twenty-four barrels and room for twelve more. Machinery powered by new steam engine, to supplement water wheel. Six reverberatory furnaces. Thirty-eight horse-driven *arrastres*. One twenty-two–inch-cylinder rotary steam engine, to power barrels; its two boilers; machinery to power twenty-four barrels.[25]

A more detailed comparison of the two inventories would further confirm the basic fact that the British company inherited the wreckage, or at best the residue, of a once-impressive operation and bequeathed a functioning establishment that was both larger and better equipped than its predecessor, especially in terms of power-driven machinery. Looked at in this light, must the British Real del Monte adventure be termed a "failure"? Notwithstanding a heavy financial loss suffered by the firm's stockholders, the English built the foundation of a great and profitable mining enterprise that is still in existence. The two documents quoted above show conclusively that almost all the foundation was laid between 1824 and 1849, not before the former year. Moreover, these bankrupt foreigners left behind them in Mexico two technological advances that were instrumental to the success of the Mexican concern that worked the Real del Monte mines for the remainder of the nineteenth century. The steam-engine drainage of the entire complex of mines at the Real and barrel amalgamation for treating low-grade, rebellious ore opened the way for profitable exploitation of old mines in Real del Monte and for new ones in neighboring Pachuca.

[25] Nota y Inventario, in Acta de socios, 1849, RdM, Accounting Dept. File IV-C-1, pp. 5–15, 17–32.

APPENDIX A

Contract between the Third Count of Regla and the British Real del Monte Company for the Working of the Regla Mines in Mexico, 1 July 1824[1]

A contract for a mining company having been entered into on 6 March 1824, in London, England, by Mr. Thomas Kinder, representing the Count of Jala and of Regla, and by Mr. John Taylor, representing the Society of Adventurers, which had been established in the British capital for the purpose of undertaking this type of activity in North America, several modifications were introduced, such changes, upon review by the count's staff in . . . [Mexico City], being ratified jointly by the count and the newly appointed trustees of the company, Messrs. James Vetch, John Rule, and Vicente Rivafinoli, in a deed executed before the notary public García Romero, on 1 July 1824, . . . pursuant to which the signatories bind themselves to the observance of the following articles:

1. The count shall turn over to the trustees of the company, in whose hands shall be placed the management and administration thereof, the mines of Guadalupe, Santa Teresa and annexes, Lomo de Toro and annexes, and such other mines as at present form a part of the count's enterprises at Real del Monte and Real de Zimapán, together with those that may, at a future date, be discovered through the operations and workings of the company, it being incumbent upon the count, on the advice of his agents, to claim the latter mines, and, should he be granted title thereto, to place them at the disposal of the company, so that all may be included within the terms of the twenty-

[1] Translation of El preliminar con que la Sociedad de Aventureros en Londres convino celebrar la compañía por 21 años, in Libro en que se hallan, el preliminar con que la Sociedad de Aventureros formada en Londres convino celebrar una compañía . . . con el S. D. Pedro Terreros Conde de Jala y de Regla . . . ; la escritura pública con que se afianzó el contrato, y los ynventarios judiciales . . . , RT, pp. 1–21.

one–year agreement, which is to enter into effect on this date and to expire on the same day in the same month of the year 1845, it being understood that the costs of such arrangements shall be defrayed by the company.

2. The administration and management of the aforesaid mines, and the exclusive privilege of working them, shall be transferred to the company and to such of its commissioners, superintendents, or agents as may be dispatched for that purpose.

3. The company shall immediately take possession of the mines, which shall thereupon be turned over to the commissioners or agents, who shall proceed to exploit them by means of steam engines or other apparatus capable of rehabilitating, draining, and placing them in working order, as is done in England, or in the manner best suited to local conditions.

4. The company shall be entitled to the unrestricted use of, and benefit from, the haciendas of Tepezala, Ixtula, and Rancho del Guajolote, belonging to the Count [of Regla], and that of San José, belonging to the Count of El Valle, by leasing the first three and subleasing the fourth, the total annual rent amounting to 1,000 pesos [dollars].

5. So that the company may enjoy the use of the above-mentioned hacienda of San José, which is not in the possession of the Count [of Regla], it shall be incumbent upon the latter to make every effort to ensure its owner's leasing it for nine-year periods, permissible under Mexican law; should the count fail in his attempt, whether because the owner be unwilling to make the hacienda available or for any other reason, the sum of 300 pesos shall be deducted from the aforesaid rental fee of 1,000 to be paid to the count.

6. The company shall be permitted to continue work on the Aviadero adit, should the commissioners or agents decide to do so, in which event it shall be the responsibility of the company to determine the measures, means, and time to be employed in that task.

7. The count shall, in accordance with the laws of Mexico, fully, effectively, and validly cede to the company, or whosoever takes the place thereof, all the mines and veins belonging to him at Real del Monte and Real de Zimapán and all the ore to be found in, or extracted from, those mines, during the twenty-one years beginning with the date of this contract, and all the haciendas and reduction plants in his possession, namely, Regla, San Antonio, San Miguel, Sánchez, San Juan, and San Francisco Javier, known also as La Nueva, and such similar establishments as he may own in the vicinity of the above-mentioned Reals. As for the main residence at the San Miguel hacienda and the pasture adjacent to the Ojo de Agua spring, it is agreed

that the count shall retain unrestricted access thereto, provided the company be permitted to draw upon the spring water; should the count, at a future date, wish to lease the residence and pasture, he shall allow the company to rent them for a moderate fee. Such expenses as the company may incur in repairing the reduction establishments at the aforesaid haciendas during the first year shall be charged against the initial capital invested in the enterprise, whereas those incurred in subsequent years shall be charged against the regular quarterly expenses.

8. The count shall, at the company's expense, draw up such reports and documents as may serve the above-stated ends and ensure the unhampered control of the mines by the company, and its commissioners or agents, during the period specified.

9. Should custom, the laws of the nation, or the Mining Code be considered as opposed to the establishment of the company herein provided for, the count shall immediately prevail upon the Mexican government to alter the situation, by means of special decrees, so as to ensure the company's full possession of those mines for twenty-one complete years; in the event that such actions delay the start of operations, the duration of the contract shall be lengthened for a period commensurate with the time lost.

10. Written accounts shall be duly kept of all work accomplished; of the quantity of ore produced and the method of its disposal; of the reduction operations carried out; of the costs incurred in the working of the mines; and of all other matters necessary to give a current and true picture of the state of the mines and of the profit resulting from the working thereof.

11. A general quarterly report shall be prepared, in writing, to show the expenses, income, and balance for the preceding three months, the count being furnished a copy of the said report signed by the chief commissioner or agent of the company; upon review and approval by the count or his agents, the company documents shall be considered definitive, no objections being entertained beyond one month from the date of their submission. Should a difference of opinion arise regarding the reports, it shall be settled in the manner prescribed below [Art. 20].

12. At such time as the enterprise yields a profit, one seventh thereof shall be credited to the company against the capital invested by it in the rehabilitation of the mines, and the remaining six sevenths shall be divided equally between the count and the company.

13. In the event that one seventh of the profits obtained during the third year be less than one sixteenth of the capital invested by the company, not only shall the said one-seventh part be deducted from

the profits, in order to repay the capital invested, but also the amount necessary to cover the said one-sixteenth part of that capital, provided such sum does not exceed one fourth of the profits; and the remaining, liquid portion, after the above-mentioned deduction has been made, shall be divided equally between the count and the company, in the manner prescribed.

14. So as to ensure exactness in the reporting of the capital invested by the company and in the payments or credits granted it, in accordance with the terms expressed above, the following shall be credited to the company and considered as an increase in its capital investment, such credit being made to its account in the manner prescribed herein: the cost of all steam and other engines shipped from England, the cost of transportation and insurance thereof, and all other costs connected with the placement of such engines at the mines and with the work performed in the establishments and installations, together with the costs of sending commissioners, agents, and artisans, and their salaries during the first year of their contract, and also the sum arising from excessive expenses incurred in the operations of the concern, as reported at the end of each quarter.

15. When the capital invested by the company shall have been repaid in full, the total profits shall be divided equally between the count and the company.

16. The count may, at his expense, appoint an inspector to survey the working of the mines and examine the company accounts; in performing that function, the inspector shall be free at all times to enter the mines and call for the account books, but he shall in no way intervene in the management or administration of the mines.

17. If, at the end of the twenty-one years, the capital invested by the company shall have been repaid in full, the mines, together with the steam engines and other apparatus installed and employed therein, shall be placed at the disposal of the count, for his use, benefit, and gain, the company retaining solely property and ownership rights to the movables found in the surface plants and smelting establishments, where they shall remain for such time as necessary to reduce the ore therein and to permit disposal of the other removables belonging thereto.

18. If, at the end of twenty-one years, the company shall have been unable to recover the entire capital invested in the mines, these shall revert to the count, as described in the preceding article; however, in such event, the company shall be free to remove and dispose of such machines, pumps, instruments, etc., as are sufficient in value to cover the deficit, with the exception of the instruments and other equipment at present being turned over to the commissioners by the count, it

being understood that all but those worn out through use shall be returned to him, pursuant to the initial inventory. Should the count wish to obtain at their fair price some or all of the above-mentioned machines and equipment, whose removal and disposal shall be within the rights of the company, he shall be entitled to do so, the company according him preference over any other prospective purchaser.

19. The count shall lend all possible assistance to the company, or its commissioners, superintendents, or agents, by helping it dispose of its produce under favorable terms and in other ways carry forward its development and by offering suggestions on the manner of working the mines and reducing the ore; he shall, moreover, bring to bear the full weight of his influence with the present, or subsequent, Mexican government, on behalf of the company, and seek the waiving of such articles of the Mining Ordinances as might be prejudicial to the company's interests or preclude the introduction of new, and profitable, methods of working the mines.

20. Should a difference of opinion arise between the count and the company, or its commissioners, superintendents, or agents, or any one of them, with regard to the mines, the following persons shall be named to arbitrate a settlement: the British envoy or, in his stead, the British consul or vice-consul or chargé d' affaires, and the director, or the highest-ranking officer, of the executive branch of the [Mexican] Mining Organization, in their capacity as public officials, with the right to name a third person by common assent; the decision of the arbiters shall be final and the parties shall be bound thereto, availing themselves of no recourse, either regular or extraordinary, as recognized by present or future laws and renouncing all such recourses as though they were enumerated separately herein.

21. The company shall pay the count 12,000 pesos each year, in quarterly installments, on condition that in a year, or years, in which there are liquid profits accruing to the count in excess of 3,000 pesos during each quarter, the excess shall be held back and charged against such installments as may have been paid in advance, until full repayment on those installments shall have been made.

22. Should the company make use of one or more of the haciendas belonging to the count for the purpose of reducing ore from mines other than those covered by this contract, it shall credit the resulting rent or fees to the joint profits in a manner amicably agreed upon by both parties.

With regard to the stipulation that the count remove any obstacle to the permanence of this contract, owing to a property entailment, family deed, or law of this country, the only one being the establishment of the Regla primogeniture over these mines, in order to satisfy the commissioners that the said entailment could in no way constitute a barrier to the present agreement, the count showed them the Royal Cedula of 18 May 1775, in which His Catholic Majesty granted the entailment license and which contains the following statement: "But with the express provision that [with] the establishment of primogeniture over the said silver mines of the Vizcaína vein and the lead mines of the Real de Zimapán, and such others as you may acquire, you shall impose upon your progeny and successors the ineluctable obligation of working such mines, in accordance with the mining laws and ordinances, it being understood that otherwise they shall at all times be subject to the reversion and denouncement provided for in the event of inoperation or abandonment." [The Royal Cedula of 22 December 1777, together with clarifying statements issued on 12 February 1779, are then cited in connection with the Regla family's obligation to maintain the mines in continuous operation or risk losing them.] The count thereupon produced the claim executed in July 1816 before the Deputation of Pachuca, together with the decree of adjudication handed down by that Mining Deputation on 9 December of that year, pursuant to which he was granted anew the said enterprises listed under the title of the San Pedro de Regla [Aviadero] adit, subject in all instances to the Mining Ordinances, Title XI, Article 11, of which contemplates imparting hereditarily a contract for a mining company and for the provision of financial assistance for the working of mines. Having seen those documents, the commissioners expressed their satisfaction at the validity and permanence of the contract, continuation of the primogeniture notwithstanding, and they therefore stated their belief that no difficulty remained for the count to overcome.

APPENDIX B

Regulations Drawn up by the British Real del Monte Company
for the Underground Working of Its Mines, with Respect
to the *Partido* and the Obligations of the Miners,
1 September 1827[1]

1. In each and all of the mines, the administrator and operators shall inspect such workings as may be found, the quantity and grade of the ore yielded, and the width of the ground containing such ore; each mine shall be assigned a name and a number and, without exception, recorded in tabular form in a ledger, a copy of this list being given to every timekeeper for purposes of information.

2. On Monday, or on the first day a work force enters a mine, the required number of *barreteros*, whose arrival shall have been duly recorded, shall be assigned by the captain to the respective workings, whether these be abundant or deficient in ore, rich, poor, or dead works.

3. A *barretero* assigned on the first day to rich ground designated by the number 1 shall, on the following day, be transferred to an area designated by the last number, leaving his place to a *barretero* initially assigned to the number 2 station; the rotation of operators shall thus follow numerical order, and none shall be given cause to complain of not being permitted to work rich ground.

4. *Barreteros* duly registered for work in any of the mines shall be paid the customary daily wage of four reales [$.50], and it shall be incumbent upon them to deposit in the gallery to which they are assigned such ore as they have broken away; this ore, cleaned and in good condition, whether of high or low grade, shall be thoroughly mixed in the gallery and divided into eight equal portions, one eighth

[1] Translation of Reglamento que la Compañía Inglesa del Mineral del Monte ha formado para el laborío de las minas que trabaja, con respecto al partido y obligaciones de los operarios, de conformidad en la mayor parte con lo que han indicado los mismos por conducto de los indicados, AEM, expediente concerning 1827 strike at Real del Monte, doc. 50.

being granted to the operator and the remaining seven eighths to the mine owner; the mine owner shall, moreover, furnish the operators such tools, blasting powder, candles, bags, and iron as they may require, the distribution of this material being entrusted to the captains, so as to ensure the greatest possible economy.

5. It shall be incumbent upon the captains to inspect all the workings, in order to ascertain that the *barreteros* are complying with their assignments, that the supplies furnished them are distributed with all due economy, and that the operations are conducted in a proper manner, as regards cleanliness, duty stations, and safety; they shall not receive a *partido*, but shall be paid a fair wage.

6. An operator may sell his share of the ore to the company or to whomever he chooses, no restrictions being placed on this right.

7. An operator assigned to a duty station within a mine shall neither break away ore from another area nor mix his ore with that of another area, for by such action he shall forfeit his *partido*.

8. *Barreteros* who sign in for their shift with the intention of being paid without working are hereby advised that, even though they may be assigned to poor ground, it is incumbent upon them to deliver ore equal in value to the wage paid them and to such expenses as they may have incurred, whether or not they receive a *partido*; if they are assigned to dead work, they shall perform such tasks as assigned them by the captain.

9. The watchmen stationed at the pit head shall inspect everything that is taken into or out of the mine, searching everybody who leaves the mine, without exception; and they shall not permit metal, powder, tools, candles, or any other article belonging to the mine to be removed, not even a candle stub to be carried away under the pretext of darkness.

10. The timbermen's tasks being so important and, at the same time, so arduous, these workers shall be permitted a place on the ore ground on Saturday nights, and such ore as they break away shall be divided under the same conditions as those granted the *barreteros*.

11. Should a mine be so rich as to attract all the workers in search of good ore, the labor force of that mine shall be rotated by the assignment of *barreteros* from each of the other mines, it being incumbent upon the company to see to it that all the *barreteros* benefit equally and are given no cause for complaint.

BIBLIOGRAPHICAL NOTES

Manuscript materials

Real del Monte Papers. The most important source of material used in the preparation of this study is the collection of unpublished papers belonging to the Real del Monte and Pachuca Mining Company. It is housed in the headquarters of the Mexican government-operated company, a building known as Las Cajas, in Pachuca, Hidalgo. A storage room, or vault, on the ground floor of Las Cajas contains the majority of the holdings that deal with the British and Mexican periods of the company's history, some records related to the first years of the American firm, and material pertaining to the present concern (mainly old account books). Most of the papers in the vault are in bound copy books, ledgers, oversized account books, loose-leaf binders, and individual file boxes. Some are simply bundled together in Manila paper. There are 775 copy books, ledgers, and account books relating to all three periods, some 550 of them to that of the Mexican company alone. An additional 500 loose-leaf binders contain papers dealing mostly with the Mexican period but also with the early years of the American firm. A small number of loose papers, wrapped and tied, referring again to the Mexican and American periods, complete the collection dealing with the Real del Monte Company proper. Moreover, there are in the vault some 300 volumes of copy books and loose-leaf binders pertaining to the several subsidiaries of Real del Monte during the American period.

A little-used wing of offices on the second floor of Las Cajas also holds some of the historical records used in this study. Eleven three- or four-drawer metal file cabinets and 177 individual file boxes contain the bulk of the correspondence and various reports and accounts on the period in which Real del Monte was operated by the United States Smelting, Refining and Mining Company. Filed according to two different systems, for which indexes are available, the papers cover the period 1906–1947.

Unpublished historical records are also stored in the safe of the present firm's accounting department. There may be found some of the most important individual documents dealing with the Mexican and American companies, particularly the originals and copies of contracts, stock ledgers of both periods, and unpublished transactions of the boards of directors of the American firm and of the present Mexican government-operated concern.

Owing to the large volume of material on the various periods of the Real Monte Company's history, a selection of the documents to be given special study was necessary. The vast majority of the bound and loose-leaf books in the vault and of the filed papers in the second-floor offices record in too-minute detail the day-to-day operations of individual mines and mills or of the Mexican concern's salt works at Lake Texcoco. Furthermore, there is a great deal of duplication: for example, the vault contains, in loose-leaf binders, the originals of letters sent from the director and subordinate Mexican company officials at Real del Monte to the Board of Directors in Mexico City and, in bound copy books, copies of these same communications.

The largest block of material used in the inquiry into the British firm is the incomplete collection of copy books, located in the vault at Las Cajas, under the heading of Correspondencia General (abbreviated CG). Irregularly numbered from 8 through 89, the volumes in this series cover the years from 1825 through 1910. Twenty-three of them deal with the British period and contain, for the most part, copies of letters that Real del Monte officials sent to the London office and to various parties in Mexico. Handwritten in both English and Spanish by unidentified persons, doubtless clerks or scribes, they bear the signatures of the chief commissioners, treasurer-cashiers, and other officials of the British establishment in Mexico. During their many years at the Real del Monte headquarters, first in the Casa Grande at Real del Monte and later in Las Cajas at Pachuca, some of the CG volumes have been water-damaged. (Approximately 20 per cent of the pages in five of the volumes are partly or wholly illegible.) Inasmuch as twenty-one of the twenty-three hold copies of outgoing correspondence, a study of them gives a thorough picture of the activities of the mining concern in Mexico. Moreover, many of the letters, especially those sent to the London management, include detailed acknowledgements of communications received at Real del Monte, thereby making up, to a large extent, for the absence of the originals of dispatches from the home office.

Among the other unpublished company papers that shed light on the history of the British company are the Acta cesión de trapaso de derechos and the Acta de socios, both drawn up in 1849. The first, a copy of the instrument by which the British concern transferred its rights and possessions to the Mexican firm, is particularly valuable in that it sets forth in detail the terms by which the mining concern passed from the hands of the British Real del Monte to its Mexican successor. The second original document is the one by which the parties that were to form the Mexican company bound themselves into an association to acquire the Real del Monte mines and mills. It explains the relationships between the British company and the various mine owners whose property it worked for twenty-five years, especially the Regla family. Both of these documents include an inventory of the property and a summary of the contractual arrangements transferred to the Mexican group. The inventory given in the Acta de socios is more detailed, going so far as to list and appraise the machinery, equipment, and stores on hand in mid-1849.

Romero de Terreros Papers. The bases on which the British concern worked mines not belonging to it are set forth as a collection of papers in Mexico City, in the possession of Manuel Romero de Terreros, the Marquis of San Francisco and a descendant of the counts of Regla. One of those documents (Libro en que se hallan . . .) contains copies of the July 1824 contract between the British Real del Monte and the third count, of the various revisions of that contract concluded between 1825 and 1831, and of the contract for the leasing of certain mines partly owned by the count. Inasmuch as the Regla contracts served as a model for subsequent agreements entered into by the British firm and by other mine owners, these documents are invaluable. Furthermore, in presenting an inventory of the mines, haciendas, and equipment turned over to the first British party that reached the mining camp, they furnish data given in full in no other place. An excellent source of information on the working of the Real del Monte mines between 1739, when the Vizcaína vein and adjacent properties were claimed by José Alejandro de Bustamante, and 1764, when a royal *cedula* Pedro Romero de Terreros' possession of Bustamante's original claim and additional properties was confirmed, is found in a leather-bound volume of manuscripts entitled "Títulos de la veta Vizcaína."

Archivo del Estado de México. The Archivo del Estado de México in Toluca, Mexico, contains only a few documents used in the preparation of this study, but they were extremely valuable. Two *expedientes* deal with the labor disputes of 1827 and 1828, the first including one document that deserves special mention—a copy of the 1827 labor contract between the British company and its Mexican working force.

Archivo de Notarías. Although the Archivo de Notarías in Mexico City is not organized for research—to find a document one must know the name of the notary who drew it up—it proved to be the depository of vitally important documents used in the present work, including the

1743 agreement between José Alejandro de Bustamante and Pedro Romero de Terreros and the July 1824 contract between the third Count of Regla and agents of the British Real del Monte.

Archivo General de la Nación. The Archivo General de la Nación in Mexico City is not yet well organized for research in the early national period of Mexican history and was not a major source of information used in the preparation of this study. The 230 volumes in the section of that archive entitled "Ramo de Minería," however, do contain a considerable amount of data on mining in the colonial period.

Papeles de los Condes de Regla. The library of Washington State University, Pullman, Washington, has a collection of Regla family manuscripts bearing dates from the sixteenth to the nineteenth centuries. Grouped under the heading "Papeles de los Condes de Regla," the manuscripts are in part catalogued in a "Calendar of the Unbound Papers and Documents in the Papeles de los Condes de Regla," compiled by Jacquelyn M. Melcher Gaines when the institution was still known as the State College of Washington. Almost all of the documents in the collection concern landholdings of the Regla family, but a few deal with its mining properties. These include copies of the contracts between the third Count of Regla and the British Real del Monte, which are similar to the documents found in the Libro en que se hallan of the Romero de Terreros Papers.

Published Documents

Proceedings, RdM Papers. The most important printed documents found among the Real del Monte Papers in Las Cajas is a collection, though incomplete, of the *Proceedings* of the stockholders' meetings in London. They are located in one of the file cabinets in the second-floor offices. The records of business transacted at stockholders' meetings between 1830 and 1845 are but one part of the valuable data contained in the *Proceedings.* Narrative reports on the progress of the firm's operations summarize the main line of development in mining and milling carried out in Mexico and at the same time present a changing interpretation of the company's fortunes as they were viewed by the London management. A report of the home office's only inspection of the works at Real del Monte, made by Secretary Phillips in 1840, may also be found in the *Proceedings.*

John Buchan's 1855 report as the Director of the Mexican Real del Monte Company is a highly informative document and an indispensable source for the account of the Mexican successor to the British firm. In an appendix, itself the director's report for 1852, Buchan sketches the history of the Real del Monte mines and gives valuable information on their working by the British firm, information that he gained both from company records and through his experience in the company's service in various capacities from as early as 1825, including the post of the last chief commissioner.

A lively first-hand account of the British entry into the town of Real del Monte in June 1824 is given in an unsigned journal written by a member of the original party; the document was printed by the American-owned company in 1939.

Mexican government documents. In 1961 the Council of Nonrenewable Natural Resources in the Ministry of National Patrimony issued a reprint of two basic documents on mining law: José Olmedo y Lama, comp., *Ordenanzas de minería y colección de las leyes y órdenes que con fecha posterior se han expedido sobre la materia* (México, D.F., 1873), and Francisco Javier de Gamboa, *Comentarios á las ordenanzas de minas* (México, D.F., 1874). The latter volume had originally been published in 1761. This valuable work contains the text of the 1783 *Ordenanzas de minería,* which was the basic set of mining laws in Mexico from its issuance up to 1882, and of such modifications of that code as were made during the life of the British Real del Monte in Mexico.

Four compendiums of laws, decrees, circulars, and other materials, two for the national government and two for the government of the state of Mexico, give the texts of legislation and executive directives affecting the mining industry in the nation as a whole and also in the state in which the Real del Monte Company operated. Arrillaga's contains a copy of the 1836 law granting Real del Monte a silver-bullion export privilege, the only piece of legislation applying exclusively to the British concern.

The *Memorias,* or annual reports, of various departments of the Mexican national government are more informative on the blasting powder monopoly and on the operation of the decrepit Mexico City mint, both important to the British Real del Monte, than on the mining industry. Reports of the government of the state of Mexico dealt on occasion directly with the British concern at Real del Monte and frequently with the mining industry as a whole in that state. They not only provided valuable information on such institutions as the Tlalpám mint and the *fondos de rescate* of the state but also shed light on the relationship of Real del Monte with what was an influential governmental unit. Moreover, they give an insight into the state government's attitude with regard to the British company, which changed from one of enthusiastic cooperation in the late 1820's to one of indifference in the 1830's and 1840's.

Other published documents. An indispensable supplement to the British concern's own accounts of expenditures and income in Mexico is found in *Real del Monte Mining Company (Ex.-Debt.)*, a prospectus issued in 1848 for the resuscitation of the dissolved Real del Monte; inasmuch as this statement of the company's outlay and income for the years 1841–1844 coincides exactly with the data found in the Real del Monte *Proceedings*, credence was given the figures for the following three years, especially since such authorities as John Buchan and Joseph Burkart disagree on the level of expenditures and income in Mexico for that period.

Written for the purpose of encouraging the formation of a company in Mexico to finance the rehabilitation of the Real del Monte mines, José Rodrigo de Castelazo's 1820 and 1823 manifestoes helped promote the British company that actually carried out the task of reviving those mines. For that reason alone the documents would be an important source of information in the preparation of this study. But they also contain much valuable data on the working of the Real del Monte mines under the three counts of Regla. Moreover, the 1820 version includes a copy of an 1801 report on the state of the deep workings of the Vizcaína vein that served as a guide for the British firm's intial plan of mining operations.

Periodicals

Three British periodicals used extensively in the preparation of this study warrant special mention. The first is the *Law Journal for the Year 1825*, which carries a full account of Thomas Kinder's suit against John Taylor, heard in the Court of Chancery in March and April 1825. This report provided the author with the most valuable single source of information on the establishment of both the Real del Monte and the Bolaños companies.

The second is the *Quarterly Mining Review*, of which five numbers, brought out in 1830–1832 and 1835, were available to the author. They contain transcriptions of correspondence from the chief commissioner to the London office of Real del Monte during 1830 and 1831; reports on stockholders' meetings held in London during those years, including occasional texts of the reports of the Court of Directors and the manager; and, most important, a "Review of the Real del Monte Mining Association" from its formation to February 1830 (this retrospective view of Real del Monte is based largely on the transactions of the annual and special stockholders' meetings held in that five-year period). The *Quarterly* also provides data on the price of Real del Monte shares on the London market between 1830 and 1834.

The third periodical that proved valuable, indeed indispensable, was the *Mining Journal*. Brought out under various titles (all of them including the words "Mining Journal") from 29 August 1835 to the present, the *Mining Journal* furnishes a wealth of information on the Real del Monte Company and on all the other British mining concerns operating both in Great Britain and abroad. Besides publishing communications sent by the overseas administrators to the home office and proceedings of stockholders' meetings held in London, some of them verbatim, the *Journal* carried, for the period under review, weekly columns showing the price of mining shares on the London market, lists of the price of various metals in England (among them quicksilver, silver, and gold), and articles on mining in Mexico. A comparison between the Real del Monte correspondence published in the *Journal* and copies of letters in Volumes 39 and 48 of Correspondencia General of the Real del Monte Papers shows that, except on rare occasions, the periodical accurately reproduced the words and data sent to London by the various chief commissioners; considerable reliance was therefore placed on the *Journal* as a supplement to the company records. Having been found to be no less exact in reporting on stockholders' meetings for which *Proceedings* were available to the author, the periodical's accounts of the meetings held after June 1845 were drawn upon extensively. Those reports are, in fact, an essential source of information on the dissolution of the British firm.

Joseph Burkart's study on the working of mines in Pachuca and Real del Monte contains much useful general information on the operations of the British company and is an indispensable supplement to the firm's own records as a source of data on the production, expenditures, and income during the 1824–1849 period. A Spanish translation of the German mining engineer's work was carried in the first, and only, issue of the Mexican scientific periodical *Anales de la minería mexicana*.

Among the other Mexican periodicals consulted, *El trimestre económico* is noteworthy for its inclusion of Miguel O. de Mendizábal's "Los minerales de Pachuca y Real del Monte en la época colonial," a study presenting a good, but by no means exhaustive review of mining in the Real del Monte–Pachuca district prior to Mexican independence. The official Mexican government newspaper, appearing under various titles, and two independent newspapers, *El sol* and *El siglo XIX*, occasionally carried articles dealing with Real del Monte and advertisements and notices inserted by the company or its agents.

Scientific Studies

The importance of Baron Alexander von Humboldt's *Political Essay on the Kingdom of New Spain* to the subject of mining in colonial Mexico is too well established to be repeated. It is, however, worth noting the use made of that work by the promoters of British mining ventures in newly independent Mexico. Prospective investors were urged to consult Humboldt for proof of the existence of great mineral wealth awaiting the English enterprise. Despite its title, Burkart's *Aufenthalt und Reisen* is less a travel account than a mining treatise. Though it deals only briefly with the Real del Monte enterprise, it is invaluable as a source of information on the Bolaños Company; indeed, the author was the mine manager of Bolaños' Zacatecas operations between 1828 and 1834.

St. Clair Duport's highly esteemed account of Mexican mining and minting deserves special mention, not because of its observations on the Real del Monte Company but, rather, because of its all but complete disregard of that British enterprise. The author purports to describe the "principal mining districts" of Mexico, covering in his treatise such relatively minor areas as Nieves, Charcas, La Blanca, and Ojo Caliente. Yet he makes but three passing references to Real del Monte. The cause of Duport's myopia is obvious. In 1836 he became, as he says in his introduction, the "owner of the parting establishment where ingots of gold and silver presented to the mint of Mexico were refined"; that very year the British Real del Monte was engaged in a bitter struggle with the parties supporting the Mexico City mint against the British firm's right to export uncoined and unrefined bullion under an act of the Mexican congress.

Travel Accounts

Much useful information regarding the Real del Monte district and the nearby reduction haciendas was set forth by the many foreigners who, during their sojourns in nineteenth-century Mexico, did not fail to visit that mining area. The fabled wealth of the counts of Regla— the third count himself received some of the travelers at his Mexico City home or at one of his country estates, including Real del Monte's San Miguel hacienda—and the Real's close proximity to the capital may explain that attraction. While many of the visitors, the most famous of whom was Madame Calderón de la Barca, merely recorded their personal reminiscences, some showed a more technical interest in the mine's operations. Henry Tudor, for example, presented data on the expenditures and earnings of the British firm during the 1830's, provided him by Commissioner John Rule. Both William P. Robertson and Robert A. Wilson sketched the history of the mining concern at Real del Monte; Robertson incorporated in his book the entire 1852 report prepared by Real del Monte Director John Buchan. One of the most informative travel accounts of the era was written by a Real del Monte and Bolaños official, George F. Lyon. Though he devoted more attention to the latter concern's establishments at Bolaños and Zacatecas, Lyon nevertheless described in some detail his visits to workings at

Ozumatlán and at Real del Monte; his retracing of the company's carriage route between the mining camp and Veracruz is particularly valuable in filling certain gaps in the Real del Monte Papers. In a sense a travel account, Henry G. Ward's *Mexico in 1827* goes far beyond the others as a source of data on mining in Mexico. Not only did Ward visit and describe Real del Monte, but, in his capacity as British chargé d'affaires, he received from Captain James Vetch two reports, long excerpts of which he published in his book. He may have considered Vetch's prediction of the amount of profit to be gained from the Real del Monte mines somewhat too "sanguine," but he defended the British concern and its first commissioner against the "little justice" done them by the Mexicans.

Dissertations

One unpublished doctoral dissertation contains information used in the writing of this work. Newton R. Gilmore's "British Mining Ventures in Early National Mexico" devotes considerable attention to the British Real del Monte. His study was based mainly on microcopies of documents in the British Foreign Office. Most of the data related to the Real del Monte Company, therefore, came from letters written by company officials in Mexico to British diplomatic representatives in that country and from dispatches sent by those representatives to the Foreign Office in London. Some use was made of travel accounts and secondary sources. Gilmore briefly tells the story of the British Real del Monte, but his work leaves periods virtually untouched, contains some errors in fact, and draws unfounded conclusions on the basis of scanty information. For example, his contentions that the British were forced to accept the *partido* and were unable to improve on the patio amalgamation process appear to have been based on statements made by officials or on letters written by British representatives in the 1820's. Neither conclusion is borne out by my review of the company papers, particularly those of the 1840's. The Gilmore dissertation was helpful, however, on the subjects of British diplomacy immediately before the recognition of Mexican independence, the mania in London in 1823 and 1824 for mining ventures in Mexico, and the action taken on some of the appeals made by Real del Monte officials to British diplomatic representatives in Mexico.

Other Published Sources

Henry English's *Guide* contains a verbatim copy of the British firm's original prospectus, not available elsewhere, and data on the company's formation and early operations. The attitude with which Real del Monte regarded its entry into the field of Mexican silver mining is stated no better than in Manager John Taylor's introduction to the works of Humboldt.

Two of the collections of documents compiled by Luis Chávez Orozco, his *Conflicto de trabajo con los mineros de Real del Monte* and *Documentos para la historia económica de México*, proved to be indispensable aids in writing Chapter 1 of this work. They were particularly relevant in connection with the long (1766–1775) Real del Monte strike. It must be noted, however, that in the introductions to his *Documentos* Chávez Orozco seems more interested in proving that a proletariat existed in colonial Mexico than in placing the source material in its historical context.

SELECTED BIBLIOGRAPHY

Manuscript Material

Mexico City, Mexico. Archivo de Notarías.
Juan Antonio de Arroyo, 1743.
Manuel García Romero, 1824, 1825.
Mexico City, Mexico. Archivo General de la Nación.
Ramo de Minería, vols. 29, 137, 192, 212, 218.
Mexico City, Mexico. Romero de Terreros Papers.
Libro en que se hallan, el preliminar con que la Sociedad de Aventureros formada en Londres convino celebrar una compañía por 21 años con el S. D. Pedro Terreros Conde de Jala y de Regla para el fomento y laborío de sus minas del Mineral del Monte y Zimapán; la escritura pública con que se afianzó el contrato, y los ynventarios judicialies de las haciendas de beneficio de metales y de labor por el que asi como las minas recibieron. D. Jayme [James] Vetch, D. Juan [John] Rule, y D. Vicente Rivafinoli, comicionados para la ratificación del pacto, Año de 1824. 180p. (Incorrectly dated, inasmuch as documents for the years 1825–1831 are included.)
Títulos de la veta Vizcaína [1756–1765]. 119 fols.
Pachuca, Hidalgo, Mexico. Real del Monte Company Papers.
Acta cesión de trapaso de derechos, 4 de julio de 1849. 9 fols.
Acta de los socios del Real del Monte, 1º de junio de 1849: Acta de la primera junta celebrada para la formación de la "Compañía de Minas del Rl. [Real] del Monte" entre los Sres. Alej[andro] Bellangé, Nicanor Béistegui, Ml. [Manuel] Escandón, E[dwin] C. Mackintosh, P[alamede] de la Roche y Juan [John] H. Buchan, con la nota de las contratas de minas, haciendas de beneficio, maquinaria y otros bienes pertenecientes a la Compañía Inglesa del Ml. [Mineral] del Monte, 1º de junio de 1849. [40 p.]

Correspondencia General.
 Vol. 8, 20 April 1825–1 November 1825. 188 p.
 Vol. 12, 24 July 1827–6 July 1832. [451 p.] (Incorrectly dated, letters beginning 20 July 1827.)
 Vol. 13, 23 August 1827–1 December 1830. [510 p.]
 Vol. 14, 3 January 1828–18 January 1834. [59 p.]
 Vol. 15, 2 January 1828–14 February 1834. [293 p.]
 Vol. 16, 7 January 1828 (Ozumatlán y Zimapán)–28 November 1832. [89 p.]
 Vol. 23, 4 January 1830–7 June 1832. [271 p.]
 Vol. 26, 4 January 1830–7 December 1833. [118 p.] (Also contains letters written between 29 May and 15 July 1827.)
 Vol. 28, 10 December 1830–7 July 1834. 735 p. (Incorrectly dated, letters ending 4 March 1835.)
 Vol. 33, 20 March 1834–20 April 1835. 280 p.
 Vol. 34, 3 March 1835–20 February 1836. 472 p.
 Vol. 35, 10 April 1835–31 August 1838. 455 p.
 Vol. 36, 21 April 1835–17 April 1847. [698 p.]
 Vol. 37, 22 April 1835–19 January 1847. 550 p.
 Vol. 38, 8 February 1836–30 December 1837. 452 p.
 Vol. 39, 30 August 1836–13 February 1843. [1,256 p.] (Incorrectly dated, letters ending 4 August 1843.)
 Vol. 40, 2 January 1838–12 February 1839. 541 p.
 Vol. 44, 17 February 1839–22 September 1840. 538 p.
 Vol. 45, 14 December 1839–31 March 1849. 165 original letters.
 Vol. 46, 26 September 1840–10 September 1842. 544 p.
 Vol. 47, 13 September 1842–14 September 1844. 540 p.
 Vol. 48, 26 August 1843–10 April 1848. 383 p.
 Vol. 65, 31 December 1838–3 October 1846. 475 p.

Pullman, Washington. Washington State University. Papeles de los Condes de Regla.

Copias de las contratas de las negociaciones de minas de la veta Vizcaína y sus anexas con la compañía ynglesa abiadora de las minas y la casa de Regla, año de 1849. [Two bound volumes, one of 60 folios and the other of 72 folios, contain two separate copies of the contracts.]

[Expediente concerning the entailing of the Regla mining properties in 1775], [126 p.].

Testimonio del testamento que ortogó al Señor Don Pedro Romero de Terreros, Conde de Regla, el dia 9 de septiembre de 1775.

Toluca, Mexico. Archivo del Estado de México.

[Expediente concerning the 1827 strike at Real del Monte, 60 docs.]
[Expediente concerning the 1828 uprising at Morán mine, 6 docs.]

Published Documents

Alamán, Lucas. *Documentos diversos (inéditos y muy raros)*. 4 vols. Colección de Grandes Autores Mexicanos, vols. 9–12. México, D.F.: Jus, 1945.

Arrillaga, Basilio José, comp. *Recopilación de leyes, decretos, bandos, reglamentos, circulares y providencias de los supremos poderes y otras autoridades de la República Mexicana*. January–June 1836. México, D.F.: n.p. 1836.

Auld, Thomas R. [Report of the Director, the Real del Monte Mining Company, April 1859.] México, D.F.: n.p., n.d.

Balanza general del comercio marítimo por los puertos de la República Mexicana, 1825–1827. 3 vols. México, D.F.: n.p., 1827–1829.

Buchan, John H. *Report of the Director, the Real del Monte Mining Company, Mexico, March 1855*. London: n.p., 1855.

Castelazo, José Rodrigo de. *Manifiesto de la riqueza de la negociación de minas conocida por la veta Vizcaina, ubicada en el Real del Monte, jurisdicción de Pachuca, de las grandes obras que en ella se hicieron, y del estado actual en que se halla, para la compañía de accionistas que desea celebrar á fin de continuar su laborío bajo las condiciones que se expresan, su actual poseedor el señor D. Pedro . . . Romero de Terreros*. México, D.F.: Ontiveros, 1820.

———. *Manifiesto de las riquezas que han producido y actualmente contienen las celebradas minas de las vetas Vizcaina y Santa Brigida, ubicadas en el Real del Monte, jurisdicción de Pachuca, de las grandes obras que en ellas se hicieron y del estado en que actualmente se hallan; siendo su actual poseedor [Pedro Romero de Terreros]*. México, D.F.: Ontiveros, 1823.

Colección de decretos del Congreso Constituyente del Estado libre y soberano de México, espedidos en su primera reunión, los años de 1824, 1825, 1826, y 1827, y en su reinstalación en 1830. 5 vols. Toluca, México: n.p., 1850. (Titles vary from volume to volume.)

Decretos del Congreso Constituyente del Estado de México revisados por el mismo Congreso é impresos de su órden. Vol. 1. México, D.F.: n.p., n.d.

Dublán, Manuel and José María Lozano, comps. *Legislación mexicana ó colección completa de las disposiciones legislativas expedidas desde la independencia de la República*. Vol. 5. México, D.F.: n.p., 1876.

Journal Descriptive of the Route from New York to Real del Monte by Way of Tampico: By One of the First Detachment Sent by the Real del Monte Company [1824]. Reprint. Pachuca, Hidalgo: Real del Monte Company, 1939.

Manifestación comedida que hace la comisión de barreteros del Real del Monte a la Compañía Aviadora de Minas de aquel distrito. México, D.F.: n.p., 1874.

Mateos, Juan A., ed. *Historia parlamentaria de los congresos mexicanos.* Vol. 11. México, D.F.: n.p., 1887.

Memoria de las secretarias de relaciones, guerra, justicia, negocios ecclesiásticos, é instrucción pública, del gobierno del Estado de México. Toluca, México: n.p., 1849–1852.

Memoria en que el gobierno del Estado libre de México da cuenta de los ramos de su administración al congresso del mismo estado, a consecuencia de su decreto de 16 de diciembre de 1825. México, D.F., and Toluca, México: n.p., 1826–1835. (Titles of the reports vary.)

Memoria en que el secretario del ramo de hacienda del Estado libre y soberano de México, da cuenta al Congreso Constitucional de todos los ramos que han sido a su cargo en el año de 1848; comprendiéndose noticias relativas á los 4 meses de 1846 y todo el año de 1847, que volvió á regir el sistema federal. Toluca, México: n.p., 1849–1852. (Titles of the reports vary.)

Memoria presentada al soberano congreso mexicano por el secretario de estado y del despacho de relaciones ynteriores y esteriores. México, D.F.: n.p., 1822–1827, 1833. (Titles of the reports vary.)

Memoria sobre el estado de la hacienda pública, leída en la cámara de diputados y en la de senadores, por el ministro del ramo. México, D.F.: n.p., 1825–1851. (Titles of the reports vary.)

Proceedings at the Annual and Special General Court of Proprietors of the Real del Monte Mining Company. London: n.p., 1835–1843.

Proceedings at the Annual General Court of Proprietors of the Real del Monte Mining Company. London: n.p., 1831–1845.

Proceedings at the Special General Court of Proprietors of the Real del Monte Mining Company. London: n.p., 1828–1845.

Real del Monte Mining Company (Ex.-Debt.). London: n.p., 1848.

Taylor, John, ed. "Introduction," in *Selections from the Works of the Baron de [sic] Humboldt, Relating to the Climate, Inhabitants, Productions, and Mines of Mexico.* London: Longman, Hurst, Rees, Orme, Brown, and Green, 1824.

Webster, Charles K., ed. *Britain and the Independence of Latin America, 1812–1830: Select Documents from the Foreign Office Archives.* 2 vols. London: Published for the Ibero-American Institute of Great Britain by the Oxford Univ. Press, 1938.

Other Published Works

Almaraz, Ramón, ed. *Memoria de los trabajos ejecutados por la Comisión Científica de Pachuca en el año de 1864.* México, D.F.: Secretaría de Fomento, 1865.

Bargalló, Modesto. *La minería y la metalurgia en la América española durante la época colonial.* México, D.F.: Fondo de Cultura Económica, 1955.

Bernstein, Marvin D. *The Mexican Mining Industry, 1890–1950: A Study of the Interaction of Politics, Economics, and Technology.* Albany: State University of New York, 1964.

Bobb, Bernard E. *The Viceregency of Antonio María Bucareli in New Spain, 1771–1799.* Austin: University of Texas Press, 1962.

Bullock, W. *Six Months' Residence and Travels in Mexico.* 2 vols. London: John Murray, 1825.

Burkart, Joseph. *Aufenthalt und Reisen in Mexico en den Jahren 1825 bis 1834.* 2 vols. Stuttgart: E. Schweizerbart, 1836.

———. "Memoria sobre explotación de minas de los distritos de Pachuca y Real del Monte de México." *Anales de la minería mexicana,* 1 (1861), 6–25, 41–65, 81–113.

Calderón de la Barca, Frances. *Life in Mexico.* 2 vols. Boston, 1843. Reprint (2 vols. in 1). Garden City, N.Y.: Doubleday, Dolphin Book C93, n.d.

Casasús, Joaquín. *La cuestión de la plata en México.* México, D.F.: Oficina Impresora del Timbre, 1896.

"Cases Argued and Determined in the Court of Chancery . . . March 1825, Kinder v. Taylor." *The Law Journal for the Year 1825,* 3 (1825), 68–84.

Chávez Orozco, Luis, ed. *Conflicto de trabajo con los mineros de Real del Monte, año de 1766.* México, D.F.: Instituto Nacional de Estudios Históricos de la Revolución Mexicana, 1960.

———. *Documentos para la historia económica de México.* 11 vols. México, D.F.: Secretaría de la Economía Nacional, 1933–1936.

Descripción de las minas de Pachuca. In *Colección de documentos inéditos, relativos al descubrimiento, conquista y organización de las antiguas posesiones españoles de América y Oceanía* (Madrid, 1868), vol. 9. México, D.F.: Biblioteca de Historiadores Mexicanos, 1951.

Diario del gobierno de la República Mexicana, 1842, 1847.

[Disraeli, Benjamin]. *An Inquiry into the Plans, Progress, and Policy of the American Mining Companies.* 2d ed. London: John Murray, 1825.

Duport, St. Clair. *De la production des métaux précieux au Mexique, considérée dans ses rapports avec la géologie, la métallurgie et l'économie politique.* Paris: Institut de France, 1843.

English, Henry. *A General Guide to the Companies Formed for Working Foreign Mines, with Their Prospectuses, Amount of Capital, Number of Shares, Names of Directors, etc. and an Appendix Showing Their Progress Since Their Formation, Obtained from Authentic*

244 *Selected Bibliography*

Sources; with a Table of the Extent of Their Fluctuations in Price, up to the Present Period. London: Boosey and Sons, 1825.

Gaceta diaria de México, 1825.

Gaceta imperial de México, 1821–1822.

Geyne, A. R., et al. *Geology and Mineral Deposits of the Pachuca–Real del Monte District, State of Hidalgo, Mexico.* Mexico City: Consejo de Recursos Naturales no Renovables, 1963.

Gilmore, Newton R. "British Mining Ventures in Early National Mexico." Ph.D. dissertation, University of California, 1956.

Howe, Walter. *The Mining Guild of New Spain and Its Tribunal General, 1770–1821.* Harvard Historical Studies, vol. 56. Cambridge, Mass.: Harvard University Press, 1949.

Humboldt, Alexander de [*sic*]. *Political Essay on the Kingdom of New Spain.* Translated by John Black. 3d ed. 3 vols. London: Longman, Hurst, Bees, Orme, and Brown, 1822.

Humphreys, R. A., ed. *British Consular Reports on the Trade and Politics of Latin America, 1824–1826.* Royal Historical Society, Camden Third Series, vol. 63. London: Royal Historical Society, 1940.

Instituto Geológico de México. *El mineral de Pachuca.* México, D.F.: Secretaría de Fomento, 1897.

———. *El Real del Monte.* México, D.F.: Secretaría de Fomento, 1899.

Jenks, Leland H. *The Migration of British Capital to 1875.* New York: Knopf, 1927.

Lerdo de Tejada, Miguel. *Comercio esterior de México desde la conquista hasta hoy.* México, D.F.: Rafael Rafael, 1853.

Lyon, G[eorge] F. *Journal of a Residence and Tour in the Republic of Mexico in the Year 1826, with Some Account of the Mines of That Country.* 2 vols. London: John Murray, 1828.

Mendizábal, Miguel O. de. "Los minerales de Pachuca y Real del Monte en la época colonial." *El trimestre económico*, 8, no. 2 (July–September 1941), 253–309.

The Mining Journal and Commercial Gazette, vols. 1–20 (1835–1850).

The Morning Chronicle (London), 1824.

Morton, Frederic. *The Rothschilds, a Family Portrait.* New York: Fawcett, 1963.

Motten, Clement G. *Mexican Silver and the Enlightenment.* Philadelphia: University of Pennsylvania Press, 1950.

Ober, Frederick A. *Travels in Mexico and Life Among the Mexicans.* Boston: Estes and Lauriat, 1884.

Olavarría y Ferrari, Enrique. *México independiente, 1821–1855. México a través de los siglos*, edited by Vicente Riva Palacio, vol. 4. México, D.F.: Cumbre, 1953.

Ordenanzas de minería otorgadas por el Rey Carlos III de España, seguidas de la legislación minera vigente hasta 1874; comentarios á las ordenanzas de minería por Don Francisco Javier de Gamboa. México, D.F.: Consejo de Recursos Naturales No Renovables, 1961. (Each section in the work is numbered separately.)

Pletcher, David M. "The Building of the Mexican Railway." *Hispanic American Historical Review*, 30 (1950), 26–62.

[Poinsett, Joel R.] *Notes on Mexico, Made in the Autumn of 1822.* Philadelphia: H. C. Carey and I. Lea, 1824.

Potash, Robert A. *El Banco de Avío de México: El fomento de la industria, 1821–1846.* México, D.F.: Fondo de Cultura Económica, 1959.

The Quarterly Mining Review, vol. 1, nos. 3–4 (September 1830–January 1831), nos. 5–7 (April 1831–July 1835).

Ramírez, Santiago. *Noticia histórica de la riqueza minera de México y de su actual estado de explotación.* México, D.F.: Secretaría de Fomento, 1884.

Reeves, John. *The Rothschilds, the Financial Rulers of Nations.* London: Sampson Low, Marston, Searle, and Rivington, 1887.

Rippy, J. Fred. "British Investments in Latin America, End of 1913." *Journal of Modern History*, 19 (September 1947), 226–234.

———. "Latin America and the British Investment 'Boom' of the 1820's." *Journal of Modern History*, 19 (June 1947), 122–129.

Rives, George L. *The United States and Mexico, 1821–1848: A History of the Relations between the Two Countries from the Independence of Mexico to the Close of the War with the United States.* 2 vols. New York: Charles Scribner's Sons, 1913.

Robertson, William Parish. *A Visit to Mexico, by the West India Islands, Yucatan and United States, with Observations and Adventures on the Way.* 2 vols. London: By author, 1853.

Romero de Terreros, Manuel. *El Conde de Regla, creso de la Nueva España.* México, D.F.: Xochitl, 1943.

El siglo XIX, 1841–1844, 1848–1849.

El sol, 1824–1828.

Stephen, Leslie and Sidney Lee, eds. *The Dictionary of National Biography.* London: Oxford University Press, 1921–1922.

Tamayo, Jorge L. "La minería de Nueva España en 1794." *El trimestre económico*, 10, no. 2 (July–September 1943), 287–319.

Tayloe, Edward T. *Mexico, 1825–1828; . . . Journal and Correspondence.* Edited by C. Harvey Gardiner. Chapel Hill: University of North Carolina Press, 1959.

Tudor, Henry. *Narrative of a Tour in North America; Comprising Mexico, the Mines of Real del Monte, the United States, and the*

246   *Selected Bibliography*

British Colonies: With an Excursion to the Island of Cuba. 2 vols. London: James Duncan, 1834.

Velasco Ceballos, Rómulo, ed. *La administración de D. Fray Antonio María de Bucareli y Ursúa.* 2 vols. Publicaciones del Archivo General de la Nación, 29–30. México, D.F.: Archivo General de la Nación, 1936.

Ward, H[enry] G. *Mexico in 1827.* 2 vols. London: Henry Colburn, 1828.

Wilson, Robert A. *Mexico: Its Peasants and Its Priests; or Adventures and Historical Researches in Mexico and Its Silver Mines during Parts of the Years 1851–52–53–54.* Rev. ed. New York: Harper and Row, 1856.

Zavala, Silvio and María Castelo, eds. *Fuentes para la historia del trabajo en Nueva España.* 8 vols. México, D.F.: Fondo de Cultura Económica, 1939–1945.

Bibliographic Aids and Guides

Aguilar y Santillán, Rafael, comp. *Bibliografía geológica y minera de la República Mexicana.* México, D.F.: Secretaría de Fomento, 1898.

Gaines, Jacquelyn M. Melcher, comp. "Calendar of the Unbound Papers and Documents in the Papeles de los Condes de Regla." Typewritten. Pullman: State College of Washington, 1950.

"Glossary of Mexican Mining Terms." In American Institute of Mining Engineers, *Transactions. Vol. XXXII, Containing the Papers and Discussions of 1901, Relating to the Mineral Resources and Industries of Mexico.* New York: American Institute of Mining Engineers, 1902.

Harvard University, Bureau for Economic Research in Latin America. *The Economic Literature of Latin America: A Tentative Bibliography.* 2 vols. Cambridge, Mass.: Harvard University Press, 1935–1936.

Hill, Roscoe R., ed. *The National Archives of Latin America.* Joint Committee on Latin American Studies, Misc. Publication no. 3. Cambridge, Mass.: Harvard University Press, 1945.

Ker, Annita Melville, comp. *Mexican Government Publications: A Guide to the More Important Publications of the National Government of Mexico, 1821–1936.* Washington, D.C.: Library of Congress, 1940.

———. *A Survey of Mexican Scientific Periodicals, to Which Are Appended Some Notes on Mexican Historical Periodicals.* Baltimore: Harvey Bassler Foundation, 1931.

Millares Carlo, Agustín, comp. *Repetorio bibliográfico de los archivos mexicanos y de los europeos y norteamericanos de interés para la historia de México.* México, D.F.: Biblioteca Nacional de Mexico, 1959.

Parsons, Mary D. and Roberto A. Gordillo, comps. *Directorio de bibliotecas de la Ciudad de México: Directory of Mexico City Libraries.* Mexico City: Mexico City College Press, 1958.

INDEX

Acosta mine: yield from, 94; ore produced in, 94–95; and steam engine, 106; comparison of, in 1824 and 1849, 217–218

Acosta vein: condition of, 60–61; work on, 88, 94–95; map of, 94; depth of, 106

adit: begun and constructed, 1739–1849, 11; clearing of, 62; and drainage tunnels, 103; and Mexican mining, 103–104

Alamán, Lucas: 29, 57

alcabala: definition of, 29; amount of, 186; and Real del Monte Company, 186–187

alimento: and the third Count of Regla, 48 and n., 49 n., 64; and Tomás Murphy, 49; and Santa Inés and Carretera mines, 49; and Morán mine, 49, 97; Phillips's appraisal of, 78; amount of, in 1840, 78; and reduction of, 95

amparo: 9

Anglo-Mexican Mining Association: 34, 50, 137

Antón Lizardo: 53–54

Apám (town): 58

Areche (Audiencia attorney): 26

arrastre: description of, 21; increase of, 113; and Mexican operation of, 130

Atlangatepec (town): 58

Atotonilco el Chico: 176

Atotonilco el Grande (plain): 7

Aviadero adit: location of, 18; construction of, 18, 102–103, 104 n.;

abandonment of, 27; importance of, 30; and plan to complete, 38–39; and contract agreement of 1825, 64; and ventilation shaft, 71; need for, 102; cost of completion of, 205–206

aviadores: 12

Azcárate, Juan Francisco: 28

azogue: description of, 20; and Vizcaína vein, 92; and Sacramento mine, 93–94; and supply of, 112. SEE ALSO quicksilver

azoguero: 23, 127

Azoyatla (valley): 7

Azoyatla adit: 12–13

Bank of England: 42

barley: 165

barrel amalgamation: and Pachuca region, 98–100; and Real del Monte Company, 118–125; history of, 119, 120 n.; cost of, 119–120; and low-grade ore, 119–125; description of, 120; nonexpansion of, 122–123; loss of silver from, 124; use of, by Mexican Mining Company, 125 n.; and fuel consumption, 163

barreteros: description of, 23; and labor disputes, 24–25, 137–152; and Terreros mine, 90; and Acosta mine, 95; and Morán mine, 95; and Aviadero adit, 103; work days of, 131; and European workers, 131–132; recruitment of, 134–137; hostility of, toward workers from other districts, 136 and n.; and tutwork, 141, 143;